ƒP

Praise for The Leader in Me

What Parents Are Saying

"The *7 Habits* philosophy at the school has promoted an atmosphere of leadership, communication, respect, and time management. By teaching the skills of self-discipline, self-reliance, and self-confidence, the teachers are fostering the opportunity to learn life skills that are required to be productive adults. My children are being educated to open the door to their future rather than waiting for the door to open."

—*Jennifer Collins, Parent, Stuard Elementary, Aledo, Texas*

"I feel very privileged to be a parent of a child who goes to school at English Estates because of the habits that are taught in the leadership program. It teaches my children practical skills like how to get along with others and things beyond academia. Of course, we also expect the academics, but the habits teach them practical things. I was twenty-four years old and into my career a few years before I had the opportunity to learn these things."

—*Laura Carroll, Parent, English Estates Elementary, Fern Park, Florida*

"In Singapore, kids are facing a lot of distractions, be it through the media or mixing with the wrong friends. So many parents worry about their children making wrong decisions in terms of character or the way they view what it means to be successful. The *7 Habits* help to lay the right foundation that will help them to make good decisions. They complement our efforts as parents to inculcate the right values of effectiveness at this very impressionable age. Speaking for myself, I wish I could have learned the habits earlier, rather than when I entered the corporate world."

—*Lai Fong Yee, Parent, Chua Chu Kang Primary School, Singapore*

"My son was very shy when he first came to A.B. Combs Elementary. But they identified his strong areas and gave him opportunities to use them. One thing he is amazing at is memorizing, so he was given opportunities to memorize and give public speeches, like at the Chamber of Commerce. It brought him out of his shell because it was an area in which he could do very well. It turns out he is quite bright, and this school gave him the opportunity to blossom."

—*Paul Zevgolis, Parent, A.B. Combs Elementary, Raleigh, North Carolina*

"My four-year-old is already versed in the *7 Habits*. She hears them at home from my second-grader and from attending school assemblies. I didn't know the *7 Habits* until my kids started teaching me. My second-grade daughter used to sit in the corner and read. She was quite introverted. The *7 Habits* have helped her to be social. They help all the students to not be afraid to try something new."

—*Christi Woodward, Parent, Dewey Elementary, Quincy, Illinois*

"Sometimes we see a call coming from the school on caller ID and our heart just races with thoughts of 'What is wrong?' But then it turns out to be a teacher saying something about how great one of our daughters did that day, like, 'Oh you should have been here, Simone read this,' or 'Tiffany accomplished that feat.' They are always trying to emphasize the positive."

—*Vernon and L'Tonya Meeks, Parents, A.B. Combs Elementary, Raleigh, North Carolina*

"The confidence and self-esteem that students have acquired through the *7 Habits* is phenomenal. Recently my son had friends over to play, and some of the boys wanted to play baseball, while others wanted to jump on the trampoline. They decided to play 'trampoline baseball' because that would make everybody happy. When he told me about it, he said, 'We were thinking win-win.' And so everybody was happy."

—*Jennifer Wood, PTA, Chestnut Grove Elementary, Decatur, Alabama*

"My son is in third grade. One time we were at a day-care center and a little girl was having trouble with her shoes. Some of the kids started picking on her, but my son stood up and said, 'You guys are not being leaders. We need to think win-win. Let's help her.' He helped her put her shoes on and then they went outside and played. I thought, 'Wow, is that my kid?' It is so amazing how he learns these things from school and then uses them outside of school. The leadership program provides the foundation."

—*Joetta Moore, Parent, English Estates Elementary, Fern Park, Florida*

"When our five-year-old son started coming home and using catchphrases like 'win-win' and 'begin with the end in mind,' it hit home with me. So I decided to take the training, and now we're putting it into place 24/7 as a family. It seems to help in my son's daily routines, my daily routines, my wife's daily routines, our family's daily routines."

—Dean Harrison, Parent, Crestwood Elementary, Medicine Hat,
Alberta, Canada

"When it comes to my children, I always go with my gut feeling. And my gut feeling is, 'This is a place where there is a great nurturing environment. It is a place where I would want to be if I was a child.' "

—Helen Vozzo, Parent, A.B. Combs Elementary, Raleigh, North Carolina

"The skills taught and the inspiration gained from the leadership program are invaluable, and are also terrific parenting tools!"

—Melanie Adams, Parent, Stuard Elementary, Aledo, Texas

What Business and Community Leaders Are Saying

"*The Leader in Me* is focused on building the future leader. Starting from elementary school, students are allowed to be leaders, and truly come to believe they can be leaders in the future. So when I tell my friends about the schools we are sponsoring, I tell them we are supporting the future. In this way, we are able to pay back to a community that has really been so kind to us."

—Peggy Cherng, Cofounder, Panda Express and Panda Cares,
Rosemead, California

"When I went to school we stuck only to academics. So when I see children learning about ethics, involvement in the community, and leadership, I find it very impressive, very worthwhile."

—Kathleen Cresswell, Member, Rotary International, Florida

"The best thing about this is that it is not just for the elite kids or the troubled kids. It is for every single student. It does not matter what their economic background is or what their social history is, it is for everybody."

—Peggy Crim, United Way Board Member, City Treasurer, Quincy, Illinois

"We expect a lot of technical skills from our employees, but we also believe that successful operations require a real strong foundation of interpersonal skills. Some of our employees had taken the *7 Habits*, so when one of them heard Crestwood Elementary was teaching the habits, we saw a real win-win between what the school was trying to do and what we were trying to do at our plant. It was an opportunity for us to give back to the community. The life skills they are learning in the *7 Habits* are so critical to their future success."

—*Rick Redmond, Vice President, Criterion Catalysts and Technologies, Medicine Hat, Alberta, Canada*

"Our company sponsored the leadership program at Chestnut Grove Elementary. It was so successful the first year that we decided to hold our Decatur Morgan County Chamber of Commerce board meeting there one month. The kids came in and spoke to us. At the end of that program, there was not a dry eye in the room. It was just total quiet. The adults were so impressed with the young children's confidence. That started a broader interest in the community, and now we are working with our local industries and businesses to support this as a district-wide effort. Starting with kindergartners, in thirteen years, we've got the opportunity to change the mind-set of an entire community. In only thirteen years!"

—*Donnie Lane, CEO, Enersolv, Decatur, Alabama*

"This creates a culture in schools that is positive, yet not overbearing. It is not putting religion or some ideology into anyone. It is nonpartisan. It is no more than talking about ways that each person can empower themselves to be the best they can be. I think that is what we desire for every child, and what this leadership approach is doing."

—*David Penn, United Way Board President, Attorney, Quincy, Illinois*

"Our Chamber of Commerce does what is called 'Business After Hours,' where we showcase businesses in the area. Two years ago was something special because, instead of a business, we showcased English Estates Elementary. Over a hundred people from the business community attended. The children spoke about leadership and the *7 Habits,* and we had a tour of different classrooms. I cannot express in words what the adults experienced. A child's eyes are like windows right into their minds, and we could see that the children had been changed by what they had been learning. I hope that this is brought to the middle school and into high school, because it will be a continuum of leadership skills that we know are very important in business."

—*Carlos Giraldo, Member, Chamber of Commerce, Florida*

What Teachers Are Saying

"When I first walked into this school, I could tell it was where I wanted to be. Students have the utmost respect for adults and each other. This is all about real life skills. We do hold students to a high standard, but we do it in a loving way. I love helping kids to believe in themselves."
—Rick Weber, Third-Grade Teacher, A.B. Combs Elementary,
Raleigh, North Carolina

"When I observe children's lives these days, sometimes I feel they lack certain skills, like interpersonal skills or teamwork skills. Singapore is a fast-paced society, and our education system is very exam-oriented. Often when students go home, their parents are busy, their families tend to be small, and they have tons of homework. As a result, they do not have the chance to interact much with other children or to develop these skills through play. So as a teacher, I feel privileged to be at a school where I can teach skills like 'think win-win' and 'synergy.' They help students to be more effective as students and better able to handle life's challenges.'
—Mrs. Limmengkwang, Teacher, Chua Chu Kang Primary School,
Singapore

"We began our journey as a 'Leadership' school only a year ago. The transformation is astonishing as well as exciting. Every day I get to see empowered five- and six-year-olds truly caring about our school's learning environment. This is a win-win situation for our children and nation."
—Maggie Lozano, Kindergarten Teacher, Stuard Elementary, Aledo, Texas

"What I love about teaching the *7 Habits* is that it is not something more on my plate. This is a method, a strategy. I have been teaching sixteen years, and since teaching the *7 Habits* my students have the best test scores. And people ask, 'How can the habits increase test scores?' Well, when children are in a risk-free environment because they are applying the habits, they feel good about themselves and are more prone to pay attention to what is being taught."
—Dana Farris, Kindergarten Teacher, Chestnut Grove Elementary,
Decatur, Alabama

"The *7 Habits* greatly help with discipline and classroom management. A lot of times I do not even have to get involved when there is a disagreement between children. They know the habits and they can work through the problem-solving steps without taking my time to solve or get involved. When it does require my help, we work through the steps of asking what is most important, what is putting first things first, and what ideas can we come up with to reach an under-standing."

—*Emily Hardee, Fifth-Grade Teacher, A.B. Combs Elementary,*
Raleigh, North Carolina

"My students are three to five years old with special needs. I have children who are autistic, speech and language impaired, and physically impaired. They like being leaders and making good choices. The *7 Habits* provide a language that I can use with them in making that happen."

—*Winnifred Hunter, Pre-KVE Teacher, English Estates Elementary,*
Fern Park, Florida

"I recently received a new student along with notes from her previous school. Her previous teacher said, 'She does not follow directions or get along with peers.' I had to read it twice since I got the record a month after she enrolled. That was not the child I am experiencing. In this classroom she is wonderful. She is so anx-ious to come to school and walks in with a smile every day. Students will learn the academics, but kindness, respect, and leadership is what this school is about. It is about teaching them to be leaders and doing the right thing when no one is looking."

—*Debbie Falkner, Kindergarten Teacher, A.B. Combs Elementary,*
Raleigh, North Carolina

"As a teacher, I am in awe as I observe our student leaders step up to visitors at our school, look them in the eye, and give them a strong firm handshake welcom-ing them to our wonderful school. Their self-confidence and self-esteem has grown tremendously."

—*Waydean Waller, Reading Specialist, Nash Elementary, Texarkana, Texas*

"I think the *7 Habits* are the greatest thing that we can teach students. They teach them how to be a leader and how to function in society, including how to deal with people who do not like them or who are hard to get along with."

—*Vicki Mallory, Third-Grade Teacher, Dewey Elementary, Quincy, Illinois*

"My students are a year away from middle school, and by practicing the *7 Habits* they are gathering coping skills. They are learning what to say, and what to do. I know it will help them to deal with whatever they will face in the near future, in-cluding all kinds of peer pressure."

—*Farica Davis, Fourth-Grade Teacher, English Estates Elementary,*
Fern Park, Florida

"I have taught twenty-one years and fully believe the *7 Habits* have helped the discipline of our children. When students come into the classroom, they know we expect them to follow the leadership model, and to use the *7 Habits*. Because of that, there are less interruptions and less disruptive behaviors, which means I can really focus on whatever it is I am teaching."

—Martha Bassett, Art Teacher, A.B. Combs Elementary, Raleigh, North Carolina

"Teaching leadership skills and the *7 Habits* has changed me as a teacher, as a parent, and as a wife. It has helped me to organize my life better. It has helped me to prioritize and to put my attention on the things that are most important. I feel I have become a better teacher because I am doing more than just teaching reading, writing, and math. Those are important subjects that all my students need to learn, but more important is that they learn that someone cares about them, that they know they are special and that they matter in this world. It is more than just the academics. It is more than the test scores. It is about who they are, how they are going to act, and their character today."

—Pam Almond, Kindergarten Teacher, A.B. Combs Elementary, Raleigh, North Carolina

"After just one year of implementation, we have seen leadership skills emerge in both students and teachers. It is refreshing to see students taking responsibility and ownership for their learning and self-discipline. In addition, it is a joy to see children attempting to create win-win situations as they seek to understand others and resolve their differences."

—Marian Holder, Third-Grade Teacher, Nash Elementary, Texarkana, Texas

"Kindergarten children tend to be like sponges, and it has been no different with them learning the *7 Habits.* An amazing thing for me has been to see how the children are able to apply the habits. One day I pulled a child in from recess to do some testing and I said to him, 'I didn't have a chance to eat breakfast this morning, would you mind if I eat an apple while we work on this?' He looked at me and said, 'Mrs. Jones, did you forget to put first things first? You should eat breakfast if you want to be ready for school.' They are learning life skills that will take them through life."

—Mary Ann Jones, Kindergarten Teacher, Crestwood Elementary, Medicine Hat, Alberta, Canada

"My favorite time of the day is morning 'Leadership Time,' when a student is assigned to be a motivational speaker and share a quote. We discuss the quote and how it is relevant to our lives. In the process, we discover a great deal about ourselves and each other, and it builds cohesiveness. To quote one of my fourth-grade motivational speakers, 'Don't just follow your dreams, chase them!' "

—*Zan Thorp, Fourth-Grade Teacher, Stuard Elementary School, Aledo, Texas*

"I see a very big difference in being a social worker at Dewey, where we have the *7 Habits,* versus at other schools that do not have the habits. The biggest difference is found in the common *7 Habits* language that is used throughout the school. I can use the same words whether I am working with a kindergartner or a third-grader, because the kids all know the *7 Habits.* Also, the students at Dewey tend to know how to solve many of their own problems. I might facilitate the process using the *7 Habits,* but then I can step back as they take responsibility for solving many of their own situations."

—*Denise Poland, Social Worker, Dewey Elementary, Quincy, Illinois*

What School Principals and Other Administrators Are Saying

"This is more than character education. We are not just teaching perseverance, patience, and kindness, we are teaching leadership. We are teaching children that not only can they develop leadership traits in elementary school, but that we expect them to take these skills with them when they go on to middle school and high school, and to embrace them as lifelong skills."

—*Lauretta Teague, Principal, Chestnut Grove Elementary, Decatur, Alabama*

"As educators and parents, our ultimate goal for our children is to have them be successful in life, and to do the things we would like them to do when we are not around. Our job, therefore, is to prepare them for life, not to guide every moment of every day of their existence. What better way to do that than through teaching timeless principles?"

—*Dr. Beth Sharpe, Principal, English Estates Elementary, Fern Park, Florida*

"When we looked at the *7 Habits* and at how they might benefit students, we began by asking, 'What are the characteristics that we want our students to have when they go to the workplace? How will the *7 Habits* build in students the character traits that are needed for the twenty-first century?' We concluded that students who go through the *7 Habits* will be planners, they will take responsibility for their own learning, and they will choose to have a positive attitude. They will work together and they will have a vision for their future. These are traits and skills that will help them do better in school, in college, in the workplace, and will allow them to lead families when that time comes."

—*Jeanne Payne, Professional Development Coordinator, Decatur City Schools, Decatur, Alabama*

"When I first came to A.B. Combs, I thought, 'Can this be real or is this just a show for the day?' Spending just a little bit of time here, I realized that this is a way of life. These are people actually living their dream. The minute you walk in the door you feel something special."

—*Michael Armstrong, Magnet Coordinator, A.B. Combs Elementary, Raleigh, North Carolina.*

"A lot of times people say, 'We need to get back to the basics, or the three R's—reading, writing, and arithmetic.' We look at the *7 Habits* as a fourth R—relationships. It is an R that allows us to teach kids how to relate to themselves and how they can relate to those around them."

—*Ed Nichols, Assistant Superintendent, Decatur City Schools, Decatur, Alabama*

"We have several students who come from troubled homes, but with the use of the *7 Habits* they start to understand what they need to do to make themselves better and to make the school better. We also have new students who arrive at the start of each year very, very shy. Those same students are now leading our morning assembly. They have become leaders in our school. This is all due in large part to the *7 Habits.*"

—*Jerry Ellerman, Principal, Dewey Elementary School, Quincy, Illinois*

"It has been a joy to watch this leadership program flourish and grow at English Estates. The results of the school academically have been phenomenal. It has changed the whole spirit of the school and the community around it. I do not know that there is any greater feeling than to see students learn the *7 Habits* at such an early age. These are lifelong skills that they get an opportunity to learn at age six that many adults do not get a chance to learn in their entire lives."

—*Barry Gainer, School Board Member, Seminole County Schools, Florida*

"We serve a varied population—economically, academically, and racially—and that includes a number of students who are 'high needs' in many diverse ways. It

is a real nice mix. We see the *7 Habits* as one of the great equalizers in the school. The habits speak to everyone."
—*David George, Principal, Crestwood Elementary, Medicine Hat, Alberta, Canada*

"The *7 Habits* for students in Adams County started with Dewey Elementary and shortly thereafter at Washington Elementary, both of which are K–3 schools. Six other district schools and four county schools followed the next year with implementation. Now the preschool, parochial school, and day-care centers have also taken the training, and the intermediate schools will start this summer. We tried to put some of this off so we could do the training at a more even-keel rate over a three-year period, but the schools have been so interested that it has gone like wildfire."
—*George Meyer, retired Superintendent of Schools and Dean of the School of Education at Quincy University, Illinois*

"*Leadership* can be such an obscure term to elementary students, but the *7 Habits* break it down into 'doable' actions and concepts for students. When students are given the opportunity to practice life skills in a safe and loving environment, they eventually add those skills to their everyday skill set."
—*Robin Seay, Principal, Stuard Elementary, Aledo, Texas*

"Having a very diverse population of students, there is a great need at our school to teach students positive skills that will have a profound impact on their lives. We strongly feel that we are meeting those needs by introducing these effective habits with our students. Amazing things happen each day as our students develop stronger academic skills, as well as better skills in relationships and in decision making. This is definitely one of the most exciting things I have done during my thirty-six year career in education."
—*Bertie Norton, Principal, Nash Elementary, Texarkana, Texas*

"We have supported the leadership approach districtwide and now county-wide because it is the right thing to do. Kids need this, and the teachers and the community embrace it. It makes the kids feel good about coming to school each day, and that is a big part of what they need because there are a lot of external forces that present them with daily challenges. This is a shining star, or a light, that they can latch on to and use to help themselves and each other. It just makes sense."
—*Thomas F. Leahy, District Superintendent, Quincy Public Schools, Quincy, Illinois*

"By engaging students early on in the importance of leadership, students will develop habits in their lives that will lead to success throughout their academic career."

—*James Henry Russell, Superintendent of Schools, Texarkana Independent School District, Texarkana, Texas*

The
Leader
in Me

How Schools and Parents Around the World Are Inspiring Greatness, One Child at a Time

Stephen R. Covey

Free Press

New York   London   Toronto   Sydney

*f*P
Free Press
A Division of Simon & Schuster, Inc.
1230 Avenue of the Americas
New York, NY 10020

First Free Press trade paperback edition November 2009

FREE PRESS and colophon are trademarks of Simon & Schuster, Inc.

For information about special discounts for bulk purchases,
please contact Simon & Schuster Special Sales at 1-866-506-1949 or
business@simonandschuster.com.

The Simon & Schuster Speakers Bureau can bring authors
to your live event. For more information or to book an event,
contact the Simon & Schuster Speakers Bureau at
1-866-248-3049 or visit our website at www.simonspeakers.com.

Designed by Ruth Lee-Mui

Manufactured in the United States of America

17   19   20   18

Library of Congress Control Number: 2008032967

ISBN 987-1-4391-0326-5
ISBN 978-1-4391-5317-8 (pbk)
ISBN 978-1-4391-3646-1 (ebook)

*We only get one chance to prepare our students for a future
that none of us can possibly predict.
What are we going to do with that one chance?*

Contents

Foreword   xxi

1. Too Good to Be True?   1
2. Discovering What Parents, Business Leaders, and Teachers Want from a School   18
3. Crafting a Blueprint for Leadership   44
4. Aligning for Success   71
5. Unleashing a Culture of Leadership   90
6. Rippling Across the Globe   107
7. Moving Upward and Beyond   134
8. Making It Happen, One Step at a Time   165
9. Ending with the Beginning in Mind   191
10. Bringing It Home   207

Notes   225

Will Your School or Child Be the Next *The Leader in Me* Success Story?   229

Sponsor a School and Invest in Tomorrow's Leaders . . . Today   231

Index   233

About FranklinCovey   243

About Stephen R. Covey   245

Foreword

As much as any professional work I have embarked upon, this book comes from my heart. It both thrills and humbles me like you cannot imagine.

It involves today's young people. It involves our future. Whether you are a concerned parent, a professional educator, or a foresighted business leader, I am confident you will find it to be an invigorating breath of fresh air, a reason to celebrate and an inspiring call for action. For what you are about to read unveils a budding trend that is gaining momentum in a growing number of schools across the United States and in various parts of the world. It is an exciting trend—one that is producing tangible, sustainable results.

From the get-go, I want you to know that I am not the mastermind behind the trend. Rather, credit goes to an expanding community of committed, creative, and caring professional educators who have synergistically joined forces with parents, civic leaders, and business proprietors to bring about a new level of hope in education.

To set the context, let me take you back a few years to what seems like yesterday. In 1989, *The 7 Habits of Highly Effective People* was published. Its subtitle was "Restoring the Character Ethic." The book caught a wave that even I had no way of anticipating, particularly in organizational arenas. Today, the *7 Habits* are still thriving in boardrooms, government offices, and corporate universities around the globe.

About the same time as the *7 Habits* book was launched, I was approached by Chuck Farnsworth, who at the time was superintendent of schools for a progressive district in Indiana. Chuck felt strongly that the *7 Habits* had an important role to play in the world of education, and he was passionately determined to lead the charge. He began by taking the habits to school administrators and teachers. To date, nearly a half million professional educators have been trained in the 7 *Habits*, with many of them being certified as school facilitators.

As we brought the 7 *Habits* into schools, the focus remained on training adults, not students. That changed in 1998, when my son, Sean, wrote *The 7 Habits of Highly Effective Teens*. Sean had been a Division I college football quarterback, which created frequent opportunities for him to be in front of teen audiences. He developed a sincere interest in young people that eventually propelled him to write the teen version. More than three million teen copies have now been sold, and Student Activity Guides have carried the habits to over a hundred thousand middle and high school students.

In the latter part of 1999, the 7 *Habits* made another significant entry into schools. During a presentation in Washington, D.C., I was approached by an elementary school principal named Muriel Summers. She wanted to know if I thought the 7 *Habits* could be taught to young children. I pointed her toward Sean's book, but she came back with the reply that she was referring to *very young* children—as young as five years old. I responded, "I don't know why not," and then casually added that if she ever tried to do it to let me know how it went.

This book contains the account of what Muriel and her talented staff initiated following that brief encounter. It is a tremendous story, one that has been simmering, thickening, rippling, and gaining momentum (and even some notoriety) for some time, as the percentage of students achieving end-of-grade targets has gone from 84 to 97 percent and the school has gone from the brink of nearly being terminated as a magnet school to being named the number one magnet school in America. How? With great success they, and now scores of other schools, have been teaching the 7 *Habits* and other leadership principles to elementary school students—yes, even five-year-olds. Their approach is unique and may even surprise you. Their intent has not been to prepare students to become CEOs or world leaders, but rather to teach them how to lead their individual lives and how to succeed in the twenty-first century. I believe you will discover in their approach some highly credible and principle-based solutions to some of the most discouraging dilemmas facing schools today.

In approaching the topic of education, I am keenly aware that today's educators are constantly under a microscope and have been the targets of abundant negative press in recent years. Such is not the intent of this book. Rather than being a critic, I prefer to promote the good. I honestly believe that it is difficult to spend time in most any school these days without departing in absolute reverence of some incredible teachers—noble mentors who have sacrificed much to do what they love and what they believe will make a difference in young lives. To focus only on the negative in education while ignoring what the true heroes are doing would be a tragic act of ingratitude.

Some may view my efforts as self-serving. I acknowledge why some might feel that way, but I am willing to risk that perception because I so strongly believe in what these schools are doing for today's young people. Indeed, it is the profound successes that these schools are having that has inspired FranklinCovey to devote more of its mission toward partnering with schools, businesses, parents, and community leaders to create resources that will better enable young people to prepare for the world that awaits them—a world that none of us can fully predict. Likewise, it was the successes of these schools that ignited Sean's desire to write his recently released book, *The 7 Habits of Happy Kids*. Both this book and Sean's book—along with a whole series of new *The Leader in Me* resources and website materials—are vital components in FranklinCovey's effort to do more toward the betterment of societies and young people of all nations.

This book represents the combined efforts of many people. My partner, Boyd Craig, provided visionary leadership and direction to the entire team and project. Dr. David K. Hatch shepherded the research efforts with passion, dedication, and world class character and competence. He took my heart, put data behind it, and helped me transfer it to paper. Their efforts were competently supported by FranklinCovey's Education Solutions team, in particular Sarah Noble, Connie Spencer, Aaron Ashby, Sean Covey, Judy Yauch, Shawn Moon, and Stephanie Calton, and such road-tested consultants as Dr. Nancy Moore, Dr. Jane Knight, Gary McGuey, and Lonnie Moore, as well as Dr. Craig Pace and Dr. Dean Collinwood, who conducted early research for the book. Others such as Victoria Marrott contributed significant administrative support. The rest of my office team—Julie Gillman, Chelsea Johns, and Darla Salin—provide constant support to all of my work. More important, well over a hundred teachers, school superintendents, principals, parents, professors, and school board members volunteered extensive input and rigorous review of the work. Their practical, tried-and-refined insights substantiate each page. My heartfelt gratitude extends to all who participated.

To gain a quick overview of what this book entails, I suggest that you skim through it from front to back while looking at the pictures and reading their captions. I also recommend that you visit TheLeaderInMe Book.org online to view video clips of schools and activities spoken of in this book.

As you view the various resources and traverse the pages of this book, I hope you feel my deep, personal commitment, and behind it all my firm belief in the potential of today's young people. As a grandparent, I am delighted with the possibilities this book may create for my grandchildren, their children, and eventually their children's children. I think nothing but the highest of them and want nothing short of the best for them. Likewise, as a global citizen, I feel a vested interest in the progress, well-being, and happiness of all young people. They are the society and hope of the future—*our* future—and I firmly desire that future to be in good hands. Finally, as a business executive, I want to be able to look into the eyes of today's young people and see a vibrant coming workforce, a pool of future leaders who are well prepared for the challenges that we all know lie ahead.

Indeed, it is my sincerest hope that this book will somehow spread its figurative wings and soar with a reach that will truly make a difference in the lives of young people the world over—now and for generations to come.

STEPHEN R. COVEY
Provo, Utah
StephenCovey.com
TheLeaderInMe.org
TheLeaderInMeBook.org

1

Too Good to Be True?

We had been doing character education for years and it did not do a thing. When I first started telling people about the leadership option, there were several nay-sayers who thought it all a bunch of "fluff." But now they are believers.

—*Leslie Reilly, Seminole County Public Schools, Florida*

Today's young people, our children, belong to the most promising generation in the history of the world. They stand at the summit of the ages. They also stand at the crossroads of two great paths. One is the broader, well-traveled path that leads to mediocrity of mind and character, and to social decline. The other is a narrower, "less traveled" uphill path leading to limitless human possibilities—and the hope of the world. EVERY child can walk this latter path, if shown the way.

But who will show them the way, if not you and me? Where will they learn how, if not in their home or at their school? When will it happen, if not now?

Join me in an unfolding story of great hope.

When Drs. Rig and Sejjal Patel moved their family to Raleigh, North Carolina, they were, like most parents, interested in locating a good school—a place where their children could learn in a wholesome, safe, and mind-stimulating environment. As they sought the advice of colleagues, the name of one school kept popping up: A.B. Combs Elementary.

On paper, A.B. Combs Elementary was quite ordinary. A public school located in a quiet neighborhood, it was home to more than eight hundred students, of whom 18 percent spoke English as a second language, 40 percent received free or reduced lunches, 21 percent were placed in special programs, and 15 percent were considered academically gifted. The building that housed them was fifty years old. Some teachers had been there for years.

But while the paper version of A.B. Combs appeared to be nothing too unusual, the stories the Patels kept hearing exceeded what even their loftiest expectations would allow them to believe. They heard accounts of high and sustained test scores, friendly and respectful students, an engaged staff, and a principal who had been named Principal of the Year. Discipline issues were minimal. Students who had severe problems at other schools were progressing well at this school. Even the teachers were happy. It all sounded pretty good.

In fact, the more the Patels heard the stories, the more they began asking themselves, "Could such a place really exist?" They did not say it to people's faces, but the thought that kept drifting through their minds was "This place sounds too good to be true!"

The Patels decided to see the school for themselves, and what they discovered was that just entering the front doors at A.B. Combs can be quite an engaging experience. There is a feeling there that is not felt in many schools. It is a feeling a person can see, can hear, and can touch. In fact, if you happen to be at the school for its annual International Food Festival, you might even be able to taste a bit of the feeling, since the students there represent fifty-eight countries and twenty-seven languages. The school is clean. Students passing in the halls look adults in the eyes and greet them. Things on the walls are cheery and even motivational. Students treat one another with respect, and diversity is more than just valued, it is celebrated.

During their visit, the Patels learned of the mission and goals of A.B. Combs. They learned of the school's traditions, particularly the tradition of caring. They walked the hallways and saw quotes and murals promoting high standards. Inside classrooms they spotted empowered, hardworking teachers. They discovered that all students are assigned leadership roles and that many decisions are made by students, not teachers. All this the Patels found quite remarkable, and they departed from that first visit determined to enroll their children.

So What About for You?

So what about for you? Are the descriptions of A.B. Combs sounding "too good to be true"?

I believe the main reason the Patels (and perhaps even you) found the reports about A.B. Combs "too good to be true" is that they are in such stark contrast to what we are used to hearing. We are so inundated with stories of bullying, poor teachers, graffiti, rude manners, low test scores, disrespect, lack of discipline, campus violence, poor graduation rates, and so forth, that we have become calloused skeptics when hearing of anything so positive. Either we find it flat out too hard to believe or we question its sustainability.

I must admit that if I had not seen A.B. Combs with my own eyes, or if it were the only school enjoying such successes, I too might doubt the viability, transferability, and sustainability of the school's approach. But a growing number of other schools have now replicated its approach and are enjoying equivalent successes. As a result, I have wholeheartedly joined other business leaders, parents, and teachers across the globe in becoming a firm believer in what these schools and great educators are doing.

A.B. Combs Elementary is located in a quiet residential neighborhood of Raleigh, North Carolina.

In short, what these educators are doing is teaching basic leadership principles to young students—as young as five years old. They are teaching oft-neglected skill sets for making good choices, for getting along well with others, and for managing time wisely. In addition, they are providing authentic opportunities for students to *apply* them by giving students leadership opportunities in the classroom, in the school, and in the community. All this they are doing in a way that is improving student achievement and restoring discipline and a character ethic in the classrooms and on the playgrounds. What delights teachers is that they are doing it in a way that does not create "one more thing" for them to do, but rather offers a methodology that many describe as "a better way of doing what we were already doing."

> This is not a school that is about making nine hundred little business leaders. This is a school about creating a well-rounded student who knows their strengths. We are here to help them find their strengths and unleash their potential to influence others.
> —*Michael Armstrong, Magnet Coordinator, A.B. Combs Elementary*

As the book progresses, you will learn why schools like A.B. Combs have chosen to teach these basic leadership principles, how they go about it, and what results they are achieving. But in preview, what these schools are reporting in near unison is:

- Improved student achievement
- Significantly enhanced self-confidence and esteem in students
- Dramatic decreases in discipline problems
- Impressive increases in teachers' and administrators' job satisfaction and commitment
- Greatly improved school cultures
- Parents who are delighted and engaged in the process
- Business and community leaders who want to lend support

What has adults who have visited or worked in these schools talking most is the visible increase in students' self-confidence, their ability to get along with each other, and to solve problems. A sharp reduction in discipline problems is one of the most frequent outcomes that teachers are quick to point out. Having fewer quarrels and acts of disrespect to deal with has allowed teachers to focus more on academics and is restoring a sense of vigor to their jobs. Parents are ecstatic about what is happening at these schools. They not only speak highly of what is happening at school but also report improved behavior at home. In fact, after observing their children, many parents have sought out training in the same leadership principles so that they can integrate the principles into home activities. Most of these results are being reported within the first year of implementation.

Of course, in education circles the biggest question has been, What has this done for test scores? Naturally, that answer will differ from school to school. Some of the schools mentioned in this book were already high academic achievers prior to engaging in the process, so their test scores had limited room to improve. But even with that, essentially all of the schools are reporting improved test scores. Perhaps the most encouraging data is coming out of A.B. Combs, which has been implementing the approach the longest. They first piloted the approach using one teacher per grade level, and that year the percentage of students passing end-of-grade tests jumped from 84 percent to 87 percent, primarily due to the improved scores of the pilot students. The next year the entire school took on the leadership approach and the percentage of passing students took another significant leap, this time to 94 percent. That was no small feat, given its widely diverse student population. What makes the increase in scores truly validating is that A.B. Combs has been able to maintain those elevated scores for a steady sequence of years, ultimately peaking at 97 percent, which certainly was one

---

People often ask us, "Does our child have to be a leader to go to this school?" We tell them absolutely not. This school is for all children, regardless of ethnic backgrounds, socioeconomic status, or academic ability.

This morning a special needs student was assigned to be the first person to welcome visitors to our site visit. He may not run a huge corporation one day, but he has unbelievable interpersonal relationship skills and there will be a job somewhere out there for him. He sees himself as a leader in manners. He feels so good about who he is despite his academic limitations. That is what this leadership model does for all children.

—Muriel Summers, Principal, A.B. Combs Elementary

of the primary factors in their being named the top magnet school in America. But awards aside, the real importance of what this suggests is that the leadership approach is indeed sustainable.

All these results are promising signs in the ever-challenging world of education.

Greatness to Match Today's Realities

But something is happening at these schools that I believe is greater than any of the results mentioned above, including the rise in test scores and the smiles on parents' and teachers' faces. Students coming out of these schools are equipped with a type of "greatness" and the skills they will need not just to *survive* but to *thrive* in the twenty-first century.

Let me explain.

Students representing fifty-eight countries and twenty-seven languages unite to create a diverse population at A.B. Combs.

It is no secret that we are at the forefront of one of the most exciting and promising of all ages in human history. The exploding advances in technology and the globalization of markets have created unprecedented opportunities for growth and prosperity for individuals, families, organizations, and society as a whole. Of course, there are also many problems and challenges—there always have been and always will be—but gaze in any direction and opportunities to progress and make a difference are everywhere. Yet amid this climate of opportunity, a question tenaciously nags at the minds and hearts of parents, educators, and employers alike: Are today's young people being adequately prepared to take advantage of the expanding opportunities and duly equipped to deal with the accompanying challenges?

Until recently, we were living in an era known as the information age. In that era, individuals who had the most information—the most "facts" in their heads—were the ones who became the fortunate few to ascend to the tops of their professions. During that era, it only made sense that the primary focus of parents and schools was on pumping as many facts into students' brain cells as possible—assuming they were the right facts for the right tests. After all, "facts in the head" is what allowed students to score high on the right "fact-based" tests, which got them into the best "fact-based" universities, and that in turn set them up for an accelerated climb up the right "fact-based" career ladder.

But that era is now being transcended as the global economy has entered another phase of speed and complexity. While factual information remains a key factor for survival in today's world, it is no longer sufficient. With the massive spread of the internet and other digital resources, facts that at one time were closely guarded trade secrets and only available from the top universities can now be accessed in most every nook and cranny on the globe at the click of a mouse. As a result, many of the so-called elite professions that once required extensive schooling are today being passed on to computers or to people at far lower education levels and wages across the planet. Factual knowledge alone is thus no longer the great differentiator between those who succeed and those who do not.

> The last few decades have belonged to a certain kind of person with a certain kind of mind—computer programmers who could crank code, lawyers who could craft contracts, MBAs who could crunch numbers. But the keys to the kingdom are changing hands.
>
> —*Daniel Pink*, A Whole New Mind

Instead, the individuals who are emerging as the new "winners"—the new *thrivers*—of the twenty-first century are those who possess above-average creativity, strong analytical skills, a knack for foresight, and—surprise, surprise—good people skills. As Daniel Pink and others are asserting, it is the right-brainers who are taking over the present economy. They are the inventors, the designers, the listeners, the big-picture thinkers, the meaning makers, and the pattern recognizers—those who know how to optimize and creatively maneuver the facts, not just memorize or regurgitate them. All this they do while knowing how to effectively team with others. And, in case you have not noticed, people with such talents are popping up on every continent, even in remote villages. As Larry Sullivan, former superintendent of schools for the Texarkana (Texas) Independent School District, points out, "Today's students are no longer merely competing for jobs against students in neighboring towns, states, or provinces, they are competing with students in China, India, Japan, Europe, South America, Madagascar, and every island and continent in between."

Yet while these are the new realities, how often do I hear today's business leaders grimacing about the new MBA or PhD they just hired who has "no clue" how to work with people, how to make a basic presentation, how to conduct themselves ethically, how to organize their time, or how to be creative—much less how to inspire creativity in others? How many times do I hear executives talk about how their company is poised to pursue a great new opportunity but cannot get out of the starting blocks because they are mired in ethical breeches or infighting between employees or subcontractors? How many times do I hear parents bemoaning the fact that their newly crowned high school graduate excelled on all the college entrance exams yet does not know how to take responsibility for their actions, to vocalize their thoughts, to treat people with respect, to analyze a decision, to empathize, to prioritize, to resolve conflicts maturely, or to plan? If you were to ask these people if they felt students were being properly prepared for the present reality, I think you would hear an unequivocal, unified, and boisterous, *"No!"*

The more I have such conversations, the more my own thoughts turn to my grandchildren, and their future children. I find myself asking, "What does the future hold for them? What can I do to prepare them better for the new reality?" Indeed, in this age, when they read far more text messages than they do textbooks, I find myself worrying less about what facts my grandchildren are studying in school than I do about what their peers—and even their teachers—are telling them about life and how to handle it. I have spent more than half of my career as a teacher and know all too well how a teacher can either cement mediocrity or inspire excellence in a student, regardless of what subject is being taught.

As I struggle to distill the essence of what the new business environment is telling me, what educators are telling me, what parents are telling me, and what my own heart is telling me, the concept that keeps surfacing in my mind is *primary greatness*. I recognize that "greatness" is a term that is intimidating to many people. To some it is even a negative or arrogant term. I think this is because many people equate it only with what I call *secondary greatness*. Secondary greatness has to do with positions or titles, awards, wealth, fame, rankings, or rare accomplishments. Almost by definition, secondary greatness can only be attained by a select few, an extremely small percentage of a population. Secondary greatness is largely determined by comparing one person against another.

Primary greatness, on the other hand, is open to everyone. Every single person can have it; there are no bell-curve limits. Primary greatness has to do with a person's integrity, work ethic, treatment of others, motives, and level of initiative. It also has to do with a person's character, contributions, talents, creativity, and discipline. It represents who people are—every day—as opposed to what they own or temporary achievements. Primary greatness is measured not by comparisons with other people, but by adherence to timeless, universal principles. It is humble.

> If we are putting all of our efforts on the almighty test score alone, I am quite afraid that we are going to create a generation of children who know how to do nothing but take a test well.
> —*Muriel Summers, Principal, A.B. Combs Elementary*

Sometimes, primary greatness is a precursor or companion to secondary greatness. In other words, a person having primary greatness ends up also having secondary greatness. Other times, secondary greatness comes alone. We all know of people, for example, who have secondary greatness but who lack any semblance of primary greatness. At the same time, many people with primary greatness never achieve secondary greatness, and even prefer to avoid the limelight of secondary greatness.

The reason primary greatness keeps coming to my mind is that I sincerely believe it is what business leaders, parents, and educators are begging for in their employees, in their children, and in their students. I will lay out *why* this is so in far more detail in chapter 2, but suffice it here to say that, truly, today's realities present a new and global playing field, one that demands far more than just having a set of facts lodged in one's head. It requires new skills, though in reality some of them turn out to be quite "old" skills. And it requires a new level of primary greatness, with a firm character foundation.

So, yes, it *is* nice that the schools mentioned in this book are reporting improved achievement scores and increased student self-confidence, and, yes, it *is* good that parents and teachers are reporting higher satisfaction ratings. But higher test scores and happier parents are not what is going to enable students to survive and thrive in this new reality. They need more. And that is what excites me most as a grandparent, as a business leader, and as a member of society about what you will read in this book. Students are exiting these schools far better prepared with the mind-sets, the skill sets, and the tool sets they will need to meet today's new realities.

A Moral Imperative?

After completing the initial year of teaching the leadership principles to students, the pilot teachers at A.B. Combs stood before their peer teachers and administrators and declared, "Every child deserves this."

Dewey Elementary in Quincy, Illinois, was the first of ten elementary schools in Adams County to model its approach after A.B. Combs. When the decision was being made, the school's principal, Christie Dickens, says most of the teachers were strongly in favor. But one particular teacher was quite reluctant and displeased. So in the beginning she mostly sat back and observed from a distance as her colleagues engaged in teaching the leadership skills. But once she saw how the approach was impacting students' lives both in and out of the classroom, she readily came on board. In fact, at the start of the second semester, she approached Christie and said,

"I know you are trying hard to collect data and monitor this to see if it is working, but I could care less about the test scores or what the data says. This is the *right* thing to be doing!"

After visiting A.B. Combs, Peggy and Andrew Cherng, founders of the highly successful Panda Express chain of restaurants, determined to start out by sponsoring six Southern California schools with the specific purpose of helping them implement the leadership approach before expanding to additional schools. However, a key leader in one of the school districts voiced strong objections. It was the term *leadership* that was causing him to react. "Let's face it," he vehemently announced, "not every one of these students is going to grow up to be a CEO or prominent leader. It is just not going to happen!" But then he visited A.B. Combs and observed their students, and once he realized that the leadership principles were focused on helping students to take responsibility for their lives, to work with others more effectively, and to do the right thing even when no one is looking, he quickly became one of the leading advocates for the approach. "This is the *right* thing to be doing for students," he now insists.

In Guatemala, years of civil strife and economic turmoil left many young people (and teachers) without any sense of hope or vision. This was very apparent and disturbing to María del Carmen Aceña when in 2003 she took over as minister of education. She knew that if the country's students and educators had little hope, then the entire country had little hope of elevating its standards of living or cultural ambitions. So she assembled a research team and after careful investigation they initiated a "Path of Dreams" program that teaches many of the same leadership and life skills that A.B. Combs teaches, only their focus is at the high school level. Today, more than two hundred thousand high school students have been taught the leadership principles, and it is with a refreshed smile that María now reports that "students are leaving school with skills for life, and committed to changing Guatemala." All along, her team's resolve was "We simply felt this was the *right* thing to do."

When asked to identify the biggest pain educators are feeling these days, one outstanding elementary school principal narrowed her reply to a single word: "Regret." When asked to explain, she said, "Educators are feeling enormous regret from the realization that over the past decade so much emphasis has been placed on raising test scores that it has come at the expense of students not learning some of the most basic skills needed for everyday life. They also regret that in the process of focusing on academics they have failed to pass on to students more of a love of learning and a love of life. And that is why," she noted, "our school decided to teach these leadership skills. It is simply the *right* thing to be doing."

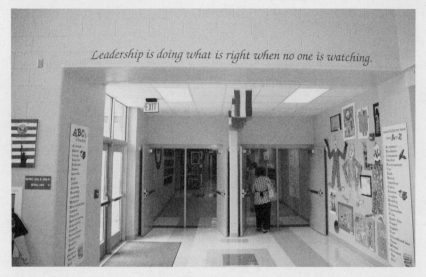

Leadership is not seen as a position at A.B. Combs. It is a way of living and leading one's own life.

In these few examples, did you notice the common phrase . . . the *right* thing to be doing? As you delve into what the schools mentioned in this book are doing, here are questions I hope you keep at the forefront of your thoughts: Do we as adults have a moral imperative to be teaching these leadership principles and basic life skills? Is this the *right* thing to be doing? Do you think young people are being adequately prepared for today's realities? If not, what do you think ought to be done to prepare them better? What do you think are the *most* important things to be teaching them? How would you go about doing it?

Keep those thoughts and questions in mind as you go through the pages of this book.

Three Themes to Look For

Of course, my wish would be that parents, educators, and business leaders of all types—especially skeptical ones—could travel to A.B. Combs or any one of the other schools to see, hear, and feel for themselves what is happening. But not even a school like A.B. Combs could absorb such an onslaught.*

So as you might surmise, one objective of this book is to share enough of what these schools are doing so that you can gain a feel for what is happening without having to travel any farther than a comfortable chair. Indeed, this book will take you to English Estates Elementary in Fern Park, Florida, which was named the most academically improved school in its district after only one year of implementation. It will take you to Chestnut Grove Elementary in Decatur, Alabama, where a local business leader has funded the school into becoming a top leadership campus. It will take you to Dewey Elementary in Quincy, Illinois, where the school's progress has motivated the local United Way to lead the charge in getting the same caliber of training to all ten thousand students in their county. It will take you to Texas, California, Kentucky, Oklahoma, and other U.S. states. Furthermore, it will take you to Canada, Guatemala, Japan, Singapore, Australia, and Europe. It is more than a heartwarming story. It is a pragmatic, creative approach that is giving rise to a new level of hope in the world of education.

As you journey from location to location, I challenge you to observe three overarching themes that I feel are foundational to the results these schools are achieving:

First, observe **the universal nature of the leadership principles** that are being taught at the schools. The principles are timeless and, in most cases, commonsensical. I did not invent the principles; they have been around for ages and are familiar to all cultures. So whether a student is stepping out of a sizable home in an upscale neighborhood or out of a thatched hut in a rain forest, the principles will enable them to make better choices today and improve their tomorrows. You will notice, however, that while the principles being taught are basically the same at each school, *how* the principles

---

* Video of some of the schools can be viewed at www.TheLeaderInMeBook.org.

are put into practice will vary—sometimes significantly—since each school has applied the principles according to what is the best fit for its specific needs, abilities, and resources. Yet as you observe the uniqueness of each school's approach, I challenge you to keep your keenest eye on the *principles*, not the *practices*. If you do, I am convinced you will discover more similarities than differences in the schools' equations for success. People and practices come and go, but principles of effective leadership will always remain the same—everywhere.

> All children smile in the same language.
> —*Quote displayed in an A.B. Combs hallway*

Second, observe **the universal nature and unique potential of children**. Children are born global. No matter where I travel, as I look into the eyes of children, particularly infants, I see the same kinds of energies and sparkles of hope. There is something common in them all. They are also born with great potential, some of which is unique to them. No two are born completely alike. Yet almost immediately following birth, their environment begins to shape them, and they begin taking on a sort of cultural DNA, or *sameness*. Much of that cultural DNA is good and even necessary for survival, but in too many cases it contains mutations that can ultimately rob them of their unique identity. I refer to them as "mutations" because they can *mute* a child's true potential. What a tragedy. In contrast, *The Leader in Me* is aimed at preventing or overriding some of these culturally embedded mutations. *The Leader in Me* assumes that all young people are good and that within each child are gifts to be unleashed. *The Leader in Me* assumes that every child is important and has something of worth to contribute. *The Leader in Me* assumes that within every child (and every educator) there are to be found true leadership qualities. Many such qualities are already visible and fully engaged in students' attitudes and behaviors, while others wait to be nurtured. These assumptions are not only foundational to the philosophy behind *The Leader in Me* but to the successes of these schools.

Third, observe that **the same principles and approach being taught at these schools can also be taught at home**. One of the great things about the

A.B. Combs has created a unique approach that has greatly enhanced the school's culture and improved student achievement, but, more important, is preparing students for life.

leadership approach is what it is doing to enhance the parent-school partnership. For starters, it is bringing more parents into the schools to volunteer and support school and classroom activities. But even more important is what is occurring as students apply the principles to their daily tasks and behaviors at home. In other words, it is not just teachers who are reporting better behaviors and reduced discipline issues. Parents are reporting the same kinds of positive results. This is particularly true in families where parents have come to know the principles for themselves and have made conscious efforts to reinforce and teach them. Bottom line: this book is not just about what schools can do, it is about what you can do in your own home. If you are a parent, I promise that if you open your mind to it, you will have endless ideas of how you can apply what these educators are doing to your home. So regardless of whether your child's school applies the leadership approach, you can apply it within the walls of your own home. (See chapter 10: Bringing It Home.)

Schools across the United States and various parts of the world, such as Chua Chu Kang Primary School in Singapore, are now implementing the leadership approach.

How the Book Is Organized

You may note by the book's size that it is not intended to pour out extensive detail. Rather, it is a starting place.

Since the leadership approach originated at A.B. Combs, and since it has the longest history of success, I have focused the first few chapters—chapters 2 through 5—on A.B. Combs. The biggest advantage of this is that it allows you as the reader to focus on one school and one overall approach without being forced to track multiple scenarios and strategies. These four chapters highlight why A.B. Combs chose to pursue the leadership approach and how it got under way, and provide key insights that they have learned along their journey. But do not let this emphasis lead you to think this is in any way a one-school or a one-country phenomenon. It is happening in multiple schools and in multiple parts of the world.

It is primarily in chapter 6 that I will give a sampling of what other elementary schools are doing to place their unique signatures on this evolving story. It is intriguing how creative the teachers and administrators have been at these schools.

While this book is intentionally centered on elementary schools, in chapter 7 we will briefly preview what is happening in some middle and high schools. I will also introduce what some creative districts are doing to use the leadership principles to redefine their cultures. In chapters 8 and 9, I provide a framework and insights for any school or district to consider when contemplating how it might go about implementing and localizing such a leadership approach. Finally, in chapter 10, I share some thoughts on how to bring the principles home.

So, yes, I must forewarn that some parts of what you are about to read may sound a bit "too good to be true." But I make no apologies because I am convinced that the stories coming out of these schools are not only *true,* they are *good*. And though none of the schools claim to be perfect or to have all the answers to the many dilemmas facing schools today, I also firmly believe that what these schools are doing is indeed bringing us closer to the *right* thing to be doing in preparing young people for today's realities and tomorrow's challenges.

2

Discovering What Parents, Business Leaders, and Teachers Want from a School

The research is clear: nothing motivates a child more than when learning is valued by schools and families/community working together in partnership . . . These forms of involvement do not happen by accident or even by invitation. They happen by explicit strategic intervention.

—Michael Fullan

I can think of no better way to introduce why A.B. Combs Elementary first got started teaching leadership principles to students than to share a few recollections from the school's principal, Muriel Summers. She has attempted to capture in a few words some of her best memories of the early days and how this all evolved. As you enjoy portions of her account, I think that you will quickly come to see that she clearly stands out as one of the great pioneers among the many educators and modern-day miracle workers referred to in this book. Here is Muriel's story in her own words:

My name is Muriel Thomas Summers. I grew up in Lilesville, North Carolina. My father died when I was ten years old, and my mother raised my sister and me, and continues to be my role model.

I went to the University of North Carolina at Chapel Hill. My early experience was hard since I did not know what path I wanted to take. I recall sitting on a bench one day literally praying for someone to tell me what to do. I felt a "calling," if you will, to go into teaching. I had always loved working with young children, and at the time I was working with preschoolers in one of the university's day-care centers. The moment I started my pursuit toward a career in education, I knew I had found my voice.

After graduation, I returned to Lilesville and taught for five years before moving to Maryland where I taught another seven years. There, I worked with many wonderful people including Joann Koehler, who said she saw in me something that I had never seen in myself—the potential to become a school administrator. Before that time, I had never envisioned myself out of the classroom. Her faith in me inspired a master's degree.

Eventually my family returned to North Carolina to be closer to our roots. Year one was spent as a first-grade teacher, after which I became an instructional resource teacher. The position of assistant principal came next.

I share a portion of Muriel's personal story because I firmly believe that the history and culture of any school—any organization—is largely grounded in the combined histories and philosophies of the people who walk its hallways. Surely, who Muriel and her colleagues are and where they came from plays an integral role in the history and culture of A.B. Combs, as will become more evident as Muriel's narration continues.

In 1998, I became principal of A.B. Combs Elementary in Raleigh, North Carolina. A.B. Combs was a good school, but not a high-performing school. It was a magnet school, which means there was supposed to be something unique about it that would attract students from outside normal boundaries. Unfortunately, the particular magnet being promoted at the time was not attracting many students. Only 350 students were enrolled.

In 1999, I attended a Stephen R. Covey presentation in Washington, D.C. I had been exposed to his work during my graduate studies in leadership, and was looking forward to hearing him in person. At one point during his speech, I became very emotional. I was looking around the room and saw that it was full of people who looked very successful. Everyone was hanging on to every word being said. I believe they were sensing the very same thing that I was sensing, that what Dr. Covey was sharing was a set of timeless, universal principles.

I found myself listening with the head of an administrator and the heart of a parent. And the more I listened, and the more I looked into the eyes of the people around me, the more I kept thinking, "Muriel, if you could teach this to young children, they would not have to wait until they were adults to learn these principles. If they looked through such a lens at an early age and continued to look through that lens for the rest of their lives, how different not only their lives might be, but how different our world might be."

Every break, I tried to muster up courage to ask Dr. Covey what his thoughts were about teaching the principles to young children. It was not until the last break when I finally got my nerve up. I caught him as he was exiting the stage and asked, "Dr. Covey, do you think these 7 *Habits* can be taught to young children?" His response to me was, "How young?" I said, "Five years old." He paused briefly, then let out a smile and said, "I don't know why not." To that he added, "Let me know if you ever do this." And that was the end of our conversation.

While I recall Muriel approaching me that day in Washington, D.C., I must confess that I failed to fully see the fire stirring in her eyes—in her heart—until I met her sometime later, when she was well on her way to achieving her vision at A.B. Combs. In fact, at the time of that first meeting, I do not believe that Muriel herself grasped the full measure of the flame that was beginning to grow within her. As she continues her story, observe how that flame surged the moment she and her staff were presented with a daunting challenge.

Little did I know of the influence that brief exchange with Dr. Covey would eventually have on my life. A few months later, our district superintendent called me in for a "reality chat." He informed me that our school was not attracting enough students to warrant its continuance, and either we had to come up with a new magnet theme or we would have to go back to being a traditional school. In other words, "Reinvent yourselves or be demagnetized." One week was the time he gave us to come up with a new theme, and "you will have no additional resources to do it with" was his parting encouragement.

My staff and I went to work trying to dream up the right school-saving solution. We talked to parents and we talked to community leaders about what they wanted in a school. We discussed with our teachers what they wanted for their own children. What was interesting was that they were all sending the same message. They wanted children to grow up to be responsible, caring, compassionate human beings who respected diversity and who knew how to do the right thing when faced with difficult decisions. Not once did we hear in all of our focus groups, "We want the best academics." I guess that strong academics were assumed, but the input we received had little to do with academics and much to do with character and basic life skills.

The 7 Habits of Highly Effective People

As Muriel sat among business leaders, she could not help but think, "If children learned the *7 Habits* at an early age, how different their lives might be and how different our world might be." Read the following synopses of the *7 Habits* and see if you come to the same conclusion.

Habit 1: Be Proactive

I am a responsible person. I take initiative. I choose my actions, attitudes, and moods. I do not blame others for my wrong actions. I do the right thing without being asked, even when no one is looking.

Habit 2: Begin with the End in Mind

I plan ahead and set goals. I do things that have meaning and make a difference. I am an important part of my classroom and contribute to my school's mission and vision, and look for ways to be a good citizen.

Habit 3: Put First Things First

I spend my time on things that are most important. This means I say no to things I know I should not do. I set priorities, make a schedule, and follow my plan. I am disciplined and organized.

Habit 4: Think Win-Win

I balance courage for getting what I want with consideration for what others want. I make deposits in others' Emotional Bank Accounts. When conflicts arise, I look for third alternatives.

Habit 5: Seek First to Understand, Then to Be Understood

I listen to other people's ideas and feelings. I try to see things from their viewpoints. I listen to others without interrupting. I am confident in voicing my ideas. I look people in the eyes when talking.

Habit 6: Synergize

I value other people's strengths and learn from them. I get along well with others, even people who are different than me. I work well in groups. I seek out other people's ideas to solve problems because I know that by teaming with others we can create better solutions than any one of us alone. I am humble.

Habit 7: Sharpen the Saw

I take care of my body by eating right, exercising, and getting sleep. I spend time with family and friends. I learn in lots of ways and lots of places, not just at school. I take time to find meaningful ways to help others.

When Muriel left the superintendent's office knowing she had only one week to come up with a new magnet theme, she literally cried all the way back to A.B. Combs. She called her assistant principal, Gailya Winters, who, according to Muriel, "does not allow us to wallow for one minute in anything but excellence." Gailya's response was "Snap out of it. We will figure this one out."

> The world is very complicated and changing. The challenges we face today are not the same challenges young people will face tomorrow. So we felt the best way to anchor our students was through teaching timeless principles.
>
> —Mr. Francis Foo, Principal, Chua Chu Kang Primary School, Singapore

Together they went to the teachers and said, "We want to remain a magnet school." They felt strongly about that because they prized the rich level of diversity they enjoyed as a result of being a magnet school. The teachers agreed and met to discuss options. What is impressive is that instead of sitting around a whiteboard or going off for team-building exercises, they made it their first order of business to go to their stakeholders and find out what they wanted most from a school. What follows is some of what they discovered, as well as brief references to confirming research.

What Parents Want from Schools

Naturally, one of the first stakeholders A.B. Combs went to for input was parents. After all, parents have a huge say in what school their children will attend, so who better is there to approach for feedback on how to increase enrollment? Muriel arranged for some one-on-one conversations and a few focus groups. These were frank discussions. As noted previously, what parents said they wanted their children to gain from school was the ability to get along with others and to be responsible. They wanted their children to be tolerant of people's differences, to become problem solvers, and to learn to be creative. These parent responses were no big surprise to Muriel or her team; they had heard it all before. What did surprise them, however, was what the parents left out of their comments. Not one parent mentioned anything about academics. Not one.

Keep in mind that the time frame for all of this getting under way was the latter part of 1999. The 1990s is sometimes referred to as the "back-to-the-basics" decade in education. Emphasis during those years was narrowed to the three Rs—reading, writing, and arithmetic—mostly at the insistence of parents. But as the 1990s were coming to a close, change was in the air. Some believe it was the gunshots of Columbine High School in Littleton, Colorado, in April 1999 that rattled parents and educators into once more thinking beyond the three Rs, as many parents started becoming more concerned about their child's physical and emotional safety at school than they were about their academics.

But in hindsight, it is clear that trends were beginning to sway well before the Columbine incident, and they were not unique to A.B. Combs. In fact, I find it interesting that at about the same time the *7 Habits* book was being launched in 1989, university researchers were beginning to reveal a dramatic shift in philosophy in terms of what parents want for their children. The shift was being tracked by University of Michigan sociologist Duane Alwin, who was comparing "modern" data to data collected in the 1920s. Alwin noted that in the 1920s, parents emphasized obedience, conformity, respect for home and religion, and good manners as being top traits they desired in their children. But by early 1990s, what parents desired even more for their children was the ability to think for themselves, to take responsibility for their lives, to show initiative, and to be tolerant of diversity. Basically these were the same types of things the A.B. Combs parents were requesting.

What do you suppose was behind the shift in parents' thinking?

Alwin concluded that the changing global economy was at the heart of the shift. "It's an increasingly complex world," he said. "Parents want their children to succeed in it, to survive in it. They know that good jobs require being able to think for yourself." He added that parents themselves had become more educated and able to think on their own feet, and they wanted that same level of empowerment to be passed on to their children.

Parent buy-in and involvement lends beauty to the sustained success of A.B. Combs.

Nearly two decades have passed since Alwin reported his findings and we have now crossed into the twenty-first century. If anything, the need for young people to be more self-reliant and more responsible has increased— exponentially. And the trend is global. In fact, the level of change that has engulfed North America, Europe, and the South Pacific over the past few years is absolutely mild when compared to the changes that have hit Central and South America, Africa, the Middle East, and Asia. In Asia, for example, where several countries have shifted almost overnight from being mere assemblers and exporters of technology to heavy users of technology—especially among their cyber-savvy youth—vast cultural transformations have taken place. Wages have increased, working hours have increased, the number of mothers in the workforce has increased, and a whole array of Western influences have gushed in, including clothing styles, music, fast food, and new, more independent ways of thinking.

In reaction to the speed and breadth of these changes, Asian parents have become more concerned about their children's education, with an emphasis on four areas: 1) *Technology:* Asian parents want their children more versed in technology; 2) *Global skills:* Asian parents recognize the global nature of their new world and want their children prepared to meet the world, including knowing how to work with people of diverse backgrounds; 3) *Analytical and life skills:* Parents want their students able to get beyond factual knowledge by gaining strong analytical, creativity, and team skills; 4) *Asian values:* while Asian parents want their children astute in each of these first three areas, they know that all three carry potential downsides. Little panics them more, for example, than the downsides of technology, such as addictions to games or pornography. Their concern about the global skills is the fear they have of losing their children to the world as they forget their home roots. But more than anything, the one common thread in parents' concerns is their sense that long-standing, traditional mores of their society—what they call "Asian values"—are being weakened amid the haste and complexities of today's world. These include such values as honesty, respect, and close family ties.

> We want our children to have Malaysian hearts, global minds.
> —*Dato' Teo Chiang Quan, Chairman, Paramount Corporation, Malaysia*

What parents are experiencing in Asia is being felt by parents everywhere. In the place of Asia, I could substitute the name of almost any country or city in the world and not be far off in my description. It is a global tsunami. No matter where I go, I hear parents echoing the same issues: "The world has changed. I want my child to keep up with technology, to be more creative, to make better decisions, and to be better able to team with people of varied backgrounds. At the same time, I want them to be good, honest, well-mannered, self-directed, respectful, disciplined, and honorable citizens."

Another reflection of what A.B. Combs was hearing from parents is found in a recent study of American adult attitudes on education commissioned by the Partnership for 21st Century Skills and titled *Beyond the Three Rs*. (See table below.) What borders on "stunning" is where adults rated as a nine or ten on a ten-point scale the importance of such subjects as problem solving, teamwork and collaboration, self-direction, leadership, creativity, and global awareness in relation to some of the more traditional subjects such as math and science.

Adult Attitudes on Education

	% who rank this skill as a **9 or 10** in importance on a scale of 0 to 10
Reading comprehension	75
Computer and technology skills	71
Critical thinking and problem-solving skills	69
Ethics and social responsibility	62
Written communications	58
Teamwork and collaboration	57
Oral communications	56
Lifelong learning and self-direction	50
Mathematics	48
Leadership	44
Creativity and innovation	43
Media literacy	42
Global awareness	42
Science (biology, chemistry, and physics)	38

In the same data, note where "ethics and social responsibility" are ranked. I find this interesting in light of the fact that not long ago, terms such as *ethics* and *character* and *social responsibility* were almost banned from the field of education. The prevailing attitude was "Those are to be taught at home; they are not the school's business." And indeed, I think most people still agree that parents shoulder primary responsibility for teaching ethics and social responsibility. But in too many cases that simply is not happening. As Principal Dan Jeffers of Lemon Bay High School in Englewood, Florida, pointed out, "Basic character traits and life skills used to be taught to young people at home, at church, and at school—all three. But nowadays the home can no longer be assumed reliable, church attendance by youth is at a minimum, and many schools are no longer teaching character-related topics or interpersonal skills due to heavy pressures to focus on core subjects."

> People ask, "Don't students come to you with these habits? Don't they learn them at home or at church?" But students don't always come with these habits. So why leave it to chance whether or not a child has these skills? Why not level the playing field and give every child the opportunity to have these skills?
> —*Jeanne Payne, Professional Development Coordinator, Decatur City Schools, Alabama*

I have reported here a few of the research findings that match what A.B. Combs was hearing parents say they wanted from a school. But in my mind, the real evidence that signals what parents at A.B. Combs want from a school is not so much what parents are *saying* as much as it is what parents are *doing*. In other words, it is evidenced by the fact since the leadership theme was implemented, enrollment at A.B. Combs has increased from 350 to over 800 students. It is evidenced by parents who drive forty minutes each way or stay in cheaper homes than they can afford to keep their children at A.B. Combs. It is evidenced by the tears that flow as parents tell of what A.B. Combs staff members have done for their children. It is evidenced by the parent (and several have done this kind of thing) who said to Muriel, "Look, I am a physical therapist and I will come in and volunteer my services or do whatever I can if my child can get in this school." Yes, these types of things speak volumes about what parents want from a school.

What the Business Community Wants

Another key stakeholder that A.B. Combs approached in identifying their new magnet theme was the local business community. Many educators would say that was a gutsy move. Entrepreneurs, MBAs, engineers, programmers, sales folks, lawyers, CEOs, and the like can combine to make for a cocky, ornery, and opinionated crowd. That is why many educators prefer to shy away from them, unless of course they are looking for a sponsor to fund an activity. That attitude by itself, as you might imagine, does little to enamor business leaders who are weary of being told, "We appreciate your interest, but we do not need your opinions. Your money will suffice."

For sure, relations between schools and business leaders have not always been fully cordial. Most educators do not make a lot of noise about it, but quietly they will tell you they do not like businesspeople meddling in their affairs. They feel that too many businesspeople talk about students as if they are widgets that can be mass-produced with zero defects. They are quick to point out that while businesses can hire who they want and when they want, schools are compelled to take whoever walks in the door and must do it whenever they happen to arrive. It does not matter if a new student speaks only a foreign language, just came from juvenile corrections, has a learning disorder, has emotional issues, or flat out does not want to be in school. None of that matters. Schools feel an obligation to give them every chance to receive an education, which means schools do not have the luxury of laying off 30 percent of their lowest-performing students to improve their end-of-year, bottom-line results. So, no, educators do not always appreciate businesspeople acting like the experts and saying, "What's wrong? Can't you figure it out? Let us tell you how to educate kids."

At the same time, many business leaders do feel a frustration with schools. A good portion of them view schools through bifocals, one lens being the view they get as parents or grandparents, the other being the lens through which they view the coming workforce. Regardless of which lens they are gazing through, what they want to see and what they are getting are often not one and the same.

For years, business leaders have been content to remain at arm's length and merely point fingers, but that is another thing that is changing in the new economy. Invited or not, more and more corporate entities are getting off their spectator chairs and becoming involved with schools.

Take for instance the U.S. Chamber of Commerce, which has begun publishing an annual state-by-state report card on schools called *Leaders and Laggards*. Listen to the tone of a recent report:

The United States in the twenty-first century faces unprecedented economic and social challenges, ranging from the forces of global competition to the impending retirement of 77 million baby boomers. Succeeding in this new era will require our children to be prepared for the intellectual demands of the modern workplace and a far more complex society. Yet the evidence indicates that our country is not ready. Despite decades of reform efforts and many trillions of dollars in public investment, U.S. schools are not equipping our children with the skills and knowledge they—and the nation—so badly need.

It has been nearly a quarter century since the seminal report *A Nation at Risk* was issued in 1983. Since that time, a knowledge-based economy has emerged, the Internet has reshaped commerce and communication, exemplars of creative commerce like Microsoft, eBay, and Southwest Airlines have revolutionized the way we live, and the global economy has undergone wrenching change. Throughout that period, education spending has steadily increased and rafts of well-intentioned school reforms have come and gone. But student achievement has remained stagnant, and our K–12 schools have stayed remarkably unchanged—preserving, as if in amber, the routines, culture, and operations of an obsolete 1930s manufacturing plant. . . . Only about two-thirds of all 9th graders graduate from high school within four years. And those students who do receive diplomas are too often unprepared for college or the modern workplace.

Despite such grim data, for too long the business community has been willing to leave education to the politicians and the educators—standing aside and contenting itself with offers of money, support, and good will. But each passing year makes it clear that more, much more, is needed. America's dynamic and immensely productive private sector is the envy of the world. Are there ways in which business expertise, dynamism, accountability, and problem solving could improve our schools? . . . The Chamber and its partners firmly believe that the traits that have long made the American private sector an engine of global prosperity—its dynamism, creativity, and relentless focus on efficiency and results—are essential to tapping the potential of our educators and schools.

The chamber's report mirrors much of what worries the business world about both the economy and education in general. And the more that global pressures put the heat on businesses, the more vocal the business leaders are becoming about the education of its oncoming workforce. So what we have is a business world that is frustrated with schools and educators who are annoyed with what they see as arrogant and naïve business leaders. Fingers are being pointed in both directions.

In contrast, neither A.B. Combs nor its community of business leaders is pointing fingers at anyone. Rather they are putting their heads and hearts together to focus on the common goal of helping young people. Muriel sees her business community not as ornery customers, but as friends and partners. They in turn are not only applauding what is happening at A.B. Combs, but are asking, "How can we help?"

So what is it about A.B. Combs that is attracting business leaders? Part of the answer goes back to what Muriel and her team learned when they asked local business leaders what they wanted from schools. One of their responses was to hand over a list of the Top 10 Qualities & Skills Employers Seek. It was their way of saying, "These are the traits we want in our employees, so it would be nice if schools could somehow produce these same traits in their students and graduates." The list:

- Communication skills (verbal and written)
- Honesty/Integrity
- Teamwork skills
- Interpersonal skills
- Self-motivation/Initiative
- Strong work ethic
- Analytical skills
- Technology skills
- Organizational skills
- Creative minds

Such lists seem to be growing both in quantity and in similarity. Most educators, for example, are familiar with Daniel Goleman's research demonstrating that Emotional Intelligence (EQ) is a better predictor of both academic and life success than is IQ. Goleman is now reporting similar evidence in the workplace that suggests that along with technical and intellectual skills, corporate leaders need the following types of traits and competencies if they are to succeed in the present business climate:

Displays and reminders are scattered throughout classrooms to remind students of the leadership theme.

Personal Competence

Self-awareness

Self-assessment

Self-confidence

Self-control

Transparency

Adaptability

Achievement

Initiative

Optimism

Social Competence

Empathy

Organizational awareness

Service

Inspirational leadership

Developing others

Creating change

Conflict management

Building bonds

Teamwork and collaboration

Whether one looks at the "Top 10" list, Goleman's list, or one of the many other such lists in existence, it is quickly apparent that what the business community wants and needs schools to produce in students goes well beyond the ability to read, write, and use a calculator. What they want can be captured in two words, *character* and *competence*, which also happen to be the core components of primary greatness. Most business leaders know all too well that deficiencies in both character and basic life skills in their employees are costing their companies dearly every day, and they are desperately hoping that schools can help out in both regards. In most cases, they sense they can teach competence, but find character tough to tutor. In fact, my friend Jim Collins reports in his book *Good to Great* that when hiring or promoting people:

> . . . the good-to-great companies placed greater weight on character attributes than on specific educational background, practical skills, specialized knowledge, or work experience. Not that specific knowledge or skills are unimportant, but they viewed these traits as more teachable (or at least learnable), whereas they believed dimensions like character, work ethic, basic intelligence, dedication to fulfilling commitments, and values are more ingrained.

> **The first thing I look at when hiring is skills. Skills get people in the door to be interviewed. But what gets them hired and what keeps them hired is character.**
>
> —*Donnie Lane, CEO, Enersolv*

I read about A.B. Combs in *The 8th Habit,* so when I was in Raleigh I made arrangements to visit the school. What I saw was beyond any preconceived expectations.

Near the end of my visit, I was asked to speak to the students, and I was telling them a number of things that really impressed me about them and their school. It was a lengthy list. At one point, one of the students, I believe he was a third-grader, raised his hand and politely asked, "Mr. Cherng, you have told us about the good things we are doing at our school, but what about the 'deltas'? You know . . . the things we need to do better."

The young man was totally serious. He sincerely wanted to know how they could improve the school. He spoke as though he was one of the leaders of the school who could potentially enact the changes. The great thing is that he was, as were all the students at A.B. Combs. They are all leaders, and all are taking ownership for the school.

—*Andrew Cherng*

When we recruit leaders, we like to see people who are able to project their passion, who have self-confidence, and who have the right attitude to really face the unknowns and the uncertainties that we all face every day in our personal or career lives. I saw all those traits in the children at A.B. Combs.

—*Peggy Cherng*

Peggy and Andrew Cherng, Founders, Panda Express (A video of the Cherngs can be found at TheLeaderinMeBook.org).

But do not be misled. While the demand for character is at some of its highest levels ever, it is not just more character that business leaders are seeking. They are also pleading for basic life skills. Look again at the lists. What about planning and goal-setting skills, decision-making skills, conflict management skills, teamwork skills, time management skills, self-assessment skills, listening skills, presentation skills, and creativity skills? Where do students get such everyday life skills? In too many schools, the answer is "Not here." At these other schools that you will soon learn more about, such skills and traits are at the core of everything they do.

What Teachers Want

We hear so much about what parents and businesses want from schools that it is easy to forget to ask, "What do teachers want?" But A.B. Combs was quick to involve teachers in the decision of what the new magnet theme would be.

To be sure, what A.B. Combs's teachers did not want was "one more thing" to have to teach. Yet when Leslie Reilly from the Seminole County Public Schools District in Florida visited A.B. Combs, it was a matter of minutes before she declared, "This is exactly what I have always wanted as a teacher!" The interesting thing is that she did not view what she was seeing as another subject matter being added to an already compact menu of things to teach. Instead, she saw it as a place where students could thrive and where teachers' creativity was unleashed while doing the same types of activities and the same amounts of work as any other typical teacher.

> This is not "one more thing" we have to do. This is a better way of doing what we already do.
>
> —*Bertie Norton, Principal, Nash Elementary, Texarkana, Texas*

Before they enter the profession, teachers have a good sense of what types of issues await them. Yet despite the realities, including challenges with students and parents, still they choose to join the teaching ranks. More often than not, what propels them is a combined interest in both teaching and in working with young people. But what underlies and truly fuels that interest is teachers' genuine desire to make a difference. Many look back to their own schooling and remember a teacher who had a significant, if not life-changing, influence on them. Their chief desire is to be that same type of influence for good on individual students, if only in a small way.

Yet teachers do not want to teach just for the sake of teaching. They want what they teach to be relevant—lessons that will help students successfully engage in life both in and out of school. They are not naïve about what parents and business leaders are asking for, and, if anything, they want the same. After all, many teachers have children of their own in school. So that is one reason why many teachers are joining forces with parents and businesses to address these very issues. For example, the Partnership for 21st Century Skills, mentioned earlier, is a joint undertaking between businesses and educators. Working in tandem, they also have identified many of the same subjects already discussed as being vital to the futures of today's students, as illustrated in the following framework:

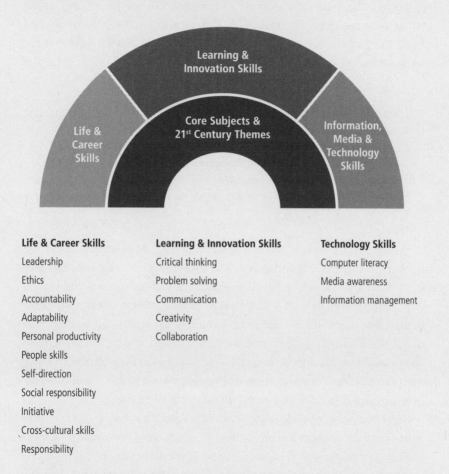

Life & Career Skills

Leadership

Ethics

Accountability

Adaptability

Personal productivity

People skills

Self-direction

Social responsibility

Initiative

Cross-cultural skills

Responsibility

Learning & Innovation Skills

Critical thinking

Problem solving

Communication

Creativity

Collaboration

Technology Skills

Computer literacy

Media awareness

Information management

Smack in the center of the illustration are "core subjects" traditionally taught in schools, such as math, science, reading, writing, history, geography, health, arts, and language. Indeed, no one is advocating removing these subjects from the curriculum. But the partnership *is* promoting greater integration of these core subjects with other topics relevant to the twenty-first century, such as financial management, global awareness, economics, entrepreneurship, and civic awareness. Additionally, they are advocating that more attention be given to the outer bow, which contains subjects that for years have been on "nice-to-do-if-you-somehow-miraculously-find-the-time" lists or offered as electives. The partnership is asserting that they no longer see the outer bow subjects as optional. Glance particularly at the topics designated under the Life & Career and Learning & Innovation Skills categories. Are those not essentially the very same subjects that the business leaders and parents were requesting?

> I have taught school for over thirty-one years and I can say without hesitation that this is the best thing I have ever been involved with professionally. These are principles kids can take with them for the rest of their lives. They discover for themselves who they are and what they can do. In the process it has helped me to organize my own life.
>
> —*Vicki Mallory, Teacher, Dewey Elementary, Quincy, Illinois*

But let us also be real and not forget that as noble and heroic as most teachers' intentions are, and as much as they do want to make a difference in students' lives, they also have some personal wants that go beyond issues of pay for performance. Teachers want to enjoy a sense of dignity and pride in their profession. They want to be treated with respect. They want good collegial relationships. They want to be organized and to feel some semblance of control over their time and what happens in their classroom. They want their talents utilized and developed. They want to enjoy their life outside the classroom. What teacher does not want these things?

But once again, the real sign of what teachers want in a school is less what they are *saying* as it is what they are *doing*. And just as with parents, one thing that many A.B. Combs teachers are doing is driving long distances to get to the school even though closer options are plentiful. In a day when it is increasingly common for public school teachers to send their children to private or charter schools, at A.B. Combs several teachers bring their children with them because they believe so strongly in the culture of the school. In fact, thirty-five of the students at A.B. Combs belong to teachers. And though a few teachers have chosen to leave A.B. Combs for various reasons, when a teacher position opens up there are literally hundreds of teachers who have heard of A.B. Combs and who apply to fill the vacancy—a far cry from so many schools who search far and wide for teacher candidates.

What Students Want

A.B. Combs's primary focus with stakeholders was to ask parents, business leaders, and teachers what they wanted from a school, and clearly it was those stakeholders' input that steered the school toward its new magnet theme. But what do students want from a school? How often do they even get asked?

> What students need to succeed in the twenty-first century is an education that is both academically rigorous and "real-world" relevant. This objective of rigor and relevance is not just for some students, it is for all students.
>
> —Dr. Willard Daggett

Not long ago, a young boy walked into Muriel's office wanting to talk. Soon tears were flowing. His father was serving in the military in Iraq, and the boy missed his dad dearly. The boy had an interesting assessment of the situation. He looked at Muriel through dripping eyes and said, "If everyone in the world was taught how to live like we are taught to live at A.B. Combs, my daddy would not be in Iraq."

We do not need to travel to far-off countries to find battle zones. With all the violence, swearing, cheating, drug issues, graffiti, hazing, bullying, and emotional batterings that go on, many schools (and even homes) have become virtual war zones. Some campuses are scary to walk onto. Yet I firmly believe that most students are good kids. All most of them want from a school is to get a good education, to be with some friends, and to have a little fun—though admittedly not always in that order. But above all they want peace of mind, and they are quick to notice if it is not present.

Whenever the opportunity presents itself, which is quite often at A.B. Combs, students are given the chance to share their talents and become comfortable performing around adults.

Peace of mind shows up on students' faces, in their behaviors, and in their test scores. It comes as a result of four basic needs being met:

- *Physical:* Safety, good health, food, exercise, shelter, and hygiene
- *Social-emotional:* Acceptance, kindness, friendship, the desire to love and to be loved
- *Mental:* Intellectual growth, creativity, and stimulating challenges
- *Spiritual:* Contribution, meaning, and uniqueness

Since not all four of these needs are met in every home, many students come to school hungry for them—in some cases practically starving. Though educators like to imagine their profession being focused on the mental need, one of many teachers' first career surprises is just how much effort and time they must put into meeting students' physical needs. Many schools, for example, have a large percentage of students who must be fed breakfast before any classroom time can be reasonably logged. It is tough to teach an empty stomach. Some schools have laundry facilities and showers so students can have a chance of enjoying good hygiene. And at all schools, teachers spend a significant amount of time dealing with safety issues— protecting kids from adults, from one another, and from natural disasters.

On top of the physical needs are the social-emotional needs. Any teacher can tell of the hours they spend mending emotional wounds. Many cases involve trivial if not downright humorous matters, while others are outright tragic. A critical factor in student achievement is what educators call *connectedness.* When students do not feel socially or emotionally connected to school or to life in general—whether it be through a peer, a parent, a teacher, a coach, or some other person they can trust or turn to for help— chances of them doing well in school diminish rapidly and the likelihood of delinquent behavior increases.

So along with the mental needs, teachers must clearly be prepared to address the physical and social-emotional needs. But perhaps the greatest need that teachers impact each and every day is the spiritual need. The word *spiritual* has its roots in *spirit,* for which dictionaries provide many definitions, most of which are nonreligious in nature, such as "disposition of mind or outlook" or "a mental disposition characterized by firmness or assertiveness." Thesauruses likewise put forward many synonyms for *spirit,* including *disposition, courage, determination, vigor, will, moral fiber, heart, enthusiasm, inner self, fortitude,* and *strength.* Combine the dictionary definitions with these synonyms, and that is what I am referring to here when speaking of young people's spirits, or spiritual needs.

Many teachers underestimate the role they play in either nourishing or draining students' spirits. Too many young people lose a lot of their spirit before they leave the school system. It is a tough world they face and often the crudeness of it seeps into their feelings of self-worth. They want to feel appreciated, but too often the world tells them they are not. I strongly believe that the most harmful form of identity theft in today's society is not what is happening in our economy but in our youth. Today's young people are constantly pressured by the media and peers into becoming somebody other than who they in their heart of hearts want to be. To be "cool" they are told they have to act a certain way. To be "hot" they sense they need to wear a specific fashion or hang out with a certain crowd. Some get labeled only by their test scores. What deplorable messages to be sending to young people! Depriving young people of their feelings of worth and uniqueness is, in my mind, the worst imaginable form of identity theft. Sometimes it is only a caring, perceptive teacher who can prevent that crime from occurring.

> Treat a man as he is and you make him worse than he is. Treat a man as he has the potential to become and you make him better than he is.
>
> —*Goethe*

After speaking with stakeholders, A.B. Combs chose leadership as its new magnet theme.

Every young person wants to grow and to be appreciated—to have all four needs addressed, to be treated as a whole child. These are natural longings of the human spirit. And so young people are quick to attach themselves to teachers and principals who know how to bring out the best in them, who help them feel unique and important, and who build their feelings of self-worth. One of my favorite definitions of *leadership* that I have used over the years is this: "Leadership is communicating people's worth and potential so clearly that they are inspired to see it in themselves." Is that not also the essence of good teaching?

Developing Leaders One Child at a Time

Muriel concludes her account of how it all began at A.B. Combs and of their visits with stakeholders with the following statement:

> As we listened to what parents and business leaders were saying, I could not help but reflect on my experience with Dr. Covey and how closely the *7 Habits* matched what the parents and community leaders were wanting us to teach students. I shared my D.C. experience with the staff and one thing led to another. In short, the theme that kept surfacing in all of our discussions was *leadership*. "That's it!" we thought. "We will use leadership as our theme."

Soon the school had a new mission statement: *To Develop Leaders One Child at a Time.* They wanted the clear message sent to each child that his or her worth exceeds anything that is ever placed on any grade report or any score on a test. They wanted to ensure that no student of theirs would ever feel so hopeless or desperate to consider being a part of any action so tragic as those at Columbine. And those are the reasons, the purposes, and the account behind how and why "leadership" was chosen as the school's new magnet theme and how the early seeds of success took root at A.B. Combs. *Leadership* was the umbrella term they would use to encompass the many character traits and basic life competencies that parents, business leaders, educators, and even students were all voicing in common.

I believe that, as a whole, today's young people represent the brightest and most talented generation ever to walk the planet earth. They have more adaptability, knowledge, ingenuity, and resources to access than any prior generation on record. But as I travel the world, my mind cannot help but pause occasionally to ponder, What kind of future awaits these great young people? What is in store for them?

A.B. Combs determined that its mission would focus on developing leadership qualities in students, one child at a time.

Nobody fully knows what the future will encompass, but it does not take a great visionary to foresee that it will be an adventure like none other. Already the world of business has taken on a new shape, as technology has "flattened" the global playing field and stiff competition is rearing its head in every industry and impacting every household. The caliber and pace of such trends have every concerned parent asking, "Will my child have the competencies and qualities of character necessary to succeed in the future?" They likewise have dedicated educators scrambling to determine, "What must we do to better prepare students for what lies ahead?" And I assure you that the same trends have corporate executives and government leaders seriously wondering, "Will the coming workforce have what it takes to keep our organization competitive in the new era?"

But forget the future for a moment. What about today? After all, are there not enough challenges facing young people today without bringing up tomorrow? Are not most parents' greatest concerns more immediate, such as, "What choices will my child make when he goes out the door and out of my sight, today?" Are not most teachers more fixed on, "What lesson plans do I need to have ready, today?" than they are on "What future career will best fit Susie in ten years?" I can say with confidence that most executives are more concerned about today's bottom line than they are about tomorrow's workforce. Surely most young people are far more interested in "What's for lunch, today?" or "Who will I hang out with after school, today?" than they are about what company will hire them out of college. That is exactly why I believe that parents, teachers, business leaders, and even students are so enthused by what is happening at A.B. Combs and these other schools. Not only are they teaching skills that will impact students' futures, but they are teaching skills and principles that are making an immediate impact, today. Students are making better choices, today. And that, in my opinion, is what stakeholders want most from a school, and why so many feel this is the right thing to be doing.

3

Crafting a Blueprint for Leadership

> In my previous experience teaching character education, it was
> not imbedded in everything we did. We would stop and say we
> are going to talk about "being responsible" this month and next
> month we're going to talk about "kindness." I think it's
> apparent that that does not work.
>
> —*Muriel Summers*

C hoosing leadership as its new magnet theme and coming up
with a purposeful mission statement were major steps forward
for A.B. Combs. But the real beauty in it was that what started
out as a nice idea to sell to the district to keep the school's magnet status
alive quickly grew into an impassioned quest that the teachers wholeheartedly bought into themselves. And the more they researched the idea and
synergized, the more their passion grew.

The big question, however, was "How?" How would they go about
teaching leadership to students as young as five years old? In other words,
it was nice that they had a new theme and a mission, but how would they
actually pull it off?

Leadership is a broad term made up of scores of subtopics, not all of
which are well suited to elementary-aged children. So the A.B. Combs team
knew that before they got too far into their efforts they would need to sift
out what exactly leadership would mean at their school. One step they took
to add more clarity was to create a vision statement that students could relate
to and that would represent specific goals and actions students could focus
upon. It was built around the four needs, or the whole child, and it reads:

Our school's vision is To Live, to Love, to Learn, to Leave a Legacy
We <u>Live</u> by striving to be the best we can be
We <u>Love</u> by caring for others
We <u>Learn</u> by working hard in school and always doing our best
We <u>Leave a Legacy</u> by sharing our school with others and trying to make a difference in the world.

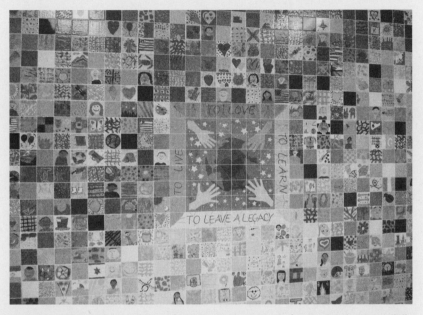

A tile mural made by students stands at the entry of A.B. Combs as a daily reminder of the school's vision statement.

Both the mission and vision statements are visible throughout the school in hallways and in classrooms. They even have a large tile mural of the vision statement mounted on the wall in the school's entry foyer. It is crafted from individual tiles designed by students and is intended to remind them of why they come to school each day.

While both the mission and vision statements were inspiring, A.B. Combs knew that the statements would only take on true value and meaning to the extent that they had a clear and viable strategy, or *blueprint,* for how they would accomplish their purposes and vision. That included knowing what leadership would mean at the school. Based upon Muriel's experience at the seminar in Washington, D.C., they felt that one of the most natural places to begin their search for what they would teach in the way of leadership was in the *7 Habits*. Some of the teachers had also been exposed to Malcolm Baldrige quality principles and had an inkling that something in those principles would fit nicely into their approach to teaching leadership. So the *7 Habits* and the Baldrige principles were two of the first places they initially went for guidance.

A *7 Habits* Fit?

What A.B. Combs quickly discovered was that the *7 Habits* are not a random list of seven discrete ideas. The habits are organized into a sequential, progressive model. The first three habits—Be Proactive, Begin with the End in Mind, and Put First Things First—combine to help a person become more *independent*. I call this the *Private Victory*. When put into practice, these three habits enable a person to be more responsible, to take more control of their life, to map out their future, to establish priorities, and to execute a plan by staying disciplined and focused. Embedded in the three habits are time management skills, planning skills, goal-setting skills, and other basic organizing skills that are foundational to independence, or *self-leadership*.

> The *7 Habits* are like vitamins. They can be found in all kinds of places and are needed whether you are aware of it or not. They can be mixed together, or taken one at a time. You don't need just the vitamins or just the *7 Habits* to live. However, you're healthier, happier, and more successful when the habits are a daily part of your life.
>
> —*Arlene Kai, Student from China, A.B. Combs Elementary*

But as the A.B. Combs staff discovered, neither the business world nor parents view independence as the ultimate "end in mind" for either their employees or their children. While being independent is important to succeed in our changed-and-changing world, people also need to be equipped to work effectively with other people and within teams. That is why habits four, five, and six—Think Win-Win; Seek First to Understand, Then to be Understood; and Synergize—are so vital. All three of these habits lead a person toward becoming more *interdependent*. They entail insights into how to communicate effectively and how to balance courage with consideration, and how to problem solve with others. Combined, they encompass conflict resolution skills, listening skills, creativity skills, and teamwork skills, and lead to what I call the *Public Victory*.

Finally, Habit 7, Sharpen the Saw, wraps around all the other habits by embracing the principle of renewal. It is the habit that enables people to stay fit for today's world in four critical areas—physical, social-emotional, mental, and spiritual. You will recognize those four areas as rooted in the four basic needs that allow young people—all people—to feel greater peace of mind.

That is a very brief synopsis of how the *7 Habits* work together. Again, I did not invent the habits. I merely organized them in a logical, meaningful sequence. They are based on extensive research I conducted while studying highly effective people via interviews and literature on leadership. They are also based upon timeless, universal principles that have been around for ages, and that transcend all cultural boundaries and socioeconomic layers. And my guess is that even from the very brief and cursory overview provided above you were able to sense that the *7 Habits* sound very consistent with what parents, teachers, and business leaders were telling A.B. Combs they wanted students to acquire. That is because they *are* very consistent (see table below). So it was no real surprise that the A.B. Combs team quickly deemed the *7 Habits* a natural fit for integration into their approach to teaching leadership to students.

What Parents, Businesses, and Teachers Want for Students	The 7 Habits of Highly Effective People
Independence	
Initiative, self-motivation	*Habits 1–3*
Self-confidence	Be Proactive
Planning skills	Begin with the End in Mind
Goal setting skills	Put First Things First
Organization/Time management	
Interdependence	
Conflict management skills	*Habits 4–6*
Communication skills (both listening and presentation skills)	Think Win-Win (balancing courage with consideration for others)

Honesty	Seek First to Understand, then to be Understood
Fairness	Synergize
Openness to suggestions	
Teamwork	
Problem solving	
Decision making	
Creativity	
Renewal	
Technical skills	*Habit 7*
Good health and hygiene	Sharpen the Saw
Emotional stability	• Physical
Analytical skills	• Emotional
Involvement in meaningful work	• Mental
	• Spiritual

In 2004, when I wrote *The 8th Habit*, which is to Find Your Voice and Help Others Find Theirs, A.B. Combs quickly added the new habit to their repertoire, largely because it fit so strategically with what they were already doing to help each individual student find their gifts and then to help them optimize and expand those gifts.

The *7 Habits* are taught to students starting in kindergarten in very basic terms and in all varieties of ways, including through posters, stories, games, toys, movies, drama, poetry, contests, writing assignments, and art. One of students' favorite methods of learning the habits is through music. Try singing these Habit One lyrics that were "proactively" created by first grade teacher Paula Everett, to the tune of "Twinkle, Twinkle, Little Star."

> *Be Proactive Every Day,*
> *Be Proactive, Stop and Think.*
> *Even though it's hard to do,*
> *I think you should try it too.*
> *Be Proactive Every Day,*
> *Be Proactive, Stop and Think.*

Baldrige Tools

For many reasons, it was also easy for A.B. Combs staff to determine they would incorporate some of the Baldrige quality principles into what they would teach students about leadership. For those not familiar with Baldrige, a little background may be helpful.

Howard Malcolm Baldrige became U.S. secretary of commerce under President Ronald Reagan in 1981. The year before he had been named Professional Rodeo Man of the Year, which undoubtedly made him something of a political novelty. At the time, the United States' economic dominance in the world was being challenged for the first time in decades, even on the frontiers of space. It was no coincidence that during this same period citizens started questioning the effectiveness of schools, as evidenced by the dreary report on U.S. education, *A Nation at Risk*, which came out in 1983.

Baldrige took a two-horned approach to reversing the decline in U.S. commercial prominence. On the one hand, he focused outward by working to open trade doors to countries such as China, India, and the Soviet Union, so that U.S. companies would have increased opportunity to expand. But he knew that just getting into those markets was no guarantee of success, since American firms would be up against competitors that paid far lower wages. The only way U.S. companies would be able to compete profitably would be through higher-quality products and greater efficiencies. So Baldrige's second approach focused inward by taking a hard look at improving the quality and efficiencies of U.S. products and services.

To do this, Baldrige assembled a team of leaders from some of the most effective U.S. corporations. One result of their efforts is still known today as the Malcolm Baldrige National Quality Award, given by the president of the United States to companies demonstrating high and consistent quality standards. In 1999, a separate category for the award was created for the field of education. Criteria against which potential district- or school-level candidates are evaluated include 1) visionary leadership, 2) valuing relationships, 3) data-driven decision making, 4) citizenship, 5) agility, 6) learning-centered education, 7) innovation, and 8) alignment to local, state, and national standards.

Another outcome of the Baldrige team's efforts was the bringing together of best practices and practical "quality tools" that had been developed over the years by a variety of experts, such as W. Edwards Deming, to help organizations be more effective and efficient. These principles were shared openly, and were intended to help leaders improve their decision-making, problem-solving, efficiency, and innovation skills. Some of the tools had been around leadership circles for years, such as force-field analysis, Venn diagrams, bar charts, and fishbone diagrams. Others were less familiar, such as lotus diagrams, spider matrices, and bubble maps.

Since many students like to learn visually, the graphic aspect of the quality tools offered a fun and creative reason for A.B. Combs to add to its blueprint for teaching leadership. But more important, the tools and principles were a timely addition for the teachers who were facing an ever-increasing push toward more accountability. The teachers knew the quality tools and principles would enable them as teachers and as a school to better

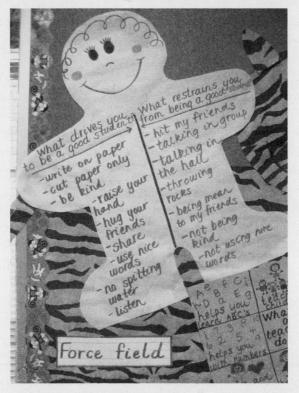

One kindergarten class uses force-field analysis to define expected classroom behaviors.

Students have fun using quality tools such as the lotus diagram (above) or fishbone diagram (below) to help them problem solve and clarify concepts.

analyze, measure, and track their progress toward key goals. As, fortu-itously, it has turned out, the quality tools and principles have also enabled them to respond to the present push among educators toward paying more attention to individual student scores. All these were added benefits to their initial purpose, which was to teach the quality tools to students to help them learn how to set goals, make better decisions, problem solve, and self-monitor their progress, all of which happen to be skills important for today's business leaders. So for those reasons, the quality principles and tools were added to the A.B. Combs leadership blueprint.

A Ubiquitous Strategy

At this point, I want to send up a rocket, launch some fireworks, and ignite a cannon to attract attention. For what I am about to describe is clearly one of the most important points of this book. It has to do with how A.B. Combs has chosen to approach teaching the leadership principles. For many schools and educators, this approach will represent a significant para-digm shift.

The approach A.B. Combs has undertaken is a "ubiquitous" approach. "Ubiquitous" means that it is built into everything the school does. It is ab-solutely integral to the school's strategic blueprint for teaching leadership. In fact, the ubiquitous approach is what has taken this from simply being a new curriculum to making it the foundation for the school's culture—a cul-ture that has proved to be conducive to higher learning, greater satisfaction, and reduced discipline challenges. It is also a culture that has been proved transferable to other schools.

Perhaps the best way to describe the ubiquitous approach is to contrast it with more traditional ones. I will use character education as an example. Most schools approach character education as a separate, stand-alone topic. For example, they might emphasize one character trait per month, such as "responsibility." They find occasional times to talk about responsibility dur-ing that month, perhaps at the start of each week in class. The principal might also place something about responsibility in the monthly newsletter or talk about it at an assembly. A poster or two might go up in a hallway. The next month, a new character trait such as "honesty" is designated.

Leadership—both character and competence—is not taught that way at A.B. Combs. Rather, the 7 *Habits*, the quality principles, and other leadership principles permeate most everything they do and most every subject they teach. Leadership is taught every day, though it often happens quite subtly and often unexpectedly. It begins in kindergarten, where the 7 *Habits* and basic quality principles are taught and retaught over a year's time in fun and authentic ways. Though occasionally the principles are introduced during stand-alone modules that are focused on one or more of the habits or quality tools, far more often they are woven into a wide variety of subjects and class activities.

Beyond kindergarten, students are refreshed regularly on the 7 *Habits* and quality principles. In fact, they spend most of the first week of school each year reviewing the 7 *Habits* as a way of establishing expectations and classroom rules—rules that the students develop in partnership with their teachers. After that initial week, students continue to be refreshed via games, lessons, and school activities. The key is that it can happen and does happen as part of any subject—math, English, science, history, art, music, physical education, and computers. Every subject.

In other words, leadership is not "one more thing" teachers have to teach. It is part of everything they teach. That is why several teachers describe it simply as a better way of doing what they were already doing. A few examples will help illustrate the ubiquitous approach.

The first example comes from Dyane Barnett, a reading coach at A.B. Combs. As part of a literature and writing module, she had fifth-grade students dissect the Langston Hughes poem "I Dream a World," which shares his vision of a better world. After discussing the poem's vocabulary, structure, and meaning, Mrs. Barnett divided students into teams and assigned each member a leadership role, such as scribe, timekeeper, or spokesperson. She then gave each team a poster-sized sheet of paper and challenged them to select one quality tool to illustrate the main points of the poem. One team chose to use a lotus diagram, another a bone diagram, two others a Venn diagram, and another a fishbone diagram. Upon completion, each spokesperson presented her or his team's creation. As a class, they then discussed which of the 7 *Habits* were evident in the poem, after which they were given personal writing assignments to describe what type of vision and dreams they had for their lives in the days ahead. The entire exercise took about thirty minutes.

This poem example is a simple one, but look at what it accomplished. Rather than merely diagramming the poem and going over its structure until the students' brains imploded and their heads got sucked facedown onto their desks, Mrs. Barnett instead involved students in teamwork and decision-making activities. She gave them speaking opportunities. She reinforced both the quality tools and the *7 Habits*. She gave students opportunities to "connect" with other students. She engaged students in thinking about who they are and who they want to become. She listened to what was on their minds and in their hearts. Furthermore, it was African-American History Week, so she linked that in as well. All of this was aside from the fact that she was teaching them about poetry, increasing their vocabulary, and working on their writing skills. So can you see how a standard literature assignment can be transformed into a robust lesson on life and leadership?

From the other side of the school comes another example where Debbie Falkner is teaching kindergartners about words that start with the letter *p*. She also happens to be simultaneously introducing a habit that kindergartners tend to like—synergize. She begins by talking about the various parts of a pizza, including the crust, the sauce, the meat toppings, and the cheeses. She explains that for the next thirty minutes their classroom will be turned into a pizza factory. About that time the phone rings and a woman (on speakerphone) asks if she can please purchase some pizzas. (Of course, Mrs. Falkner is capturing all these *p*'s on the chalkboard and overpronouncing them.)

To respond to the woman's request for six pizzas, students are divided into teams of four, with each student having an assigned leadership role. One is in charge of the crust, one the sauce, one the pepperoni topping, and another the cheese. They then go to work creating the various ingredients using construction paper and scissors. Mrs. Falkner lets them know that they must work as a team so as not to delay the woman's order. As teams hustle to make their pizza, Mrs. Falkner occasionally asks what the End in Mind is and what First Things First are—both being concepts the students have already been taught. She then introduces what *synergy* means, and why working together, valuing each person's talents, and respecting one another's roles is important. As the exercise comes to a conclusion, she uses a force-field analysis chart shaped like a pepperoni pizza to ask students what the pros (drivers) and cons (restraining forces) are of working as a team. In response, students offer answers that not only surprise the adults in the room, but demonstrate that they truly do understand the principles. Again, this is a fun exercise, yet look at what Mrs. Falkner covered. Not only was the letter *p* better understood, but students were given opportunity to learn how to work together while learning the basic concepts of synergy and while reviewing previously learned habits and quality tools.

These are two short examples of how the habits and quality tools are integrated into core subjects in a ubiquitous manner. The same types of lessons occur in specialty classes such as music, where the music selected has been carefully thought out to inspire students to envision the type of person they want to become. Art projects too have meaning. For example, fifth-grade students are asked by art teacher Martha Bassett to design a future cover for *Time* magazine that includes a self-portrait and caption indicating something they will do in life to make a significant contribution. Again, these examples all reflect things the teachers incorporate into what they are already doing, so they do not see them as "one more thing" they must do.

Examples of How Teachers in Florida and Alabama Are Applying the Ubiquitous Approach

Andrea Cohn, Third-Grade Teacher at Chestnut Grove Elementary, Decatur, Alabama.

For a class reading period, Mrs. Cohn reads to students the book *Salt in His Shoes*, a story about Michael Jordan growing up to be a great athlete, and a tall one at that. She then talks with the students about whether it was the salt that Michael's mother put in his shoes that made him grow and jump so high, or something else. She asks, "What habits did Michael learn? What leadership traits did he develop? What do you want to be when you grow up? What habits will you need to exercise to reach your dreams, or to be a leader?"

Christian Plocica, Physical Education Teacher at English Estates Elementary, Fern Park, Florida.

At the beginning of each year, Mr. Plocica works with students to create a mission statement for each class. Students then repeat their class mission statement each day during warm-up exercises. They also do a series of leg and arm stretches that have been choreographed to the *7 Habits.* True to the notion that not every child is gifted in every subject but is gifted in some way, Mr. Plocica has developed games and exercises that emphasize teamwork over competition and that reinforce synergy, valuing differences, and thinking win-win. He may say to the class, for example, "I want everyone to get into groups of $(4 \times 6) \div 8$." Inevitably a child "bright" in math but perhaps less solid in physique or athletic prowess will call out the right group size, while another will start organizing everybody, and still another will begin posturing to be the team leader. In the end, everyone—not just the class "jocks"—feel important, involved, and needed. Students are also given the opportunity to track physical goals and progress. All this is done as part of normal events that would go on in most any typical physical education class.

Gayle Fowler, Second-Grade Teacher at Chestnut Grove Elementary, Decatur, Alabama.

During a science module, Mrs. Fowler tells students about a basket of seashells she collected from the Gulf of Mexico. One by one, she pulls the shells from the basket so students can see their size and shape. Each time, she also identifies a minor flaw in the shell. She then challenges students to think about what types of things or events might have caused the flaws. As the students' minds race around the ocean floor, wildly imagining all the kinds of critters or storms that could have caused a little nick or dent in the shells, she goes on to tell them of a college roommate of hers who had some annoying traits. The traits were irritating enough that they became the focus of how she viewed her roommate. Those traits continued to bother her until an incident occurred when that roommate helped her at a time when she was in true need. The incident taught her that the roommate also had strengths. In fact, the strengths were so strong that she soon began to overlook the roommate's little flaws. She then pointed out the beauties of the shells, and how the hermit crabs and other shelled creatures found great use in them. Of course, the concluding point was that everyone has little flaws, but that we should focus on their strengths. She then passed out to each student notes that their classmates had written about their individual strengths.

Using the ubiquitous approach, from day one students are taught principles of leadership. They are told that they are leaders who possess unique gifts and that part of their expected contribution while at A.B. Combs is to share those gifts. Everywhere they turn they see hallway displays and motivating reminders of the mission and vision statements and inspiring quotes that elevate their mind-set as to who they have the potential to become. They play fun classroom games that teachers have invented and that are usually tied to some state or national education standard. They see leadership principles exhibited on the the school's morning news, which is broadcast via television to every classroom. By the time they leave kindergarten, they not only feel good about themselves, but they can converse with adults on the basics of the 7 *Habits*, the quality tools, and what leadership means to them.

Art assignments are a memorable way to motivate students to begin thinking about who they are and who they want to become.

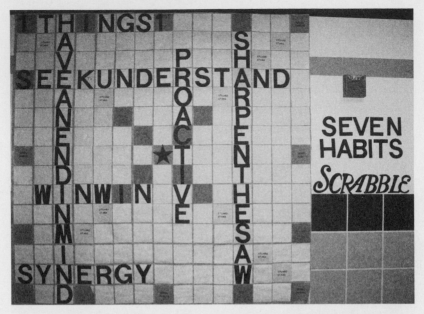

Creative teachers at the schools make a game of teaching leadership principles.

A way to illustrate how the ubiquitous approach differs from more traditional approaches is to look at how many, if not most, teachers view the relationship between traditional academics, life skills, and character education:

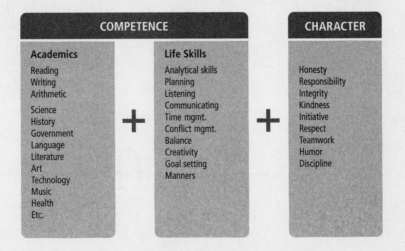

According to this illustration, most teachers view the three areas as independent boxes with plus signs in between. Their thinking is "I must teach core academics + life skills + character." Such a thought can be overwhelming given all that teachers already have to teach.

But the ubiquitous method does not approach teaching the *7 Habits* or other leadership principles in that way. Instead, they bring the life skills and character right into the mainstream of the core academics that they are already teaching. In other words, if they are going to teach reading and literature anyway, why not do it while reading books and poems about people who are responsible, proactive, or honest, or read literature that will motivate students to set goals and persevere? If they are going to teach science

My Goals

My goal is how to play bascitball.

My goal is to how to do a flip.

My goal is how to cowt Mune.

My goal is how to play football.

My goal is how to play Domnows.

My goal is how to swim.

My goal is lrn how to slep in my bed.

My goal is how to tip with owt looking.

My goal is how to play tinis.

As kindergartners such as Max learn to write, spell, and use a keyboard, why not allow them to think about their goals and consider how they can improve their life skills?

and plan to have students do reports, why not teach them basic presentation skills to enable them to present their findings confidently in front of the class? If students are required to take physical education, why not teach them skills for working in a team? If they are going to have school activities, why not let the kids do some of the planning so they can learn goal setting and planning skills?

> A nation becomes what its young people read in their youth. Its ideals are fashioned then, its goals strongly determined.
>
> —*James A. Michener, Prominent Author*

Now, if you are a parent, why not do the same thing? Once you and your child understand the essence of the habits, you can read a book, tell a story, play a game, watch a video, or go for an "adventure" walk, and invite your child to share with you which of the *7 Habits* he or she sees, and why. Simple, real life, powerful! (For more ideas, see chapter 10: Bringing It Home.)

If I were to try to illustrate the ubiquitous approach, it would look something like the following:

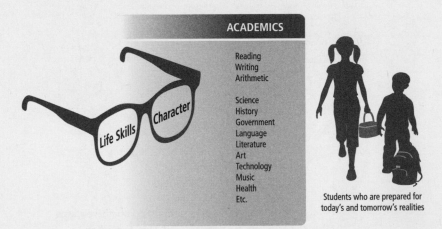

Students who are prepared for today's and tomorrow's realities

What I am highlighting is that teachers who use the ubiquitous approach keep their focus on traditional core academic subjects, but they do it while looking through the lenses of incorporating life skills and character lessons whenever possible. The entire time, however, their greater "end-result" vision is focused on preparing young people for tomorrow's realities and today's tough decisions. So, yes, it is teaching the same traditional subjects, but it is done through a whole new set of lenses—a new paradigm.

Data Notebooks

There is one more key component of the A.B. Combs strategic leadership blueprint that deserves special attention. It is a tool that ties together the *7 Habits* and the quality principles. It also links in to the ubiquitous approach and has had a tremendous impact on the success of the leadership theme.

A.B. Combs, and now a number of the other leadership schools, give each student a three-ring binder. Students call it their data notebook. They use their data notebook to record personal and academic goals and to chart their progress toward those goals. Students also use the notebooks at student-led parent-teacher conferences to explain to their parents how they are progressing. Many students treat the data notebooks like gold and are quite protective of them.

Each grade level has a customized set of graphs, charts, and diagrams that are inserted into the binders and are then kept up-to-date weekly, if not more often. A key benefit of the data notebooks is that they provide students with an ongoing, timely source of feedback, which is a known key driver of student achievement. Since the data notebooks represent only a single student's work, students use it only to compare themselves individually against their own goals and previous scores, not someone else's. What demoralizes students is when they are constantly compared to others and feel they are not up to par.

> When success in the classroom is defined in terms of competitive status with others, only a few students can be successful. However, when individual growth is the criterion for success, then all students can experience success regardless of their comparative status.
>
> —*Robert J. Marzano*, What Works in Schools

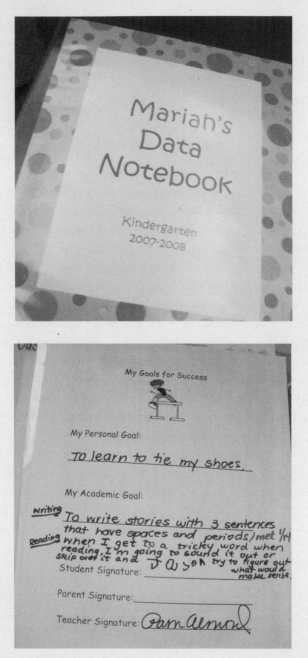

Students track progress using their individual data notebooks as pictured in the cover (above) and in the goals (below).

It is an impressive experience to sit down and have a kindergartner or third-grader share his or her data notebook and explain what it contains. It does not take long before it becomes clear that the child owns the data— and in most cases is quite proud of it.

> Data notebooks are a very important part of the process because they help students develop intrinsic desires to achieve goals. The *7 Habits*, Baldrige criteria, and data notebooks provide the perfect blend.
>
> —*Barbara Watkins, Teacher, A.B. Combs Elementary*

While student data notebooks track and enhance individual achievement, teachers keep similar notebooks for each class. Charts and graphs are also posted on walls to capture class progress. Students work together to set and achieve class goals and are big on celebrating milestones. But each student knows they must work diligently to meet their individual goals so that they can do their part to contribute to the class goals.

Students chart progress as a class to see how they are doing as a team in achieving class goals.

To continue the flow, similar notebooks, charts, and graphs pop up in administrative offices, since administrators are also keen on tracking school progress and celebrating schoolwide goals. As Muriel describes it, "It's kind of like standing naked in front of the mirror. It puts it all out there. You can't cover it up. Data drives everything we do. It lets us know what we need to improve in our school." But then she adds this qualifier: "We have learned over and over again that with data, often less is best. And our notebooks have been streamlined over the past couple of years because we are not collecting data on anything except those things that are in direct alignment with student achievement and improving the processes in our school."

So, no, the teachers do not all wear calculators on their belts, nor do they stare at histograms all day. But, yes, they do try to focus only on what is relevant, with an eye toward getting better. And they do it by leading with data.

The Blueprint Takes Shape

You now have a sense of some of the major content A.B. Combs uses to teach leadership principles and skills, including basic life skills. You also have some understanding of their method and tools. All are vital ingredients to their success. However, it is important to note that these are not the only things they are doing or teaching to teach leadership or to be successful. For example, they also incorporate other leadership content into their teaching, including insights from thought leaders in the leadership field such as Peter Drucker, Jim Collins, and Daniel Goleman. Furthermore, they gather and present stories and insights from past leaders such as Abraham Lincoln, Mohandas Gandhi, Martin Luther King, Jr., and Mother Teresa. They identify successful leadership traits and stories from current leaders in science, politics, the arts, and sports, including leaders from their community. They read about leaders, watch DVDs about them, and talk about what makes them leaders. They have also brought in leaders for students to interview, including the governor of North Carolina and an impressive array of corporate leaders. One of the students' favorites was when leaders of Lego Corporation came from Denmark to view their leadership

Around every corner are leaders who have something to say to students about their potential and what it takes to be a leader.

approach. Most often, however, teachers simply pull from classic children's literature and other fun books or captivating movies that they already have on their shelves. Basically, anything that will enable students to effectively navigate life in the twenty-first century falls within their leadership model.

> We have not created anything new. What we have done is bring together the best thinking that is out there and identified how it all aligns to create a culture of learning.
>
> —*Gailya Winters, Assistant Principal, A.B. Combs Elementary*

It is likewise important to note that "leadership" principles are by no means the only concepts shaping what happens at the school or in the classrooms. A.B. Combs is very adept at staying up-to-date with the latest research and practices in the field of education. In fact, they tend to be role models for how to put leading-edge educational research and concepts into practice. They see them as complementary to what they are doing with the leadership theme. Some of these leading practices:

- **Rigor, Relevance, and Relationships.** This reflects Dr. Willard Daggett's work and places emphasis on using real-world authentic tasks over worksheets.
- **7 Correlates of Effective Schools.** Rooted in Dr. Larry Lezotte's work and the Effective Schools Movement, these include a clear and focused mission, a safe and orderly environment, a climate of high expectations, frequent monitoring of student progress, and positive home-school relations.
- **Brain Research.** Based heavily on Dr. Howard Gardner's research on multiple intelligences and on Daniel Pink's *A Whole New Mind*, this recognizes that all children are wired differently, so educators must adapt to different styles and teach to both sides of the brain.
- **The Essential 55.** Founded upon Ron Clark's work, this emphasizes making memories for children and explains how to instill in children a desire to learn and how to help them respect themselves and believe they can do anything.
- **Professional Learning Communities.** Dr. Rick DuFour and Dr. Robert Eaker's approach emphasizes having a collegial group of educators who are united in their commitment to student learning and collaborative teamwork and development.

- **Emotional Intelligence.** Dr. Robert Cooper's work *The Other 90%* invites students and teachers to bring 100 percent of their energy and excellence to whatever they do. It covers such topics as trust, quality, living well, learning from one another, and staying calm under pressure.

The list could go on, as A.B. Combs teachers incorporate ideas from still other key thought leaders in education, such as William Glasser and Michael Fullan. The point is that the school is doing more than teaching leadership. Nevertheless, Muriel likes to position the leadership principles and approach by using the schoolhouse model illustrated below. The model has become their visual blueprint, or *strategy*, for teaching. Note that at the top is their "end in mind," which is to develop twenty-first-century skills in students. The windows represent leading practices in the field of education that will help them reach that goal. But what Muriel likes most about the model is that it places the *7 Habits* and Baldrige principles at the very foundation of the schoolhouse. As she describes it, "The secret of our success is constancy of purpose. We incorporate a lot of programs [*windows*] here, and those will change as things change in our district, in our state, in our country, and in the field of education. But what will not change

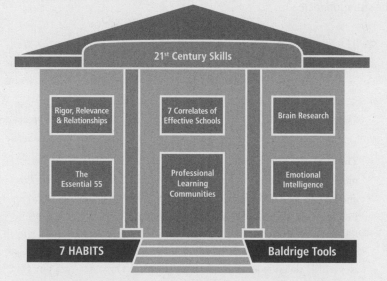

is the foundation of our schoolhouse, which is 7 *Habits* and Baldrige, and the end goal which is to equip students with twenty-first century talents and mind-sets."

But the Real Key Is ———!

So far in this chapter we have seen how A.B. Combs designed its overall strategy for *Developing Leaders One Child at a Time* by determining that they would place the 7 *Habits* and Baldrige quality principles and tools at the foundation of everything they teach and do. I have also shared their ubiquitous method and how they have used the data notebooks to bring the process together. But the real key to their strategy is yet to come.

I will tell you what the real key is by sharing one of my favorite stories from A.B. Combs. It involves a young man whose former principal contacted A.B. Combs to alert the staff regarding the nature of this young man. She revealed that he had recently "cold-cocked" her, knocked her flat unconscious. She declared that he was a problem child, a danger to the school and to its students.

A typical procedure in many schools after receiving a student with such a history might be to put the student, upon arrival, on some kind of strict action plan. But listen to Muriel describe how she and the staff approached the situation instead:

> We had just started this leadership theme and I felt that if this program really did work then it would work for a child like this young man. I never read his file, which in retrospect probably was not the wisest choice, but it was a choice from the heart to give this child a new chance.
>
> When he got off the bus there was no mistaking who he was. He walked with an attitude. I immediately went up to him and said, "You must be [name], I have been waiting for you." The guidance counselor was right beside me and added, "We're so happy you're here. I can tell you are going to be a leader." He said, "Who the . . . are you and get the . . . out of my face." I said, "We don't use that kind of language here. We use a different kind of language, but we're happy you are here nonetheless."
>
> So we began to build a relationship with him and we could see that tough exterior slowly dwindle away. We had great support systems from our team.

We told him we loved him every single day. At first when we would say, "We love you," sometimes he would curse us, and then other times he would just look at us like we had two heads, but by about October he began to tell us he loved us back.

He became one of the most popular children in the school. He had a temper and had setbacks, but his life was forever changed as a result of that one year. His grades went up to As and Bs, and he made honor roll. He eventually moved so we sort of lost contact with him. But from that experience I knew the leadership theme would help students, and that has fueled my passion to not give up on this leadership model.

In reflecting upon this great story, I go back to A.B. Combs's schoolhouse model. I am quite humbled by the placement of the *7 Habits* in the foundation because I know the role that a foundation plays in stabilizing a house. However, if I dare add anything to the model, it is this: a house, along with its foundation, is only as stable as the ground upon which it rests. Think about that. If the ground upon which it is built is unstable, a house and its foundation too will be unstable. Built upon sand or a fault line, even the strongest of foundations is susceptible to erosion, cracks, or crumbling.

> This school is successful with all students because they love them and respect who they are. When I first met the teachers the thing that I got from them was that these people really love the kids. And they have a heart for seeing them go from point A to point B to point C and finishing the year and then next year seeing them shine on.
>
> —*Patrice Hardy, Parent, A.B. Combs Elementary*

What makes the A.B. Combs schoolhouse and leadership model so strong is that its foundation is built upon solid ground. That ground consists of a firm mix of caring and love. It is made up of teachers who truly want the best for students and who care enough to take the time to discover students' individual gifts and then find ways to nurture and unleash those gifts. In other words, the young man's life was not changed merely as a result of his teachers teaching him the habits or a few nifty quality tools. Those may have helped, but the real key was that he knew his teachers cared about him as an individual. It may even have been the first time someone cared for him in that way. My guess is that in his past he had been the repeated victim of identity theft of the emotional kind. But then, at last, a few teachers who truly cared entered his life and helped him find his identity—his voice.

> Few things help an individual more than to place responsibility upon him and to let him know that you trust him.
>
> —*Booker T. Washington*

Indeed, story after story flows into A.B. Combs from parents wanting to say thanks for what the school is doing for their child beyond the academics. The stories highlight one of the most fundamental premises of A.B. Combs' philosophy: "If you treat all students as if they are gifted, and you always look at them through that lens of being gifted in at least some aspect, they will rise to that level of expectation."

The same level of love and respect is found in the way teachers interact with one another. Muriel and the other educators mentioned in this book do what they do so well because their collegial relationships are built upon trust and care. They are not built upon volatile fault lines, where everyone is eager to point out the others' faults. Rather, they have a lot of respect for and a lot of trust in one another as professional peers.

Without love and mutual respect, the *7 Habits*, the Baldrige principles, and all the other pieces of the schoolhouse model would lose much of their potency over time. And so it is upon that culture of caring that the real key to the success of A.B. Combs's strategy is founded and grounded.

4

Aligning for Success

Far and away the biggest mistake managers make is ignoring the crucial importance of alignment.

—*James C. Collins and Jerry I. Porras,* Built to Last

In the world of education, there is no lack of creativity, passion, caring, or research as to how to create a great school, a great classroom, or a great student. More often than not, the great barrier to success is that the systems and processes are not in place to sustain excellence.

The way I presented the previous chapter may have given the impression that as soon as A.B. Combs came up with its mission, vision, and strategy, the teachers immediately jumped into implementing the leadership theme by teaching students. But that would have been like planting a seed without preparing the soil. They could have done it, but the results would not have been the same—it is all part of the Law of the Harvest.

In other words, there was some preparatory work left to do before they could get fully under way. Recall that when Muriel took over as principal, not everything at A.B. Combs was in fine order. The facilities needed work. Some teachers had lost their passion; most were working in isolation. And resources were scarce. So, yes, it was good that they had come up with an inspiring new magnet theme and strategic plan, but the school as a whole was not prepared to embrace the caliber of change they knew would be required to implement the leadership theme.

Muriel describes the school's situation during that time period as resembling a scattered mass of arrows that were pointing in as many directions as there are degrees on a compass. As a school, they had numerous academic programs in place, but those programs were not tied to any common schoolwide vision or objectives. Likewise, individual teachers had "pet projects" in motion with varying degrees of success, but those too were not connected to any schoolwide goals or strategy. Everyone was just doing his or her own thing. So you can see why Muriel might describe those "old times" as being a bunch of randomly aimed arrows. In consulting terms, such a situation is referred to as lacking alignment.

Of course, in the beginning the prime culprit for the lack of alignment was the lack of clarity regarding the direction the school as a whole was trying to go in. But even after they had selected the new leadership theme and created their strategy, the A.B. Combs team knew they had some significant aligning still to do. In other words, the mission, vision, and strategy provided the "big arrow" around which all other arrows could be aligned, but there remained some critical "midsized" arrows that needed to be brought into alignment, as well as some "small" arrows that either needed to be adjusted or outright removed before they were ready to implement.

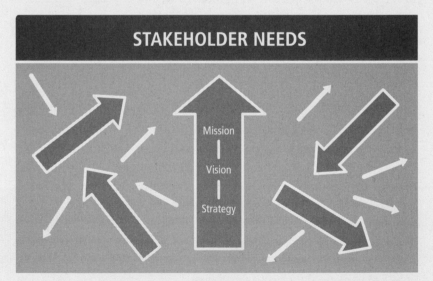

Talking with stakeholders and identifying leadership as their theme gave A.B. Combs clarity of direction (the big arrow), but still there remained other arrows to be aligned—or removed.

Four of A.B. Combs's "midsized" arrows included:

1) bringing people "on board" with the new theme
2) aligning the school's structure to match the strategy
3) training the staff in the 7 *Habits* and quality principles, and
4) aligning the reward systems so that the right outcomes would be reinforced and sustained.

This chapter will describe in broad terms how A.B. Combs went about aligning these four "midsized" arrows to their newly created mission, vision, and strategy.

Bringing People on Board

Far and away the most important and often most difficult form of alignment involves getting the "right" people on board and engaged. "All on board" beats "All are bored" any day. Teachers must have more than an owner's manual; they must have ownership.

A.B. Combs had a lot of talented people from the start. But there were a few who resisted the new leadership theme. They understood the superintendent's mandate but favored approaches that from their viewpoints were more "academic" in nature. Muriel puts it this way:

> Introducing the leadership theme dealt us some tough going in the initial stages. It was hard. Some felt that at a time when educators are faced with such high-stakes accountability and testing, "Why should we do this? We've got to stay focused on test scores because we're going to be evaluated by the scores that the children make on the end-of-grade tests." Yet at the same time, there was the majority saying, "The most important thing we do is to teach children to do 'the right thing,' and if we take this work and it goes in the direction we think it's going to go, we don't need to worry about test scores—they will come."

Those initial philosophical differences turned out in hindsight to make A.B. Combs a better place to teach as a teacher and a better place to learn as a student. They forced everyone to keep an eye on test scores and motivated the faculty to make better linkages between the leadership theme and hard-core academics.

What proved to be the more sensitive challenge was the small portion of teachers who resisted the change not because of philosophical differences, but because they simply were not willing to exert the effort. They had done things their way for years, so "Why change now?" While Muriel respected those teachers and their feelings, she recognized that the new leadership theme would have difficulty getting off the ground if all teachers were not on board. In terms of commitment, she hoped to have No Teacher Left Behind.

So even though the majority of teachers were in favor, Muriel and her team sensed that if they went to the staff and said, "We are all going to change, and everyone is going to teach the *7 Habits* and quality principles," the minority's resistance likely would have killed the effort before it got under way. So they moved into it cautiously by determining that they would initiate it as a pilot with only one teacher per grade level implementing the new leadership theme the first year. Fortunately, as that first year progressed and as teachers witnessed the increase in the pilot students' self-confidence, the decrease in discipline issues, and the increase in academic scores, one by one even some of the staunchest doubters came on board. The few who remained undecided were coaxed to at least give it a try by the pilot teachers insisting, "Every student deserves this." So it was the successes of the students and the urging of peer teachers that drove the change; it was not something that was being "forced" upon them by the principal.

Another thing that brought teachers on board was experiencing the signature *7 Habits* workshop as a staff. For several, the experience was life changing. They felt the seminar helped them to be more organized and effective, both personally and professionally. But most of all they felt that the days they spent tucked away together as a staff were an enormous bonding experience. It was more than just getting to know one another better. It gave them a common language that they could use to discuss schoolwide issues, to handle student behavior problems jointly, and to create synergy among grade-level teams. Even to this day, eight years later, those originally involved in the training experience continue to declare that it was the best thing they could have done as a school, both to create a culture for student achievement and to create buy-in.

But teachers were not the only stakeholders A.B. Combs needed to bring on board. Parents too were vital. Fortunately, bringing them on board turned out to be one of the easiest alignment tasks. Parents talk to parents, and the parents of the students in the pilot courses became some of the best salespeople for the leadership theme. The combination of higher scores and better behavior is a combination no parent ignores, and news spread quickly, even to district offices, where the improvements in test scores and the noticeable increases in enrollment brought the district on board, including the superintendent. And with each passing day, other stakeholders who heard about what was happening at the school also began joining the ranks of the enthused, such as several community and business leaders who volunteered their expertise and resources as a way of vocalizing their support for the new leadership theme.

Aligning Who Will Do What

It was also important that A.B. Combs align their organizational structure to match the new leadership theme. This involved a change in philosophy and leadership style more than it involved a change in the organizational chart. In fact, the organizational chart at A.B. Combs looks like most any other school's chart. The major difference is that everyone on the A.B. Combs chart has the word *leader* attached to his or her title, and the accountability to go with it. At the administration level, there is the leader of student counseling and the leader of media. Students know Mr. Ricky, the custodian, as the leader of keeping the building clean. Kitchen staff members are leaders of nutrition. Yes, every administrative role has a leadership component and every administrative leader is empowered and expected to be responsible for that stewardship.

At the teacher level, every teacher is considered a leader. First and foremost, all teachers are leaders of their classroom. There are also teacher-leaders for each grade level. Specialty teachers are known as leaders of art, leaders of music, or leaders of physical education. There are professional learning community leaders, and special project leaders. There is a *7 Habits* team and a Baldrige team made up of teacher-leaders who ensure that the *7 Habits* and quality principles are taught and reinforced properly. They too have leaders. But again, most of these same positions—change a word or two—exist at other schools. They are just not generally referred to or treated as leaders at other schools. Indeed, this would be nothing more than a play on semantics if Muriel did not expect them to actually be leaders and then support and hold them accountable as leaders.

It is at the student level where the leadership structure of A.B. Combs truly gets interesting and varies from the typical school. This is primarily because each and every student is also considered a leader of something. There are students who are leaders of public speaking, for example. Other students are leaders of science, leaders of music, and leaders of physical fitness. Most often, these leaders are students who excel in a particular area or who want to expand their talents in that specific area. In each classroom, there are also student leadership roles that have to do with the management and orderliness of the classroom; such roles include classroom greeter, timekeeper, team leader, cleanliness leader, and librarian.

Additionally, there are opportunities for students to take on leadership roles at the school level that go well beyond the traditional student council. At the beginning of each year, students who want to take on a schoolwide leadership role identify what role they want to pursue. They then use an application form to define the job and interview for that specific leadership role. One year more than four hundred students applied for and were given roles, such as leaders over the International Festival or leaders over the morning news program. In the process they learn interviewing skills and become more comfortable in such situations.

Because of their "gifts," several students are chosen to fill temporary and specific leadership roles. For example, Mrs. Winters chose a second-grade boy to help a certain kindergarten student learn how to behave properly at school. At a later time, that kindergartner asked for that same second-grader to help him with math and reading. These students are referred to as "peer leaders."

A.B. Combs's community and students have collected more canned goods for the North Carolina Food Bank than any other school in eastern North Carolina for the past fourteen years! As it should be, our reciprocity with the community serves both "child" and "village."

—*Katie Trueman, Guidance Counselor, A.B. Combs*

Other leadership opportunities arise for students due to the school's emphasis on community service. The school takes on some ambitious service projects each year, such as working with the Red Cross and other charitable agencies to raise funds for needy people in their community. These projects are not headed by the teachers or administrators or the PTA. Rather it is students who do the leading—as guided by adult mentors.

Students at the leadership schools apply for schoolwide leadership roles to gain experience, and to have a little fun. Below are a few examples from schools like A.B. Combs and Stuard Elementary in Aledo, Texas.

Mail Carrier	Student Council
Science Curator	Tech Help
Backstage Hand	Grounds Crew
Media Assistant	Public Speaker
Recycling Club	Announcement Team
Teacher Academy	Computer Technician
Special Event Planner	P.E. Helper
Green Recycle Team	Library Leader
Music Maestro	Lost and Found Patrol
Greeter	Leadership Cabinet
Critter Keeper	Morning News Anchor
Safety Patrol	

Another leadership role that deserves special mention is that of students involved in the hiring process for new teachers. When the list of new teacher applicants is narrowed, student leaders are given a chance to interview them. These student leaders have a reputation for being some of the toughest interviewers—and some of the most perceptive. The students have a knack for picking out teachers who like children, which is something that is often difficult for adults to assess. One applicant was quickly dismissed by the students because, as they exclaimed with disgust, "She didn't even know we were a *7 Habits* school. She didn't do her homework."

Let me give an example of how the student leadership roles affect the culture of A.B. Combs. Once a month a student leader is pulled out of

One of the more popular leadership roles for students is being a greeter when guests come. Students learn to welcome visitors, give a good handshake, and look adults in the eyes.

each classroom for an hour to represent his or her class at a chat session with the principal. During that hour, the student leaders are encouraged to bring up things they would like to see done differently. Muriel never ceases to be amazed at some of the things students bring up. For example, they used to have a student code of cooperation (as opposed to the "code of conduct" that many schools have) that was called MAGIC. The acronym stood for:

> **M** odel expected behavior
> **A** ccept responsibility
> **G** ive respect
> **I** mprove through goals
> **C** ooperate

One day a student stood up during one of the chat sessions and said, "Miss Summers, what we do around here is not 'magic.' It is hard work." He suggested that a new code of cooperation be created and even gave it a new acronym, LEAD, which stands for:

L oyalty
E xcellence
A chievement
D iscipline

Muriel could not help but be impressed with the young man's thinking, but knew that MAGIC was painted on walls and on signs throughout the school. All the students were familiar with it. So to change it would not only be a hassle but a sizable expense. Yet at the same time, she also knew the boy was right. The signs were changed.

So in essence, every administrator, teacher, staff member, and student is a leader at A.B. Combs. But again, to make this happen involved a change in philosophy more than a massive redo of the school's organizational chart. I repeat for emphasis that this is more of a change in philosophy than a change in the organizational chart. This is made evident by what Justin Osterstrom, a fourth-grade teacher at A.B. Combs, shared when he was interviewed about the benefits of the leadership theme. See if you can detect in his comments how leadership at the school is less about a position or title that a person holds than it is about the philosophy of the school and its belief in the potential of children:

> The spirit of students helping each other is very strong here. One girl, who is bilingual in Spanish and English, was asked to help a girl from Mexico. She was a great peer leader and helped the girl to be successful. She is one of those students who doesn't naturally stick out but is given opportunities here to make a difference.
>
> Another boy had behavior issues. Poverty, low socioeconomic status, and other such factors were hurting his school progress. Still he had so much good about him. He ended up in the office for discipline one day. Instead of punishing him, Muriel decided to support him by giving him responsibility and having him speak on leadership and the student data system to touring visitors. It totally changed his maturity. He blossomed and started hanging out with peers that were good for him. His grades improved. The positive influence of the school on him was incredible—just to see what a moment of leadership can do in a child. I feel privileged that I got to see the shift. He just makes me smile.

In previous schools, I saw no empowerment for the students. Power was all in the teacher. Here the students helped interview me for this job. The students' questions were more challenging than the teachers'. These students are genuine; this is not a façade.

Did you notice how a quiet student was strengthened by being assigned to be a mentor, a troubled student was lifted by being given added responsibility, and other students felt valued by being given opportunities to interview teachers?

If anything, student achievement and test scores are emphasized more with the leadership approach. They are not ignored. But the teachers know that the greater vision—the ultimate end in mind—is to unleash the potential of each child. This has brought a sense of artistry back to their careers, a feeling of being a true leader. In every child they are looking for talents, for *gifts*, and are trying to find ways to unveil, mold, and expand those gifts. And this applies to every child, not just the students labeled "gifted."

To some, this may all sound impressive; to others it might sound overwhelming. In fact, a question that Muriel and the other principals who have now taken on the leadership theme are often asked is, "How do you do all this? Where do you find the time?" No doubt they are busy. But if you look at their schedules you will note what it is that they are busy doing—they are busy looking ahead to the future, examining best practices at other schools, creating down-the-road strategies, and getting to know students and parents. In other words, the fact is that they spend far less time putting out fires and trying to make minor decisions than the average principal. Why? Because they have empowered others—including students—to do many of the leadership tasks, and because there are fewer fires to put out. So giving students leadership opportunities and unleashing teachers' talents not only is an integral part of A.B. Combs's success but can also lead to time savings—and to better leadership.

Getting People Trained

Of course, one of the major alignment tasks was to get the right training plans and resources in place for both the staff and the students. The natural place to start was with the teachers, since they would be the ones teaching the students.

From the get-go, A.B. Combs determined to train not just all teachers, but all staff members. All were to be leaders, and all would be mingling with students, so why not train them all? The first year, the training focused on the 7 *Habits* and took place over a three-day period. Training centered on applying the habits to staff members' individual lives, as opposed to focusing on how to teach the habits to students. The logic was that it would be difficult for the adults to expect the students to apply the 7 *Habits* if they as adults were not applying them. The side benefit was the unity the training generated for the staff as a whole.

The second year's training focus was on educating the staff on the Baldrige principles and on how to use the various quality tools. This involved helping the full staff to learn how to apply the principles and tools to their individual roles, and also helping teachers to better understand how to teach the tools. As a staff, they became committed to utilizing the tools in running the school and each classroom, and in holding themselves accountable. Soon charts and graphs began to appear in each of the rooms, and student data was being discussed frequently in meetings.

From that point on, each year various aspects of the 7 *Habits* and the quality tools were revisited or added to, mostly during faculty and staff development meetings. It proved to be a great way of reenergizing the leadership theme and preventing it from becoming just a short-lived program. But the best training that teachers in particular receive is what transpires inside them as they prepare to teach and as they stand in front of students and teach the principles, and as they apply and model the habits. The more the teachers teach and apply the leadership principles, the more they learn for themselves.

As for the students, you already know something of how they are taught the 7 *Habits* and the quality principles and tools. But let me note that while in the early years there were well-tested and professional training materials already in place for the adults, for the students there were none. So the teachers created everything basically from scratch. Both independently and synergistically they came up with lesson plans, parent resources, discipline methods, bulletin boards, book lists, video clips, music, science projects, games, and so forth. They worked wonders.

With the leadership model, one thing they encourage kids to do is to get up in front of their class and to speak. Recently, when our fifth-grade son, Walter, was elected student body president, he was able to calmly present his speech in front of seven hundred people in the gym. Just watching him walk into that room, go up in front, and speak in such a nice, natural voice to all those people, was like watching the leadership model coming to a grand culmination. The beauty is that it began when he was five years old in kindergarten. So it was not this big jump to do it in fifth grade. It started small and it built. It was just that next step. And it came sort of naturally to him.

—Steve and Helen Vozzo

Students like Walter Vozzo (shown here speaking to 140 adults) are given ample opportunity to speak in front of groups, as noted by Walter's parents.

Today, things are a little different. A lot of resources have been created and teachers create a swap on a continual basis. Indeed, while some of this might again sound intimidating, teachers who are replicating the leadership theme at other schools are discovering that there is less involved than they initially anticipated. They find that just about any literature, or history, or science, or geography lesson they have previously used already has components of the habits embedded. They merely need to add a comment or two to bring out those habits or concepts for the students. And in many cases, particularly with the upper grades, they do not even need to do that, as students learn to draw out the habits from the literature on their own—even kindergartners.

While many great sample lesson plans and activities are now available in resources such as *The Leader in Me* website,* I believe that most teachers would agree that the way students are taught the best or the most about the leadership principles is not just through the lesson plans or activities, but through 1) teachers modeling the habits, and 2) students being given the opportunity to practice the leadership principles. It all starts in kindergarten and continues until the day they move on to the next level. From day one, they hear the teachers and staff talking the talk and walking the walk. They work in teams, they are assigned leadership roles, and they are given ample occasion to put the principles into practice. After five or so years, it becomes second nature to them.

Celebrating Successes

One of the most complex systems for any organization to align is the reward system. No one ever seems to be entirely happy with whatever reward system is in place. Yet though they knew it would be a tricky task, A.B. Combs also knew it needed to align its reward systems with the new leadership theme if it wanted to reinforce and sustain the new theme. And, once again, this is an area where teachers' creativity shined brightly.

Let me give you an example. Two of the leadership traits the teachers wanted to reinforce in students were creativity and hard work. One method that some of them chose to use was a grading rubric they call the Hamburger Rubric. It goes something like this. When a teacher assigns a project, students receive a grade on a scale of one to four that is based on the following metaphor and criteria: A person enters a restaurant and requests a hamburger. They are then asked to rate the service they receive using a four-level scale:

* TheLeaderInMeBook.org

Level 1:	They have to wait extra time, and what they get is not what they requested. Instead they get a sack of unsalted greasy fries.
Level 2:	They get a hamburger on time, but it is only mildly warm and is missing the cheese and relish they expected.
Level 3:	They get a hot-off-the-grill hamburger that has everything they expected. They get what they asked for.
Level 4:	Their hamburger is just how they wanted it and the waiter says, "Today I am also going to give you some fries and a shake for free." It is clearly more than what was expected.

When teachers use this rubric, students know that a 3 is a pretty good score to receive on a project, but they have a real twinkle in their eye when they get a 4 because they know they have gone beyond expectations in terms of both creativity and hard work. And it pleases them to know their teacher noticed.

Here is another reward system they have established. One of North Carolina's state standards requires students to learn basic manners. Of course, the teachers could tell the students to sit down, fold their arms, shut their lips, and listen while they are taught manners. But they do not. Instead, they give students a challenge early on in the year. If they as students demonstrate good performance in specific areas over time, their class will be invited to a special silver-tray luncheon in the cafeteria with the best food the cafeteria has ever served. Students salivate at the idea and they take it upon themselves to make sure that everyone lives up to the requirements. They work hard for the honor, and once they arrive at the fancy affair they discover that before they can eat they must learn what "all those forks" are for, what to do with the napkins, when it is polite to start eating, and so forth. It is not difficult to visualize those fifth-graders lined up along the tables having a great time. Scarcely do they know they are learning manners or fulfilling a state requirement. They just think they are being rewarded— and they are, in an aligned way.

Teachers are insistent that students be rewarded for demonstrating leadership, not just academic achievement. Debbie Powell, for example, the school's Physical Fitness Leader, rewards students who exemplify the habits during physical education. There is a countywide competition called First in Fitness that top athletes can compete in as a school. Forty students are selected to represent A.B. Combs, but those students all know that athleticism alone will not get their names on the list. They must also exemplify the habits. For example, they need to display proactivity by keeping their emotions under control. They need to Begin with the End in Mind by setting goals, and Put First Things First by practicing and getting rest.

There are many other ways students are rewarded. Individual classes nominate Leaders of the Week, with all students getting a turn. Students are recognized during the daily schoolwide televised morning news. Regular schoolwide and in-class celebrations and award ceremonies are held. But aside from the parties and awards, the real reward systems at the school take us back to the four sources of peace of mind, the four basic needs—physical, social-emotional, mental, and spiritual. Students at A.B. Combs are rewarded in all four of these areas in some way nearly every day. To come five days a week to a place where they feel safe, where they are recognized and loved, where they have their creativity and minds stimulated, where they are involved in meaningful projects, where they hear teachers, administrators, parents, and friends calling them by name, calling them leaders, and pointing out their strengths, and where they know they are being prepared to lead their own lives for a lifetime, how much more could a child want in the way of rewards?

So just showing up to school each day can be a reward. As Muriel relates it: "You will hear us compliment the children all the time. You will hear us thank them. We tell them we love them every single day, and how much we appreciate them. We have nine hundred students and it is important to us that we connect with each of them every day, even if it is only through the airwaves on the morning news. That is part of our core value system here. We let children know we believe in them."

As for the teachers and staff, their rewards are mostly of the internal kind. A.B. Combs has won several awards, Muriel has been named Principal of the Year, and a number of teachers have been honored in public. But teacher after teacher will talk instead about the stories of students whose lives have changed as a result of the leadership theme or something a teacher has done to implement it. Every teacher has such stories and has felt such internal rewards. So it is with the parents as well. All see the big-

Scores of awards are presented each week in classrooms, school assemblies, and morning news broadcasts. Rewards emphasize teamwork and leadership skills, not just test scores.

gest rewards as being *not* what is handed out at an assembly or an end-of-year rating, but rather what is happening in the minds and hearts of these young students.

> One girl transferred into the school and was very shy. In one week she was up in front of the school being very confident. Her father kept saying, "I can't believe that is my daughter." It has to do with the expectations we set for the school and the students. They rise to the level of expectation we establish for them.
>
> —*Karen DeVoss, Teacher, Dewey Elementary, Quincy, Illinois*

Before concluding this section, I do not want to overlook the fact that there are two sides to reward systems: 1) the reinforcing of good behavior and 2) the disciplining of unacceptable behavior. You have likely heard the expression about the "bad" guy who was harshly punished, followed by someone saying, "He got his just reward."

Disciplining students and classroom management is an issue at any school. The good news is that one of the very first things we hear from schools that have implemented the leadership theme is that discipline issues are down—significantly down. Almost every school that has taken on the leadership theme has said this very thing. In fact, a number of teachers have insisted that the number one benefit of the leadership theme is how it helps with classroom management and schoolwide discipline.

On any given day, a handful of students are dealing with stresses at home and come to school agitated. So no one at A.B. Combs tries to hide the fact that there are occasional matters of discipline that need to be handled. But the fact is that those instances are way down, even with the enormous increase in the number of students. Teachers at all the schools will be quick to tell you what a difference it makes in the classroom. As one teacher noted, "Even if only ten minutes is saved each day by not having to stop the class to deal with a behavioral issue, what a difference that makes, not only on the amount of time that can be spent on learning, but on the conditions under which students are then allowed to learn." It is very difficult to motivate a child to learn when they feel threatened physically or emotionally. That is why A.B. Combs feels so strongly that when discipline issues arise, they should be handled proactively (nonemotionally), keeping the end in mind and first things first, while thinking win-win, seeking first to understand, and synergizing around third alternatives. And because the students have been taught these principles, in many cases the problems are resolved by the students themselves, using the *7 Habits* framework.

Aligned for Success

There were other aspects of the school that A.B. Combs needed to align with the new leadership theme before it got under way with implementation, such as communication channels, budgets, and resources. And the point that this chapter started out with was that in too many cases, such alignment efforts are hastily skipped over or ignored when implementing change. This is true whether speaking of a school, a home, or a personal life. As a result, so often it does not happen; they never get built into the systems. And that is why so many great ideas never are sustained.

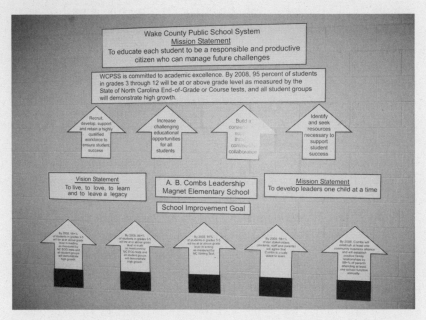

Today, A.B. Combs has its arrows aligned, as illustrated in this diagram mounted outside the administrative offices.

So in concluding this chapter, I emphasize that A.B. Combs did not simply come up with a mission, vision, and strategy and then say to everyone, "Go do it. You're empowered! Have fun! Let us know how it goes." No, before trying to implement the new theme, they first stopped and did what it took to get the right people on board. They put together an aligned structure and institutionalized a philosophy of empowerment. They provided people with the training they needed. And they put the reward systems in place that would support and sustain their efforts. This does not suggest everything had to be in perfect order, nor does it suggest that a school cannot get started without a major overhaul. It merely suggests that some thought and effort needs to go into getting the systems and processes aligned prior to full implementation for this to have its greatest impact. The absence of this step taking place is one of the most, if not the most common reasons why change efforts fail in schools, businesses, and homes. The very fact that it did take place at A.B. Combs has contributed greatly to the leadership theme being sustained for as long as it has.

And since those early days, A.B. Combs has continued to align, realign, and realign again their arrows. Today, Muriel will be the first to say that not everything is perfectly aligned. A.B. Combs is still a work in progress. But continuous improvement is what they are about. They are not resting on success. As a result, the entire staff can go to work far more at peace each day, knowing that A.B. Combs has moved a great distance toward getting the school's arrows in far greater alignment and at least pointing in the right direction.

5

Unleashing a Culture of Leadership

If you don't know how to execute, the whole of your effort as a
leader will always be less than the sum of its parts.

—*Larry Bossidy and Ram Charan*

To this point, I have shared glimpses of how A.B. Combs came
up with their mission and vision, and how they created a strategy. I have also indicated that before they jumped directly into
implementing the new leadership theme, they patiently paused long enough
to align key school components. In this chapter, I present an overview of what
happened when it finally came time to implement. Of course, in each chapter I have already given you "sneak previews" of what happened when the
teachers took the leadership theme to the students, but this chapter will give
more detail. One caution, however: it is important to understand that this
did not all happen overnight. A.B. Combs is nearly a decade into the leadership theme, and much of what appears in this chapter—and even in previous
chapters—came about piece by piece, gradually emerging over time.

You can imagine how eager the teachers were to get under way when the
time to launch finally did come. But given the fact that they had never seen
such a leadership theme implemented at any other school, getting under
way required a substantial leap of faith and came with a few unsettled
nerves. As Muriel describes it, "We were confident as can be as we prepared
to unleash the new leadership theme, yet in the back of our minds we could
not help but take an occasional deep breath and ask, 'Can we really pull
this off? Can we do this without any resources other than ourselves?' Each

time our answer was an emphatic yes. We could feel it from head to toe. Our answers were united, 'This will be a labor of love. We can do it!' " That "can do" attitude was not only contagious among the teachers, it was enough to get them over any initial bumps and glitches they encountered. What ultimately resulted was an award-winning school culture.

A school's "culture" results from the combined behaviors of the people involved in that particular school. It is sometimes referred to as "the way we do things around here." Culture is not the mission, the vision, or the strategy that is printed on a sheet of paper or mounted on a wall. Culture is not the list of school values or the school's policy manual. Culture is not what is proclaimed out of someone's mouth. Rather, culture is how people actually behave and treat each other on a consistent day-in and day-out basis. Culture can be seen, felt, and heard.

It is no secret that a school's culture has direct impact on the learning state of students. It is, therefore, unfortunate that a world-class school culture is not something that comes in a kit with a clear set of numbered instructions. It cannot be grown in a Petri dish. What adds to the challenge is that culture cannot be created by one person, and it is generally not a good sign if one person or group is trying to take credit for creating it.

Given all the other pressures lined up on their agendas, many principals will argue that they simply do not have the time even to tamper with the culture, much less create a new one. So while there have been a number of excellent books written by educators for educators on the subject of creating culture, most efforts to create or tweak a school's culture end up being either glaringly weak or serendipitous—"it just happened." In fairness, the same is true for the cultures of most businesses and work teams. So I greatly applaud A.B. Combs and the staffs of the other schools that have adopted the leadership theme for having the courage to work on their school's culture amid the many other pressures that are heaped upon them.

To describe what A.B. Combs did to create their culture of leadership, I will borrow from the approach that an anthropologist might take in trying to describe a society—ancient or modern. Though I claim no special expertise in anthropology, what I do know is that anthropologists try to observe and study a number of factors that they believe reflect the culture of a society, including:

- Behaviors
- Language
- Artifacts
- Traditions (Rituals)
- Folklore

Using these factors as a guide, let us look at what A.B. Combs has done to create a culture of leadership and student achievement.

Behaviors

I begin with one of A.B. Combs's key culture-building activities. It is where it all starts, every year. You see, A.B. Combs takes its culture so seriously that it devotes the better part of the first week or more of each school year to working with students to create or re-create it. That is right; a full week. Every year.

> We spend about a week using Harry Wong's work regarding the first days of school. It's been around for a long time, but those things that have been around for a long time have been around for a long time for a reason—because they work. So we spend the first week of school teaching the children nothing other than how they are to be leaders in this school.
>
> —*Paula Everett, Teacher, A.B. Combs*

During that first week they do not teach core subjects. Instead, they review the *7 Habits* and write class mission statements. They talk about accountability. They have students create, apply for, and interview for class and school leadership roles. They set personal and class goals and assemble their data notebooks. They have students help write classroom codes of cooperation—what behaviors "are" and "are not" acceptable. They create artwork to go on bulletin boards in the halls and in the classrooms. All these things happen during the first week in a fun, engaging way.

It may seem outlandish to spend an entire week establishing the culture, but A.B. Combs does not see it as exorbitant at all. One of the main reasons for doing it is to ensure that students get to know each other and feel "connected"—new and returning students alike. Helping students feel connected is what prevents and removes many of the discipline issues before the year is scarcely under way. They know they will only reap what they sow and so they are very careful to sow the right things from the start—making sure that they are preparing the soil and planting the right seeds. Once more, it is putting the Law of the Harvest to work.

Clearly, the *7 Habits* are not the only behaviors taught and emphasized at the school during that first week. Basic manners and etiquette are big. They are taught the wisdom of going places in pairs. They are taught that good hygiene and grooming are part of being a leader. They are encouraged to greet visitors, look them in the eye, and welcome them to the school. They are taught to say, "Yes, ma'am," and "Yes, sir." They also determine ways that good behavior will be rewarded. As a result, polite and mature behaviors have become "a way of doing things" around A.B. Combs—part of their everyday culture.

Language

Language spoken in the hallways says volumes about the culture at A.B. Combs. On a regular basis you will hear phrases such as "We dwell in possibilities here." "We tell them we love them every day." "We focus on what they can do, not what they can't do." "We focus on the positive." "Every child is important." Quotations and bulletin boards placed strategically on walls all across the school send the same message.

When two of our FranklinCovey consultants dropped by unexpectedly early for an appointment one morning, as soon as they got out of their car they could hear Muriel's voice talking to the children over the school's intercom system. "Children, you are so wonderful. Yesterday, you did such a marvelous job doing your responsibilities. I just can't tell you how much I respect you . . . how much I love you." One of the consultants turned to the other and said, "How can a child walk away from this school after six years of hearing daily messages like that and not feel somewhat special or loved?"

When students arrive at their classroom each day, both the teacher and an assigned greeter—*Leader of the Day*—are there to meet them at the door. Typically they shake hands and say the student's name, and often add something nice about how the student looks or something about a recent accom-

What students hear every day at A.B. Combs is that they are important, that they matter, and that they can be leaders every day in their own way.

plishment. It is rare for a child to slip through a day without being addressed by name or being complimented.

I have referred a few times to the school's morning news program. With money from a grant and the artistry of the technology instructor, Randall Miller, a schoolwide television broadcast is transmitted each morning to every classroom. Student leaders run the equipment and help write the script. Shortly after the bell rings, the news show begins. A student shares a brief lesson on one of the habits, after which other students announce birthdays and significant accomplishments, and recognize *Leaders of the Week*. Sometimes leadership skits are shared. If a special guest leader is visiting, all students get to see and hear from them via the broadcast. Most of the speaking parts are led by students, through time is always reserved for Muriel or one of the other administrators. But even then, the bulk of their message to students is "We love you. You are such outstanding leaders. Here is an example of how I saw a student exhibit one of the habits." And it all starts within the first fifteen minutes of the day. It is their way of Beginning with the End in Mind and Putting First Things First.

It is no different for teachers. Their mornings begin with a hallway huddle. The school has a series of motivational songs that students and faculty have chosen, and when the music goes off over the intercom system fifteen minutes before the first bell, teachers know to go out in the hallway to meet as a grade-level team. During the huddle, they share some type of inspirational quote, a great thing that happened the day before, anything special that happened in their lives, and, of course, anything they need to coordinate regarding the students. Occasionally the hallway huddles are combined so that schoolwide issues can be raised and successes celebrated. The point is that right from the start of each day it is next to impossible for a teacher to feel like an isolated island at A.B. Combs.

One of the ways the *7 Habits* language is frequently reinforced is through music. Students learn a number of songs filled with positive thoughts and values. Some songs are originals, but mostly they are popular songs that students already know. A teacher will from time to time adapt a song to fit *7 Habits* language. Each class seems to have its favorite tunes, while the school chorus has its own set of top hits. Music is one of the favorite tools for teaching the *7 Habits* in all of the schools that are doing the leadership theme.

When asked what the *7 Habits* have done for their school, clearly one of the most common things that teachers say is that the habits have given them a common language. The *7 Habits* language comes out in discussions about math, science, history, literature, physical education, or art—essentially all subjects. It comes out in nearly any meeting or activity. It is the common language when dealing with disciplinary issues. It is heard during assemblies. It has become so engrained that no one even pauses to think about it. It just comes out.

In short, celebrating and expressing belief in the potential of children is the language of A.B. Combs.

Artifacts

An anthropologist studying an ancient culture is unable to observe the behaviors of that culture or listen to its spoken language. So what they must do instead is study artifacts they uncover—buildings, pottery, art, tools, and so forth. They infer from those "things" what the culture of that ancient civilization might have been. Well, if an anthropologist were to visit A.B. Combs and try to infer its culture based only upon what "things" he or she could observe in its hallways and classrooms and on its grounds, the anthropologist could infer much.

Though some building extensions and trailers have been added in recent years, most of A.B. Combs is a fifty-year-old facility. But it does not feel the same as it did. As the Patels discovered, just walking through the front doors can be an engaging experience. Within a short distance, visitors come across posters, murals, and artwork depicting the school's mission and vision statements. Each hall is decorated with artwork that further portrays the leadership theme in one way or another. Hallways are labeled with street signs bearing the name of one of the habits or some other leadership theme. One wall displays photos of leaders who have visited the school. Another wall shows well-known world leaders whom students have learned about. International flags are displayed outside the media center to represent the various nationalities of students. In prominent places quotations drawn in calligraphy inspire and promote the potential of children. It is difficult to enter any hallway without wanting to stop and read.

In the spring, students put on an art show. Every student—not just the gifted artists—has a piece of inspirational art on display somewhere in the building. It is a magnificent display not just of art, but of hope, of dreams,

The Texarkana Independent School District has rebuilt its culture around a philosophy of win-win and seeking to understand with parents and staff.

of aspirations. The art show sends the reverberating message to each and every student: "You are important, you have gifts, and you have potential." It is a place where dreams and talents are nurtured.

When entering classrooms, visitors find posted on the walls class mission statements, more inspiring quotations, and fun uses of the quality tools, including "Issue Bins," where students can place concerns on a sticky pad for discussion at a later time. Visitors will also find artwork illustrating the habits, and charts and graphs letting students know where they stand as a class relative to class goals. Every room is filled with creative ideas and displays, but the key is that they all reinforce the leadership theme and class goals. They are not just random thoughts or crafts.

Much has also been done to clean up the school's external appearance. Besides involving student leaders in keeping the grounds clean and appealing, people in the community have joined in to make several improvements. For example, they joined with students to overhaul an open area in the center of the school. What once was mostly barren dirt is now a garden area with landscaping and large shade trees where teachers can bring students to read and share ideas. An artist's garden consisting of a mosaic of rocks and flowers was created by a professional artist. And, if artifacts could talk, the new amphitheater would tell how parents donated money and time to assemble an outdoor stage and benches so that the school would have a place where all students could gather at once.

> While organizations can pronounce a change in policy or procedures, they cannot proclaim a change in attitudes, beliefs, or behaviors . . . The concept of changing culture may seem simple enough, but changing culture is not like changing the décor.
>
> —*Richard DuFour and Robert Eaker*, Professional Learning Communities at Work

Yes, at A.B. Combs, the culture and theme of the school is visible in every direction. Virtually every picture or display has a story and a purpose behind it. This in no way suggests that the culture is only cosmetic. A school cannot change its culture merely by painting the walls or putting up some nice posters. Culture is not a decoration. Nevertheless, the beauty and surroundings of a school can contribute much toward creating an atmosphere that is conducive to academic achievement and students' peace of mind.

Traditions

Any culture tends to develop a set of traditions. A.B. Combs is no different. Over the years the school has developed a series of traditions that are intentionally designed to fulfill five purposes: 1) to give students an opportunity to be leaders, 2) to build relationships between students, faculty, family, and community friends, 3) to complete academic requirements of the district or state, 4) to reinforce school values such as service to the community, and 5) to create lasting memories for students.

Some of A.B. Combs's more popular traditions include:

Leadership Day: To respond to the many requests from educators wanting to see the school, twice a year the school is opened to registered guests for a day. Students teach visitors what leadership means at A.B. Combs. They perform musical arrangements, serve meals, give short speeches, share their data notebooks, teach the habits, guide tours, and showcase other leadership talents. Over four hundred student leaders participate in the day's events, much to the delight of guests. The number of guests is capped due to interest beyond the physical capacity of the school.

Inaugural Ball: This event takes place in the fall of each year following student body elections. It fulfills a state-mandated social dance requirement and celebrates democracy. Student leaders plan and conduct the gala's activities, which include the swearing in of the school's new student leaders. Its popularity has required that it be moved to a larger location, as over a thousand students and family members enjoy the festivities. While all students participate in one or more dances, Leaders of Dance provide the more challenging renditions.

International Festival: Food and dances from all over the world are enjoyed at this potluck event. Family and community members are invited to test delicacies from around the globe, and it too has been relocated due to bulging attendance. Student leaders are masters of ceremonies and event leaders.

Silver-Tray Luncheon: Fifth-grade students are given the opportunity to attend a special lunch where they are taught basic manners and table etiquette. Always a hit with the students, it also fulfills a state requirement—but do not tell the kids; they think it is a reward and just for fun.

Service Projects: Each grade level takes on one or more community service projects each year. From helping the local chapter of Red Cross, to donating to Oprah Winfrey's new school in South Africa, to managing canned-food drives, to an entire array of other activities, students lead the service projects under the direction of the guidance counselor, Mrs. Trueman. One project brought in $2,500 for the Leukemia Society.

Celebrate Success Day: Individual achievements are regularly celebrated in classrooms, assemblies, or morning news broadcasts. But Celebrate Success Day brings the entire school together to celebrate what they have accomplished as a school. It is a way of demonstrating what good leaders do and reinforcing why teamwork is important.

Other traditions dot the annual calendar, such as music performances and science fairs. Individual teachers have also developed their own classroom traditions, as when Barbara Watkins sets up tents in her room for reading camp. But again, all the traditions have purpose, and, in the end, students go away with new skills, added measures of confidence, and lasting leadership memories.

Favorite traditions include Leadership Day, where students are given a chance to showcase talents and be leaders.

Opportunities to think of others and give service are a tradition at every grade level with students taking the lead.

Folklore

One of the things that helps establish A.B. Combs's culture is the collection of stories that seem to hang around for years. For example, one day when the choir director, Jacquelin Keesee, was inadvertently delayed, she arrived late to class only to find a fourth-grade girl standing in front of the students and taking charge. She had the choir started and practicing their warm-ups. She had been given no direction to do it; she just did it. That is a story that has hung around for some time and has been repeated to students as an example of proactivity and leadership.

The story about the young student who challenged Muriel to change the code of conduct from MAGIC to LEAD has also stuck around and been used multiple times. To this day, Muriel takes advantage of the incident to let students know they are all leaders and can contribute.

Another story that has stuck for years involved one of the kindergarten teachers, Pam Almond. Her story is well-known by teachers who see it as a clear message of how the school respects all teachers and treats them as family. One evening, Pam was awakened at the stroke of midnight by news that her police officer husband had been shot in the head while making a routine traffic stop. As she describes it:

> As I was being rushed to the hospital, not knowing whether I would ever see my husband alive again, I tried to maintain my calm so as to not lose track of other important details, including what to do about my children who were still asleep at home and my students who I knew would be arriving at school bright and early. I soon learned that my police family had already cared for my children, and when I reached the school the next morning, I discovered that things were already cared for there. All they would say was, "Worry about you and your family first. We'll take care of your students."
>
> Putting *First Things First*, including family, is a big part of the everyday culture at A.B. Combs, not just in emergencies. I have always felt that, but even more so since we initiated the leadership theme. Gratefully, my husband miraculously survived, and many times we have used the *7 Habits* in our

Teachers like Pam Almond find leadership a joy to teach and a blessing to their individual lives.

home to help us adapt and get through this. That is what this school and this leadership approach is all about.

Indeed, stories abound at A.B. Combs. They are part of the culture; they reinforce the culture. Muriel knows the value of a good story and has herself become a bit of a master storyteller. Positive stories are what keep great cultures alive and progressing. And at the rate A.B. Combs is going, it appears there will be many more stories to tell in the years ahead.

Creating Culture: Walking the Walk

Again, culture is not just talking the talk, it is walking the walk.

At A.B. Combs, the culture begins with Susan and Karen. At Chestnut Grove Elementary it begins with Angie. At English Estates Elementary it begins with Dolores and Karen. At Dewey Elementary it begins with Kim. At Crestwood Elementary it begins with Barb or Barb.

Who are these individuals?

They are the executive assistants and receptionists. They are the first points of contact, the first impressions that visitors get when they visit the leadership schools. In many ways, they are the face of the school's culture.

But they will tell you that it is the principals, not them, who deserve the credit for the culture. After all, the principals are the ones who lead the meetings, approve the plans, and agree to the activities that will reinforce the culture.

But the principals in turn will emphatically refuse credit for the culture, channeling credit instead toward the teachers. After all, teachers are the ones who are on the front lines making it all happen.

But "No way!" will be the teachers' claim. They instead will single out the students and parents as being most deserving of the credit. After all, they could not do it without the students, and so much of the culture gets brought in from the homes. But ask any parent and they will immediately volley any credit for the culture back to the principals or teachers. And on and on it goes at the various leadership schools—everyone is passing credit.

And that is the way it should be. A school's culture cannot be a one-person undertaking if it is to succeed and be sustained. So credit rightfully goes to all involved.

But all that said, I think that most everyone involved would agree that the real credit for the successes of the leadership schools resides not in the people, but in the principles. In other words, credit is not in the principals, but in the *principles*. The *7 Habits* and the Baldridge tools are all based on timeless, universal principles. The principles apply to all aspects of life. As multiple parents have indicated, the *7 Habits* are principles that students can apply no matter what stage of life they are in or what their future career may be. The same principles can help guide a school and lead them to creating principle-based cultures. "Principals" will change from time to time, but "principles" will not.

Perhaps more than anything, the leadership principles have created a culture of confidence at A.B. Combs and the schools that have taken on the leadership theme. Story after story continues to soar out of classrooms and homes about what the leadership approach has done for students' self-confidence. Consider this example from Grey and Amy Jones, parents of three A.B. Combs students:

> Our son Michael was very reserved when he started at Combs. He had been given many opportunities to present in front of his class, but he had always resisted. The project that he did finally present was because of the leadership skills he had been taught. One day we heard something coming from his room. He was practicing his speech and making sure he was dressed properly for his presentation. Since then, he has excelled in storytelling and public speaking. In fact, he won the storytelling competition, and his class went to the national storytelling contest. Now he says he wants to be a leader.

Some of my favorite stories involve accounts of students taking the principles and culture back to their homes, such as this account sent in an e-mail to Muriel by Amy Dressel, the mother of a girl named Emma:

> Emma had such a great year last year! We can't keep books out of her hands. Above all else we see the leader in her. Being home with her this summer, I can't tell you the number of times I've heard, "Let's be proactive," or, "Daddy, can we get on the Jet-Skis? We need to have fun and Sharpen the Saw." But best of all was when my three-year-old Sam said to Emma, "Let's synergize! We can clean up and then we'll watch TV. It's a win-win!" I over-

heard this at 6:45 a.m. on a Saturday two weeks ago. Thanks for the best year a kindergartner (and her parents) could ever have!

I personally enjoy hearing of students teaching their parents about the leadership principles, thereby providing parents with a little home-schooling of their own. One father, for example, admitted that he was driving home from a sporting event recently when someone cut him off and his temper blew up. His young daughter kindly asked, "Daddy, I wonder if we can be a little more proactive in this situation." (For some thoughts on in-corporating the habits at home, see chapter 10: Bringing It Home.) Trust me. Scores of parents have shared similar stories of what the school's culture has done for their child and their homes. If I shared them all, it would not be long before you were back to thinking exactly what the Patels ini-tially thought: "This sounds too good to be true."

So I will refrain from sharing many more parent comments, though in concluding this chapter and moving on to what other schools are doing, I thought you would at least like to hear what the Patels are reporting now that they have been a part of A.B. Combs for a few years:

Mrs. Patel: Our older daughter attended a private school for kindergarten and first grade. She was a bright little girl, but was very shy. In the classroom, she would take the backseat and let others take the lead. But not anymore! A.B. Combs has given her so many opportunities to shine. They've given her leadership positions, like they do with all the students. When guests come to the school she is a greeter, and it has helped her to come out of her shell.

Mr. Patel: The *7 Habits* provide a template to help approach and organize your life. That is why I like it. It is not just an academic thing—it is an every-day life thing. Having these principles will make the students successful in all aspects of life.

Mrs. Patel: With this leadership model the children are involved in many service opportunities in the community—they even take the lead. The *7 Hab-its* provide the children with guidelines for life, not just homework. Even when they quarrel they pause, take a step back, and say, "Let's just calm down for a second and think win-win." I've heard that expression so many times. They work it through. I don't have to intervene.

The top comment visitors to A.B. Combs make is about students' self-confidence, particularly when standing and speaking in front of an audience of adults.

Since establishing themselves in Raleigh, the Patels have once again changed residences. Though there are several closer options, every day Mrs. Patel makes a forty-five-minute drive each way so that her children can remain at A.B. Combs, concluding, "It is definitely worth it."

While credit for what is happening at A.B. Combs and the other schools you will learn about truly does go to the principles, I do want to give great credit to everyone involved at A.B. Combs for what they have done in being the epicenter of the leadership theme. Part of their genius is in having the vision that this can indeed be done with elementary students. Surely many adults would have begun teaching these basic lessons of life at the middle or high school levels rather than the elementary level. But not only has A.B. Combs proven that it can be done at the elementary level, they have shown that it may be the most logical place to begin. Students seem more open and accepting of the leadership principles at the elementary level. The flexibility of elementary schools' structures and curricula are also more conducive to using the principles to implement an overarching cultural intervention.

> It always seems impossible until it's done.
>
> —*Nelson Mandela*

So I wholeheartedly applaud what A.B. Combs has done and continues to do. I admire how they care about young people and how they look for the good that is in them. The world needs more models and fewer critics; less focusing on what is wrong with today's youth. So for all these reasons, I salute Muriel, the administrators, the outstanding teachers, the staff, the students, the parents, and the entire A.B. Combs community of leaders.

6

Rippling Across the Globe

What we all are looking for when we embrace this process is
the same, but our paths are a little different given our unique
terrains.

—*Gailya Winters, Assistant Principal, A.B. Combs Elementary*

To this point, the limelight has been focused squarely on A.B.
Combs. Here and there I have made reference to other schools,
but clearly the attention has been on A.B. Combs. I have done
this intentionally so that you as a reader could concentrate on one story and
not be confused by multiple scenarios. But if A.B. Combs were the only
school having success with the leadership theme, this book would be of far
less interest and value than it is. Therefore, I am eager to highlight some of
the successes that are taking place at a sampling of other elementary schools
across the United States and other parts of the world. But first some background.

When A.B. Combs got going with the leadership approach, they did so
rather quietly. Even when they started seeing the early fruits of their efforts,
they kept their successes in reserve. It was mostly parents who first began
spreading the word about the leadership theme to other parents. But word
eventually also trickled out to other educators, and it was not long before
A.B. Combs began receiving knocks on its door from fellow educators and
curious parents who were hoping to get a peek, like the Patels.

Before long, Muriel started receiving invitations to share the school's
leadership approach at various professional conferences. From those pre-
sentations evolved an even greater lineup of visitors. Several of those visi-

tors returned to their schools committed to implementing all or portions of the leadership theme.

When my book *The 8th Habit* was published in 2004, I included a short synopsis of the A.B. Combs story, and that generated another pool of interested visitors. Though A.B. Combs was flattered by the attention, the collective smile that it generated on the staff's faces had a distinct grimace mixed into it, as if to say, "Thanks for the compliments, Stephen, but do you know how many more phone calls and visitors are now coming our way?" I suppose that when I asked Muriel in Washington, D.C., to let me know what happened if she ever tried teaching the *7 Habits* to young students, I should have warned her that I would pass the news along to hundreds of thousands of other people. With that, the ripple effect was beginning.

By 2006, when A.B. Combs was named the number one magnet school in the United States, word about the school was definitely out and more schools and educators were joining in. What is now taking the ripple effect to the next generation is that as these other schools are having similar successes, schools that neighbor them are starting to follow suit. So a second generation of ripples has begun.

No one, of course, knows for sure how far or wide the rippling will extend or how long it will continue. But, again, I would like to share highlights from a sampling of these other schools so that you can get a glimpse of what is happening on their campuses. Each of them, like A.B. Combs, uses as its foundation the *7 Habits*. Most are using some portion of the quality tools. Each has its unique look and feel. My intent is not to go into detail on each school's story, but rather to show what they are doing to put their unique signature onto the leadership approach. As you read about each school, I remind you once more to try to observe the universal nature of the principles and of children. I trust that you will be impressed not only by what they are doing, but by the speed of their success.

English Estates

I will begin with English Estates Elementary in Fern Park, Florida. It is home to Dr. Beth Sharpe, who as principal is passionate, visionary, and deeply interested in where students go in life.

The English Estates story actually began with Leslie Reilly, Choices Program Coordinator for Seminole County Public Schools. She had heard Muriel present at a model schools conference, and what she heard piqued her interest enough that soon afterward she found herself at one of A.B. Combs's Leadership Days. She says that within seconds of being inside the school she knew she wanted to create such a school in Seminole County. She admired how friendly the students were and was amazed to see their confidence, smiles, and resiliency, particularly since she knew what at least some of them must go through at home.

At the time, English Estates was a forty-year-old K–5 school that once had been a top school but had lost much of its glimmer. For some time, parents had been taking their children out of English Estates and moving them to other schools, almost in droves. The district's superintendent, Dr. Bill Vogel, was looking for a way to somehow get the school "refreshed" and thought that what Leslie Reilly had observed at A.B. Combs might be the right igniter. So the day after Beth took over as principal, Leslie "stunned" her by suggesting she go to A.B. Combs to investigate the feasibility of turning English Estates into a leadership school.

Beth is an inquisitive learner and very willing to explore. So she had scarcely settled into her new role before she and a handful of teachers were headed for A.B. Combs. This was during the 2004–2005 school year, and they too returned enlivened about the leadership theme, though Beth knew it would not be easy to replicate at English Estates.

After being principal for seven years at a school that was full of positives, it had been a shock for Beth to walk into English Estates only to find many of its 750 students and some faculty just going through the motions. There was a noticeable lack of heart. Over 50 percent of the students were on free or reduced meals. There was a wide racial mix among students, many of whom lived in apartment or condominium complexes, which meant frequent turnover. The school had not made Adequate Yearly Progress (AYP) for quite some time, and was considered a "School in Need of Improvement." Beth says she wrote out more disciplinary referrals in her first three months at English Estates than she had in the entire seven years at her previous school. These and other factors made it clear that it was going to take more than a roaring pep talk to turn things around.

Beth did not rush into anything. She invited Muriel to visit and share her story with the entire staff. That raised the energy and buy-in level of the staff to the point that Beth assembled a team and began planning a strategy with the intent to implement the leadership theme starting in the fall of 2005. They carefully planned out who would do what, when, and where. One of their first orders of business was to train all the staff in the *7 Habits*, which Beth describes as not only a lifting experience for her personally, but as a bonding, vision-stirring occasion for the entire staff.

Leadership Is Elementary is the new theme that greeted English Estates students when school was opened for an all-new year and an all-new way of teaching.

The leadership theme was launched in August 2005. When students arrived for the first day of school, they knew immediately that something was up. A bright new Roadrunner logo was painted on the front of the school with the words *Leadership Is Elementary*. Teachers spent a significant portion of the first two weeks teaching students the *7 Habits* and working to establish goals and expectations for the year. From that point on, teachers and staff kept the *7 Habits* alive by integrating them into the core curriculum, school programs, and everyday discussions—much as A.B. Combs had done.

So how did it go? In other words, what results did they see? At the conclusion of that inaugural year, English Estates received the district's award for "Most Improved Academic Scores," with test scores up as much as 35 percent in some subject areas. The state of Florida, which gives schools an A, B, C, D or F rating, moved English Estates from a B rating to an A rating. Moreover, the school met AYP for the first time.

Of course, the teachers, the district, and especially the parents were delighted with the rise in academic achievement. But . . . ! As was the case with A.B. Combs, there was more to celebrate—more fruits—than test scores. Most notably, discipline referrals dropped from 225 the previous year to 74 the year following. And, according to the annual climate survey, parents' approval of the school rose to 98 percent. Parents like Laura Carroll suggest why:

> At one point parents were literally saying, "We won't allow our children to go to English Estates." One of my friends even moved to a home that cost $100,000 more, just to go to a different school. I didn't have an extra $100K, so stuck it out and am glad I did. One night I came home and my daughters were busy cleaning their rooms—an event not too common without prodding. I kept asking, "What's going on here?" The girls said, "We're being proactive. We're synergizing. We're doing win-win." They were doing it all on their own. The 7 *Habits* are now integrated in a lot of our home activities. We ask, "What's First Things?" and then we focus on those things. It has reduced a lot of stress in our home. I learned these concepts as a manager after college. I wished I had learned them as a child.*

Teachers too are giving the leadership theme rave reviews. Sandi Johnson, a third-grade teacher who was selected to be the 7 *Habits* coordinator and certified instructor for the school, says: "When I went to A.B. Combs and saw what they were doing, I just kept thinking, 'This is everything I've ever wanted to do as a teacher.' I saw the music, the art, and the students owning their own data. Now it is my turn to do it in the classroom. I absolutely love teaching such valuable life skills to students."

One of the keys to the success of the leadership theme is that teachers love teaching the material to students. It is visible in the teachers' eyes, and they are very creative in how they go about it. So it is more than the students who are benefiting. In fact, attached to their A rating were "bonus"

---

* See chapter 10 for ideas on how to bring this home.

funds from the state to the tune of about $80,000 that could be divided according to what the parent council thought most appropriate. The parents unanimously voted to give all the money (minus 10 percent) to the teachers, feeling it was more than deserved. The teachers then voted to divide the money evenly with all staff, including custodial staff, as a way of letting everyone know that they were all in it together. The teachers said that the 7 *Habits* even played a part in dividing up the funds, as language used during their discussions was all about win-win and having an abundance mentality.

> In a day where we hear so much about bullying going on in schools, what a great process and moment this is to see kids respecting each other.
>
> —*Dede Schaffner, Seminole County School Board*

Since that first year, English Estates has primarily done more of the same, though each year they try to "up the ante a bit," as Beth says. They find ways to do regular renewal training and share best practices and successes with each other. When a new idea or activity gets added to their model, the idea typically has come from a teacher and it has been tested by a few others. Some of the new ideas or twists they have incorporated into the leadership theme:

- The "Morning News" is broadcast over television to all classrooms each day, similar to A.B. Combs. But rather than a small team being responsible for it, each fifth-grade class takes responsibility for six weeks of news. They write the scripts as part of writing assignments and include leadership insights. Students who do not stand in front of the camera take on other leadership responsibilities for the crew.

- A theme the school adopted is *Readers Are Leaders.* This is a reminder that schools that take on the leadership theme do not do so at the expense of students not excelling in core subjects.

- Each class creates a flag that represents its class mission statement.

- Each class has a *Talking Stick* to use during class meetings and discussions. Talking sticks are listening tools that allow only the student holding the stick to speak until they are finished saying what they have to say and feel understood.

- Students have fun creating a *7 Habits Trail Mix* consisting of seven tasty ingredients, each representing a habit. This emphasizes how the habits synergistically complement each other, just as the students' talents can complement each other.
- Some classes have writing exercises called *Random Acts of Leadership*. Students record ways they have seen classmates show leadership.
- Attendance at parent-teacher conferences was traditionally low. Some parents simply did not want to hear what either they or their children were doing wrong. So English Estates implemented a *Dinner-Data-Discussion* night. Dinner is provided for a small fee for those who want it, and then they visit the classroom where students lead parents through their goals and data in their data notebooks, with the heaviest focus on what students are doing right. Some classes are now experiencing perfect parental attendance.
- The Rotary Club is a great friend of English Estates and sponsors activities such as the annual *Take a Kid Fishin' Day,* which is used as an incentive for attendance, good behavior, and reading. The Rotary Club also sponsors an *Essay Contest* in which multiple schools participate, but one of the judges noted that she can nearly always tell which essays come from English Estates because they tend to be more thoughtful and often contain *7 Habits* language. Moreover, when the students present their essay they are more poised and comfortable with adults than are students from other schools.

Teachers monitor progress in reading, writing, and mathematics in *Class Data Notebooks* and then bring the notebooks together to identify "common problems" that the school as a whole can work on together. They have also created a "compelling scoreboard" of the schoolwide data titled "Leading with Data."

Early on, Beth was challenged with a question: "With all the pressure to perform academically, how did you dare choose to work first on changing the culture?" Her response was simple: "Because it felt like the right thing to do." To that she added, "The core of our school is relationships and the culture. The *7 Habits* is the catalyst that enhanced both our relationships and the new culture."

According to the teachers, the biggest influence the *7 Habits* have had on their culture is in giving them a common language that they share even with the students. A first-grade teacher seeing a fifth-grade student in the hall can say, "This isn't Sharpen the Saw time; you need to be doing..." and the student knows exactly what is implied.

We Love to Sharpen The Saw!

At all schools, one of the students' favorite habits is Sharpen the Saw and they love to share how they do it.

Clearly one of the signature pieces of the English Estates story is the district's involvement. Both Dr. Vogel and Leslie Reilly were very supportive, but so too was the district's entire school board. Board member Dede Schaffner, for example, is a retired district volunteer coordinator and says she knew a good thing the minute she saw it. With her urging, the entire board voted to offer funds to cover all eighty English Estates staff members to be trained in the *7 Habits* and helped fund a cosmetic lift for the school.

Another signature component not to be overlooked is the speed of the school's success. The quickness with which they were able to improve their culture and raise academic scores is in many ways a tribute to being able to learn from A.B. Combs. But much of the credit also goes to English Estates' combined patience and aggressiveness in getting started. Beth patiently took time to first get people on board and to develop a viable strategic plan. Only then did she go aggressively after her vision with full steam. Once under way, there was no "try a little of this" attitude in her, and that is a big reason why they accomplished so much in so little time.

Chestnut Grove

Clearly one of the signature components of Chestnut Grove Elementary in Decatur, Alabama, is its partnership with a successful local business leader, Donnie Lane. When Lane learned what was happening at A.B. Combs, he was so intrigued that he went to nearby Chestnut Grove Elementary and convinced Principal Lauretta Teague to gather a few teachers and join him in traveling to North Carolina to see firsthand what was happening.

Lauretta is a leader who always has a look of calm resolve, and when she moves forward on something people know her intent is to do what is right for the students. She describes her first visit with Donnie Lane and how the leadership theme got started at her school:

> In the fall of 2004, Donnie Lane, CEO of Enersolv Corporation, called me on the phone to discuss a matter regarding my school. He advised me that having parental and community support was important to the success of our school and that there were people in the community who wanted to make a difference.
>
> We met later in my office and he showed me a video of A.B. Combs Elementary from *The 8th Habit*. He felt our students could benefit from learning the *7 Habits* and that we should visit Combs. He chartered a small plane, and a few of us went with him, including one of our parent volunteers. After seeing A.B. Combs, the teachers all turned to me and said, "Mrs. T, we can do this." I had a vision, they had a vision, and the rest is history.

Upon returning to Decatur, the teachers who had traveled to A.B. Combs made a presentation to the staff about how they felt the *7 Habits* would benefit students, including how it would help the students to be more responsible and accountable for their learning. It was teachers convincing teachers. The staff became excited about embracing something they felt would benefit the students and would be a lift for them as teachers. The question that remained was "How?"

Once more, Donnie Lane volunteered support. He covered expenses for getting the entire staff trained in the 7 Habits. He wanted it done in a special way, so during the summer of 2005 he paid for them to go off-site to a comfortable resort area to complete the training. Two parents also joined in. During breaks and in the evenings, they brainstormed ways they could best transfer the habits to the students. Lauretta insists that "the retreat provided an opportunity for the staff to bond with each other, and to develop a new vision for the school." She adds, "The staff returned to the school as a unified team with the right attitude. There was no opposition from any of the teachers." And when the school doors reopened for the start of the new school year, the teachers were ready to go.

Chestnut Grove does many of the same things that are done at A.B. Combs and English Estates. They share leadership insights each morning as part of their televised morning news (SNEWS). Hallways are eloquently decorated with reminders of the 7 Habits, as well as the school's new mission statement and code of conduct. The Decatur Public Works Department made street signs for them so they could name each hallway after one of the habits. An artistic parent added her flair throughout the buildings in the form of murals. The habits are also reinforced in fun ways dur-

Student leaders at Chestnut Grove are eager and prepared to tell visitors all about the 7 Habits by word or by song.

ing assemblies, where a *7 Habits* song created by the music teacher is sung with gusto.

It is interesting that at Chestnut Grove the teachers do not focus on creating a lot of special lesson plans. They know the *7 Habits* so well that any time an opportunity comes up, they simply insert questions and principles as they see fit and when it feels right—no matter what the subject or what time of day it may be. It comes naturally to them. According to Lauretta,

> Implementing *The 7 Habits of Highly Effective People* into our school has made a significant difference in how we respond to each other and how we teach children to take responsibility for their own actions and behavior. We are so proud of our students and the leadership roles they now have within the school and the character that is developing within each child. It is making an impact on children and the culture of the school. Students are taking ownership for their education. It's making the teachers and students talk performance. They are all tracking their own progress. It truly is a win-win! I have not heard one negative comment from parents. All I hear from parents is about how the students are using the *7 Habits* at home. And I can honestly say that it has helped me personally in my relationships.

A big part of the Chestnut Grove story is that other elementary schools in the district are now also under way with the leadership theme; one of them is led by one of Lauretta's former assistant principals. Donnie Lane is serving as president of the local Chamber of Commerce and is coaching colleagues on how they too can sponsor and support a school. He is also involved in taking the *7 Habits* to the middle school that the elementary schools feed into, and plans are in place to take the leadership theme to all schools within the Decatur district.

As for Donnie Lane, the only payday he looks forward to in return for his generosity is when he sees the smiles on the students' faces and the confidence in their eyes. He gives all the credit for what is happening at Chestnut Grove to Lauretta and her high-quality teachers, and distances himself from interfering with school decisions. But in spite of his humility, there is no doubt that Donnie's involvement is a major element in the journey of Chestnut Grove—a journey that is making a difference in many young lives. Thanks, Donnie.

Adams County, Illinois

Nestled in the rolling plains of Western Illinois farm country and pinned against the Mississippi River lies Adams County, Illinois. There the sun rises up over the horizon each day to signal that something exciting is happening.

The story there began with Dr. George Meyer. George ascended through the education ranks first as a teacher, then as an administrator, and finally as a district superintendent. When he retired, he joined the staff at Quincy University, where he became dean of the School of Education. About that same time, he came across a book that included principles that he says he wished he had been able to teach while in the public schools. The book was *The 7 Habits of Highly Effective People.*

George began teaching the *7 Habits* to college students who were studying to become teachers. Knowing that the best way to learn a concept is to teach it, he started having his students teach the habits to students at Dewey Elementary in Quincy. Dewey is a K–3 school with about 220 students, 63 percent of whom are on free or reduced lunches. Initially, it was only the college students who were teaching the *7 Habits* once a week to students, but the more the full-time teachers listened to the habits being taught, the more they too started using the language in their classrooms. Gradually the *7 Habits* became a common language at the school.

Christie Dickens was principal of Dewey at the time, and eventually she and a few others visited a Leadership Day at A.B. Combs. They were very impressed by everything, but according to Christie the most important thing they observed was in the eyes and faces of the Combs students—they could see the eyes and faces of their own Dewey students. In other words, they could envision their students doing the same types of leadership behaviors. So even though they were a much smaller school with far fewer resources, they knew they could take on the leadership approach, mostly because they knew their students could do it. They just needed to figure out how to do it their own way—their own Dewey way.

Meanwhile, George was certified as a *7 Habits* facilitator and was able to take all the faculty and staff through the *7 Habits* training. Before long, all kinds of art, poems, and new songs with *7 Habits* lyrics were ringing out of classrooms, and students started taking on a new attitude about school.

Habit #6:
Synergize

When school pictures went awry, Christie Dickens worked with the photographer to come up with a proactive, win-win solution.

In fact, students started showing up to school early—twenty minutes early—to attend the daily before-school assembly, a favorite activity that started quite serendipitously. What happened was that more than half the students would arrive early to school each day to receive a school-provided breakfast, after which they would go out to the playground. But on days with inclement weather, many of them filled the gym instead. The gym on those days could get quite raucous, so a few teachers started conducting fun *7 Habits* activities as a way of maintaining some semblance of order. When other students heard of the activities, they too began arriving early. Soon parents were calling and asking, "Why is my child insisting on being at school twenty minutes early?" Indeed, there is no requirement to attend the assembly since school does not officially begin until 8:05 a.m., yet at 7:45 a.m. over 90 percent of the students are there. Student greeters welcome students at the door. Students sing *7 Habits* songs, perform skits, celebrate birthdays, recite the Pledge of Allegiance, and share successes. Several parents attend, including one father who brings his children to school each morning on his way to work and then stays long enough to watch the assembly, claiming, "It's the best way to start my day."

One day the school photographer came to Christie with a horrified look on his face. Something had gone wrong and all the pictures he had taken would have to be redone. Rather than being upset, Christie got an idea. She asked if—along with the standard mug shots—he would take photos of students doing *7 Habits* activities. He agreed and those photos were turned into posters that are distributed throughout the school to brighten students' faces and remind them of *7 Habits* principles.

The teachers and staff were surprised at how quickly the leadership theme impacted their culture. One of the objectives they had set in implementing the process was to increase parent involvement, and that did happen. The number of parents attending PTA meetings more than doubled, as did parent attendance at monthly parent-child activity sessions. Meanwhile, tardiness declined 35 percent, disciplinary referrals dropped 75 percent, and referrals of students for completion of work declined 68 percent. But the real delight came over the course of the year when they could see the impact the program was having on the Illinois Standards Achievement Test (ISAT) scores in both reading and math, as indicated in the following chart:

	Before 7 Habits (2005)	After three months of 7 Habits (2006)	After one year three months of 7 Habits (2007)
Reading	57.4%	72.2%	89.7%
Math	77.4%	90.3%	100%

Though the test scores represented significant improvement, it is again interesting to note that in all the interviews conducted for this book with administrators, teachers, parents, and students, not one of them mentioned a single thing about the higher test scores. All their focus was on the attitudes, the behaviors, and the confidence of the students. Third-grade teacher Lori Post noted, "The self-confidence of the third-graders rose dramatically that first year. Everyone wanted to be a leader. It gave them so much joy. Many of them started out rather shy, but at the end of the year every one of them gave a speech. The look in their eyes indicated there was nothing they felt they couldn't do."

As principal, Christie says she saw a lot of change in students during the first year. Much of it was evidenced when students were brought in from the playground to resolve disputes. On one occasion, two boys were brought to her and instead of trying to solve the problem for them, Christie simply had them talk it out. Without any coaching, one of the boys accused the other of "not being very proactive" in response to what had been done to him. But then he paused and admitted, "I wasn't thinking win-win, either." On another occasion, a boy who had difficulty controlling his emotions, yet who was looked up to as a leader by other students, approached Christie prior to making a presentation, saying, "I've got to have a plan. The kids are counting on me." In each case, what Christie is quick to point out is that it was the students who were doing the problem solving.

Denise Poland is the school's social worker and sees the *7 Habits* from a unique perspective, as she works with students who face some of the more difficult challenges. She has been at Dewey for nine years and is quick to note that Dewey was a good school even prior to the *7 Habits*. Yet when asked if the *7 Habits* had made any difference at the school, "Huge! Huge!" was her emphatic reply. The first thing that she points out is that the *7 Habits* provide a common language. "We all speak the same speak," she says. "Students hear the same language from classroom to classroom throughout the school." This means she can use the same *7 Habits* language whether she is working with a kindergartner or a third-grader. In fact, she says, "I used to counsel the students on what to do, but now in many cases I sit back and listen in amazement as the students use the *7 Habits* to come up with their own solutions."

Denise finds that Habit 1: Be Proactive, in particular, gives her language to help students understand that while they cannot control everything that adults do and not everything that happens to them is their fault, they can in most cases control what they do in response, including "Be Proactive. Call 911," if needed. She notes that some of the students come from tough home situations, including a few whose parents hated school as kids and still dislike having anything to do with school. So she has been teaching the parents the *7 Habits* in monthly lessons with as many as seventy-five of them in attendance. "It gives the parents coping tools for dealing with issues," she says.

And clearly the students and parents are not the only ones benefiting. As Christie points out, "Our focus from the beginning was on looking at how the habits could help the children. But early on we noticed that some of the real changes that were occurring were not with the students, or with their parents, but with our staff. We saw talents coming out of them that we had never seen before. And when they share the influence this has had on their interactions with each other, and the positive influences it is having on their personal lives and families, those are the moments I enjoy the most."

Dewey does many of the same things described at A.B. Combs and the other leadership schools. I have only skimmed their story. However, I want to emphasize what I see as two signature elements of the Dewey story. The first is that Christie Dickens is no longer principal. She was asked by District Superintendent Thomas Leahy to become an assistant superintendent, largely so she could mentor other principals on how to implement the leadership theme. She had strong hesitations about taking the position because the 7 Habits were only one year under way at Dewey and she did not want the initiative to lose energy. So when she turned the baton over to Jerry Ellerman, it was with some trepidation. Jerry, whose previous experience was mostly at the high school level, also had hesitations about the new role, including wondering what this 7 Habits "stuff" was all about. But today, a year into his new role, moisture comes to his eyes as he talks of what is happening with the students. He points to one student in particular who has extreme emotional issues and most likely should be in a self-contained setting. "It's only the 7 Habits that are keeping him out," says Jerry. "When his class does 7 Habits activities or uses the language, he feels something and settles right down and focuses."

At all of the previously mentioned schools, the principals have always remained the same—there has been no changing of the guard. The last thing Mrs. Dickens wanted to hear when she returned to Dewey for a visit was "Things just aren't the same." But with a year in the rearview mirror, today she is delighted to report that if there has been any change at all at the school then it has been for the better, as teachers have stepped up to take the teaching of the leadership principles to an even higher level. What this indicates to me is that the leadership theme is not solely dependent on the style of the principal or the passion of any one individual.

The second signature element is that Dewey is now only one of eight elementary schools within the Quincy Public School District that have embraced the leadership theme. From the beginning, George Meyer had aspirations of creating a principle-centered community and his wish just might come true. The United Way of Adams County had been studying for months how it could best contribute to the community, and after reviewing several options and visiting Dewey, it decided to find ways to fund taking the 7 *Habits* to all 10,000-plus students in the county's pre-K–12 schools over a period of three years. They began at the elementary level and are working their way up to the high schools, and they are well ahead of schedule. Already more than three hundred teachers have been trained in the habits. Each school has different student demographics and teacher personalities, so they are all doing it in accordance with what is most comfortable for them and adding their own twist. Washington Elementary, for example, holds a Grandparents' Day for students to teach their grandparents the 7 *Habits*. Needless to say, it is music to grandma's and grandpa's ears.

As each school finds its own niche, the United Way is right behind them all the way. It has even assembled several other business partners to provide funding not only for Quincy schools but for the entire county, including preschools and parochial schools. I cannot begin to tell you how excited and humbled I feel at the potential of what is happening, as a new ray of hope is spreading its glow over Adams County.

United Way of Adams County was seeking to take a position on an issue in the community, and to really put forth an effort to engage the community in something that could truly make a difference. We examined a number of underlying challenges in our community, such as poverty, and considered how it was leading to other things like teen pregnancies, substance abuse, and underemployment. We knew that if children succeed in school and succeed in life, they are more likely to avoid a lot of those other problems, so after doing our research and seeing Dewey Elementary, we decided to take the 7 *Habits* to all students in the county. Once we stepped up and made a three-year commitment to doing this, it was a matter of no time before local businesses were willing to step in and help with more funding, or to provide training space, or do whatever they could do.

—*Cheryl Waterman, Executive Director,*
United Way of Adams County, Illinois

These are but a few of the stories that reflect how the leadership theme is rippling across the United States. I could tell you about more schools like Rowlett Elementary in Florida, which has combined the *7 Habits* with the school's magnet theme of arts and music for more than eight years. While not doing the full leadership theme, teachers there are extremely creative in matching the habits to Florida's standards for character education. I could also tell you about Summit Academy, a charter school in Draper, Utah, where forty parents per week volunteer to teach students the habits. I could tell you about schools in Texas, Arizona, West Virginia, California, New Jersey, and other states that are now on their way. Indeed, there are many more exciting U.S. stories to share. But the title of this chapter is Rippling Across the Globe and so it's time to look at a few examples of what is happening beyond U.S. borders.

Canada

The leadership theme is beginning to ripple across the globe, though I do not wish to overstate this because it is still in the early stages internationally. But let me share a few examples, starting in Alberta, Canada.

In Medicine Hat, the *7 Habits* started off as a district initiative for teachers and administrators nearly a decade ago, when David George, principal of Crestwood Elementary, was certified to be one of two *7 Habits* facilitators for the district. The ensuing *7 Habits* training was received so well by participants that the district decided to expand the offering by adding three more facilitators. That team has now trained over 250 district personnel, including all central office staff and school principals.

During one of the sessions that David attended, someone planted an idea that took root in him. They said that it would be great if the staff of an entire school attended the *7 Habits* so that all the teachers and administrators could use the habits as a common language. As a principal, David was intrigued by the idea, but he was not sure how his staff would react. He hoped at best that 80 percent of them would get behind it, but to his delight, all but one or two voted to do it. "We're in!" they said.

Thirty teachers and twenty support staff were trained in the habits chunk by chunk over a six-week period. The habits quickly became a noticeable part of how the staff did things, particularly as *7 Habits* language was used in meetings and in other interactions. In fact, things were going very well when David came across the brief write-up about A.B. Combs in *The 8th Habit*. Immediately he was hooked on the idea of taking the habits to the students. Shortly thereafter, he and two others made a visit to A.B. Combs. They returned home inspired and brought with them two pieces of advice from Muriel. First, she said, "Do not water down the *7 Habits*. Trust that the students will understand them." Second, "Do not boil someone else's water." In other words, "Do it your own way."

When the time came to take the leadership theme to the students, they did it on a more gradual basis than the schools previously mentioned. They spent the first year just softly familiarizing students with the habits. For example, a magician came at the start of the year and did magic tricks representing all seven habits—a memorable hit with the students. Then, during September, they taught the Foundational Principles during assemblies and occasionally brought them up in class discussions. When October came, they focused on Habit 1, followed by Habit 2 in November, and so forth throughout the year. In June, they did a review of all the habits and celebrated ways that students had applied them during the year.

In the second year they began integrating and blending the habits into all subject areas, much as the other leadership schools had done. Sixth-graders, for example, had a required assignment to read a novel. As part of the accompanying writing assignment, they were given certain sections of the novel and asked, "If you were to rewrite that paragraph, how might you rewrite it so that the person was proactive instead of reactive?" They then talked as a class about how the outcomes of the book would have been different had the characters handled things according to the habits.

As the *7 Habits* gained momentum with students, the teachers also became increasingly engaged. One teacher wrote a song called "Color Me Covey," which matches each habit to one of the colors of the rainbow. David George also carved out a portion of each staff meeting for teachers to swap ideas and share successes. One idea the teachers all decided to adopt was to place a section on student report cards for giving students feedback on how well they are progressing relative to each habit.

Throughout each day, students are encouraged to "Catch Somebody

Doing Covey." They can then put that student's name on a ticket and place it into a barrel for a drawing and a prize. During assemblies, teachers recognize students who are 7 *Habits Heroes.*

When asked to identify what the 7 *Habits* have done for Crestwood, David's first response was identical to what principals at the other schools have said: "It gives us a common language that has unified us." But his greatest focus is on what it has done for the students. He says that before habits were introduced, when students were sent to his office for discipline problems they would come in pointing fingers at each other, putting all the blame on the other one. Now, he says, they come in taking responsibility for their own actions, and he can talk to them about "withdrawals in Emotional Bank Accounts" and how they can "make deposits"—and everyone immediately understands. He cites similar experiences in working with parents who come in upset about something. They too can use the habits as the common language for solving challenges.

The Crestwood staff has found what Muriel said about not watering down the habits to be true. Students of all ages understand the language. For example, the kindergarten teacher was reading a story to her students and asked for someone to describe what had happened in the story. The class was not even discussing the habits but one girl raised her hand and, referring to the character in the story, said, "She had a paradigm shift," and then went on to explain why.

Parents have been very favorable to what is happening. David George invited parents to fill out a survey on the school, and whereas before, thirty parents might fill it out and turn it in, eighty filled it out with each one giving the 7 *Habits* portion a "very favorable" rating. Meanwhile, the school's parent council has joined in and arranged for training in the 7 *Habits for Families.* Over sixty families have taken advantage of the offering.

Another indicator of parent approval arose during the summer of 2007. David found himself struggling because he anticipated that the school would lose about fifty students due to attrition, given the school's maturing population base. That meant the school would also lose two teachers, which David did not want to see happen. But he says that one by one he started getting knocks on his door from parents he had never met before. They came from outside school boundaries saying they heard the school was doing the *7 Habits* and wanted their children enrolled. It happened often enough that when the new school year began, he had a full allotment of students and he was able to keep all the teachers.

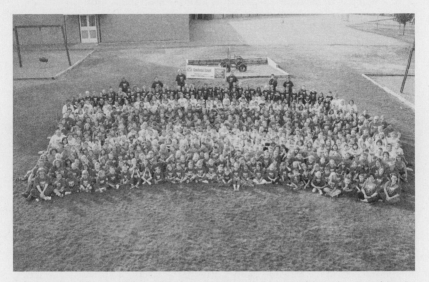

When a local business learned that Crestwood was teaching the *7 Habits,* its employees approached the school with "How can we help?"

Parents were not the only ones knocking at David George's door. He got a call one day from a local business, Criterion Catalysts and Technologies, Canada, which had heard the school was doing the *7 Habits*. They as a company were also doing the *7 Habits* and wondered if they could somehow help the school. When they learned that Crestwood was kicking off a year-long celebration in anticipation of the 2008 Olympics in Beijing, and that the school would be having an "opening ceremony" with activities built around the *7 Habits,* the company volunteered to purchase shirts for each student. The shirts arrived in all seven colors of the rainbow to match the "Colors of Covey" song. David chuckles a bit when he admits that when the company first called he was not even sure who they were or what business they were in. "They just wanted to be a part of it," he says. The association has turned into a valuable business-school partnership.

> Today's business world is very competitive, and most businesses operate
> on a global basis. To be competitive you have to have a strong
> foundation of people skills. If we can have the habits developed at this
> early age, these children will truly be the leaders and the good
> employees of the future. So it is truly an investment in the future.
>
> —*Rick Redmond, Vice President, Criterion Catalysts and Technologies, Canada*

David George and his staff are now enjoying the opportunity to mentor other schools in Alberta. Three or four public schools and a private school for Sikh students are in the early stages of implementation and are delighted to have Crestwood as a nearby resource. David was also delighted to find that another school in Red Deer, Alberta, was also well under way, having initiated the leadership theme unaware of what Crestwood was doing.

I will not go into detail about Red Deer, but one thing I find interesting about the school is that it was already a "top tier" school before it ever got started on the leadership theme. Mike Fritz is the principal at Joseph Welsh Elementary in Red Deer. He points out that the school already had strong test scores, good students, lots of parent support, and so many good things going for it. So if anything, Mike, says, "We were a great school deciding if we wanted to become even greater."

So it was with some curiosity that Mike approached the entire staff to see if any might be interested in pursuing the leadership theme. The staff's response was overwhelming. As he describes it, "They were vibrating with energy." They brought Muriel to their school to share her story and fell in love with her. Eight parents from the school council joined them in their *7 Habits* training, as well as some staff from the middle and high schools into which their school feeds. Afterward, they initiated many of the same activities that other leadership schools have implemented.

The school is in both a district and a province that are quite rigorous about collecting feedback. Their data is collected by outside professionals, and the school's first-year results, collected by Alberta Education, appear to confirm what parents want in a school:

Survey Item	Prior to *7 Habits*	After One Year of *7 Habits*
Parents who agree that students are taught attitudes and behaviors that will make them successful at work when they finish school	69.4 %	92.3 %
Staff who agree that students are taught the attitudes and behaviors that will make them successful when they finish school	77.8 %	100 %
Parents who are satisfied that students model the characteristics of active citizenship	81.4 %	90.7 %
Parents who agree that their child is encouraged at school to be involved in activities that help the community	65 %	100 %
Parents who agree that students respect each other	84 %	98 %
Disciplinary incidents referred to school administration for further follow up.		67 % decrease

In addition, a year and a half into the implementation of the *7 Habits,* Schollie Research and Consulting, which administers surveys to about five hundred of Alberta's schools to include parents, students, and staff, found the following at Joseph Welsh Elementary:

Survey Item	Disagree	Agree
Students: I feel that I get chances to be a leader in my classroom or in my school.	5 %	95 %
Parents: The Character Education Program, *The 7 Habits of Highly Effective People,* has had a positive impact on the atmosphere at my child's school.	1 %	99 %
Parents: I would like to see the Character Education Program, *The 7 Habits of Highly Effective People,* continue at my child's school.	3 %	97 %
Teachers: The Character Education Program, *The 7 Habits of Highly Effective People,* assists me in teaching students the principles needed in their daily lives.		100 %
All Staff: The Character Education Program, *The 7 Habits of Highly Effective People,* has provided this school with a useful language to communicate to students, staff, and parents.		100 %
All Staff: The Character Education Program, *The 7 Habits of Highly Effective People,* has had a positive impact upon this school.		100 %
All Staff: I would like to see the Character Education Program, *The 7 Habits of Highly Effective People,* continue at this school.		100 %

While the percentages are impressive, Mike says he sees the most amount of change in how students handle disagreements. It used to be that students came in to him often in a very defensive manner. What had started out as a fairly small problem had become a big problem by the time it got to him. But now he finds that students either work out conflicts themselves or with the help of staff using win-win language. "What we are creating," he says, "are problem-solvers."

Mike Fritz laughs when he describes how in the beginning he wondered if any of the staff would be interested in becoming a 7 *Habits* school. Now he says that, if anything, he is the one saying, "Well, let's think about this a bit," and the teachers are the ones saying, "Come on! Let's go! Let's go! Let's do more."

Singapore

Chua Chu Kang Primary School in Singapore has 2,200 students with an average of forty per class. Fortunately, its large size is matched by the teachers' energy for teaching the 7 *Habits*.

Singapore has an education force and national philosophy well suited to the 7 *Habits*. In 1995, for example, the Ministry of Education approved training in the 7 *Habits* for all teachers, and half of the twenty thousand educators took up the offer. The ministry also requires that students at all grade levels be taught character building as part of a civics and moral education section. Most students follow a standard nationwide curriculum for that class, but recently a number of K–12 (primary through secondary) schools have taken some creative steps to insert the 7 *Habits* into the national curriculum. Most notable among the elementary schools is Chua Chu Kang Primary School, where Mr. Francis Foo is principal.

Mr. Foo was passionate about bringing the 7 *Habits* to the students, but did not want to impose his will upon the staff. So he first tested the waters by inviting teachers who were teaching primary five and six (eleven year olds) to investigate the idea of taking the 7 *Habits* to students. The one question he had for those teachers was "Would you be committed to this?" Their response was so encouraging that they decided to give it a go.

A number of the teachers and some parents had been through the 7 *Habits*, but nobody had really thought much about how to teach the habits to students, and no one at the time had heard of A.B. Combs. So in 2006, under the leadership of Ms. Ho Siow Chun and Madam Ng Boon In, and with the support and vision of Mr. Foo, the team worked with Franklin-Covey representatives in Singapore to tailor a set of teacher and student guides.

The name on the front of the Singaporean school echoes the rich diversity both of the school and of the country's student population.

The first order of business was to train all one hundred teachers in the habits. Once that was complete, a plan was set out for how they would teach the habits to students. They decided to teach Habits 1–3, the Private Victory, at the Primary 4 level (ten-year-olds), while Primary 5 students (eleven-year-olds) would be taught Habits 4–7, the Public Victory. Primary 6 (twelve-year-olds) students were to be mentored in how to use all *7 Habits* to prepare for their major national exam.

While the teaching of the habits was mostly reserved for the upper grades, all grade levels are in some way exposed. *7 Habits* posters, for example, grace the school's hallways, including several enlarged photos of students exhibiting the habits. Large signs representing each habit hang in the assembly area. As part of a special week, Primary 1 students designed *7 Habits* bookmarks, while Primary 2 students created badges, Primary 3 students composed *7 Habits* rap songs, Primary 4 students did comic strips, and Primary 5 students wrote stories—all of which were tailored to reinforcing the *7 Habits*. But the real treat was the school's play. Its title was a familiar one, *Snow White and the Seven Dwarfs*, but in this version the seven dwarfs (each representing a habit) were tasked with teaching Snow White how organize her life.

The school's approach is different than those mentioned previously since the habits are only emphasized at the upper levels and are taught as a designed curriculum instead of using the ubiquitous approach. Still, the school is thrilled about what they see happening with students. In honor of their efforts, they were recently awarded the nation's Character Development Award by the Ministry of Education. And as for those national exams, Mr. Foo reports that the school has moved out of the "average" range and into the ranks of the higher-rated schools.

What is happening internationally excites me. Other schools are also under way, such as Timboon Elementary in Australia, which has been replicating the A.B. Combs model for a number of years. More schools are in the initial stages in Europe and other parts of Asia. And though the leadership theme is just getting moving internationally, I see great potential in what this can do for children across the globe. As FranklinCovey has discovered in its corporate dealings where the 7 *Habits* growth is expanding outside the United States at a pace even faster than in the U.S., these principles are universal. They span all cultures, all creeds, and all socioeconomic levels. So given my deep belief in the potential and worth of children—all children—I am delighted by the vision of where this leadership theme has the potential to travel around the world.

The Meaning of a Signature

In summarizing this chapter, I am reminded of the song lyric "I Did It My Way." In a very real sense, that is what each of these schools is singing. They are each adding their own unique signatures to the leadership approach.

In an earlier chapter I insisted that teachers must not only have an ownership manual, they must have ownership. This is not an off-the-shelf program that teachers stand up and regurgitate verbatim. First they must live and love the 7 *Habits* and other leadership concepts. Otherwise students will feel the duplicity. But more than anything, they must attach their own personality—their own voice—to what they are teaching. They must make it their own. When they do, it shows up in their eyes, in their language, and in the way they handle discipline matters. At that point, the students begin feeling it and believing it.

> In years to come, your students may forget what you taught them. But they will always remember how you made them feel.
>
> —*Sign in A.B. Combs faculty room, author unknown*

And that is what is so great about each of these schools, each of these teachers. They have all added their unique signatures to what is happening. Their schoolhouse models may, in general, look similar to A.B. Combs's model, yet ultimately they are all different. Not all of the existing schools, for example, focus as much on Baldrige principles, though most have some quality tools in place, including the data notebooks. Not all utilize the windows that A.B. Combs integrates. Instead they have their own models, their own philosophies, based on their unique needs and strengths. And that is not only okay, it is important.

Every classroom has a different feel. No matter how many lesson plans are shared between teachers, no teacher ever does it quite the same. The important thing in the end is what the students *feel*. When students *feel* the leadership theme is directed in their best interests and when they *feel* that their teacher has their potential in mind, that is the moment when students take a giant step forward being able to successfully lead their own lives well into the twenty-first century.

7

Moving Upward and Beyond

The foundation of every state is the education of its youth.

—*Diogenes Laertius, quotation on ceiling of Joliet Township High School*
Central auditorium

A fter participating in a 7 *Habits* class at their high school, two sisters decided they had what it takes to start a business, and their newfound proactivity led them to become successful teen entrepreneurs.

A young high school student was filled with venomous desire for revenge after his older brother was fatally stabbed during a fight at school. But then he was touched by a passage out of the 7 *Habits for Teens* that he read as part of a freshman class. He went home and wrote a three-page sonnet, called it his mission statement, and committed to devoting his life to doing good in honor of his brother.

In inner-city Chicago, a Latino high school student was introduced to the 7 *Habits* as part of a literature class. She says that her three-word mission statement, "Never give up," led her to become not only the first in her family to go to college, but the first to graduate.

In Singapore, a young Chinese student was struggling to keep up in school and lacked focus. But then he took to heart every page of the 7 *Habits for Teens* that he had received at school. His grades spiked upward, he now has a career plan, and he is recognized as a leader at his school.

As you are well aware by now, the emphasis of this book is on what is happening with the leadership theme in elementary schools. But as you might surmise from the above vignettes, the intent of this chapter is to take you into a few middle and secondary schools to provide a glimpse of what is happening at those levels—and there are some great things happening. There are also some interesting things happening at district and government levels that I will briefly introduce at the end of the chapter.

You might recall from the foreword that the initial introduction of the *7 Habits* into schools was focused on the adults, not students. In fact, the focus on taking the habits to students did not gain momentum until my son, Sean, authored the teen version of the *7 Habits* in 1998. But neither the initial focus on adults nor the wait for Sean's book kept a few eager high school educators from getting a head start, including a pair of educators at Joliet High School.

Joliet Township High School Central

At the time the original *7 Habits* book was released, Tony Contos was a counselor at Joliet Central High School in Joliet, Illinois. But Tony knew absolutely nothing of the *7 Habits* until a parent approached one of his colleagues and said "You need to read this book." After reading the book, the colleague passed the same challenge on to Tony: "You need to read this."

Tony was reluctant. Already he had stacks of reading material in his to-do pile, and, besides that, reading was not the most burning task on his mind. Occupying him instead were serious thoughts of abandoning his career in education. He had entered education with a resolve to make a difference, but all he was finding himself doing was battling bureaucracy, enforcing rules, and slapping bandages on a few students' problems.

Only out of respect for his colleague did Tony give the book a look. He obtained an audio version and began listening in his car on his way to and from the school. Soon he found himself going out for lunch and taking a long route back or running errands in the evenings so that he could complete another chapter. Each habit seemed to link to a particular decision he was grappling with at the office or a challenge one of his students was having.

Tony and his colleague called FranklinCovey to see if anything related to the *7 Habits* was available for students. The *7 Habits* book was just out, so at the time the answer was no. But FranklinCovey had just hired Chuck Farnsworth to start up its education division, and Chuck agreed to work with Tony in creating some lesson plans and student activities. Tony describes those days as "quite an adventure and a workout." But he loved it. It reignited his enthusiasm for being an educator. After he had been testing lessons with students over the period of a few weeks, one mother walked into the school and asked, "What on earth is going on?" The mom had seen good things happening with her daughter and wanted to find the source.

Tony did a lot of role plays using real-life examples and asking students how they would use the habits to work out solutions to the various situations. At the end of one class, a student approached him and said, "This is the first time I am allowed to talk about things that I want to talk about. I come from a family of hoodlums, but I know I can change all that, at least as far as my life is concerned." About that same time, Tony recalls having a discussion with a nun who told him, "Tony, kids want to know the path. They like direction and firm standards far more than most adults think." Tony found that to be true in the classes he was teaching. He had no intention of turning the discussions into therapy sessions, or anything close, but found that students thrived on opportunities to talk with trusted adults about real issues that were on their minds.

Tony was also certified to train the school's staff and that, too, he says, refreshed his career. He recalls challenging a set of teachers to find ways to apply the concept of the Emotional Bank Account during the ensuing week. One staff member reported back how she was assigned to stand watch each morning at one of the school's thirteen entrances. She decided to make a "deposit" for each student who entered through her assigned entrance. The very first day, a rather rough herd of boys arrived. One of them used some inappropriate language, but she resisted pouncing on him, and the boys recognized it. The next day, when the same boys arrived, she spoke to them politely. By day four they were being respectful and saying hello to her. The next week she was reassigned to a different entrance, and to her surprise some of the students who typically entered through her original door noticed her missing and sought her out. They wanted to say hello and tell her they missed her.

A challenge all along was finding funding to purchase materials. But as people in the community started hearing what the school was doing, several people stepped in to assist. One such person was an attorney in the county prosecutor's office. He told Tony that when his department sold off

Since its release, *The 7 Habits of Highly Effective Teens* has sold over three million copies and traveled to schools all over the world, including this classroom in Korea where students are learning a *7 Habits* song with actions.

confiscated goods taken in drug raids, a portion of the money would be given to the school for *7 Habits* training. The rationale was that by the time the county had investigated a murder or drug scene, pursued and arrested the perpetrator, and prosecuted and incarcerated him, it often cost the county up to a million dollars or more. "Save me one kid," he said, "and you save the county a million dollars."

Tony has since retired, but to this day he looks back on his years in education and says that teaching the *7 Habits* was the highlight of his career. I am personally grateful to Tony and other educators like him who, during those early years, so masterfully found ways to help FranklinCovey take the *7 Habits* content to teens in very practical, meaningful ways.

Noble Street Charter High School

Because of tighter curriculum requirements and the nature of how they are structured, most middle and high schools do not build the *7 Habits* into the school's culture as elementary schools do. Instead they teach the *7 Habits* as an elective class, squeeze them into an existing course, or make them part of a school event, such as freshman orientation. A glowing exception is found at the Noble Street Charter School in Chicago.

Noble Street Charter High School had its start in 1999. It was founded by Michael and Tonya Milkie, two former public school teachers, in partnership with the Northwestern University Settlement Association, a social services organization in Chicago. What started out as one school has now become seven campuses, all situated in inner-city Chicago. The schools are nonselective, which means there is open enrollment and no special entry requirements (unlike many private schools). Eighty-five percent of the approximately five hundred students at each campus come from low-income homes. Most are of Latino or African-American descent.

From the beginning, Michael and Tonya envisioned the school as something that would be different. They have set high standards, including insisting that students tuck in their shirts and dress conservatively. Breaches in rules result in demerits, which can lead to detention or jeopardize promotion to the next grade level. This may sound a little "tough," but what the Milkies and the faculty remind students is that they want them ready to enter the workforce when they graduate—whether that be from high school or college—and proper dress and hygiene are all part of that.

Despite the high expectations, the school does not feel overly strict. Visitors will see students who are happy and getting along with each other. Pictures on walls are of Noble students having fun and engaged in meaningful projects. Though students are required to participate in a set number of service hours, typically they do so willingly because the events are fun and are done with fellow classmates and teachers. Student leaders are involved in school decisions and are instrumental in maintaining the upbeat school culture.

When asked what makes the culture so rich at their campuses, the teachers give credit to the *7 Habits* and the school's approach to character and discipline. Each campus is given the freedom to determine how the habits will be taught based on what works best for their situation. At the original campus, for example, the *7 Habits* are taught as part of the year-long freshman literature class. Students read the *7 Habits for Teens* as a class at the start of the first semester, then for the remainder of the year they read a series of "personal journey" books that promote taking charge of one's life and overcoming opposition. These include *We Beat the Streets, Tuesdays with Morrie, Chinese Cinderella*, and *The Catcher in the Rye*. (Traditionalists need not fret: Shakespeare gets his turn in later grades.) In the book discussions, the *7 Habits* principles are reinforced. Many class writing assignments also embed concepts found in the *7 Habits*, such as the writing of a personal mission statement and journal. Students also write the script for a fun play that depicts the habits in action, and then perform it for the entire school at the end of the year.

At Noble's Pritzker campus, the habits are taught as part of Miss De-Guia's social studies class that all freshmen take. They too read the *7 Habits for Teens* together as a class, and then apply the habits to various social issues. Students are more than willing to share their opinions on controversial issues and can get quite serious when discussing how they might use the

Posters of students past and present are hallway reminders for Noble students of who they have the potential to become.

habits to resolve social dilemmas or address personal challenges, such as dealing with drugs, sex, and alcohol. The key is that they trust Miss DeGuia and know she is interested in their lives, both now and in the future.

What makes the Noble Street Charter School campuses stand out among most high schools that teach the 7 *Habits* is that their delivery of the habits does not stop at the freshman year, nor is it restricted to one class. All teachers are versed in the habits and use them on a regular basis as part of advisory classes. Advisory classes are set up so that students are assigned an advisory teacher at the start of their first year, and then that advisory teacher and the same group of students remain together for the full four years. They meet every day and often include in their discussions one or more of the habits. In this sense, the advisory teacher acts as a life mentor.

One of the school's athletic coaches said she had to laugh when her team was behind in a basketball game and some of the players started to get upset and lose their composure. She heard students in the crowd chanting out things like "Settle down. Be proactive. Take control." But of course not everything goes entirely smooth at the school. For example, one student complained that her father had taken her copy of the 7 *Habits for Teens* and would not give it back until he was finished reading it, so she did not have her copy to bring to class.

What Noble Street Charter School is most proud of is its college attendance rates. And they should be! They are strikingly higher than most neighboring schools. One of their graduates, Angelica Alfaro, was in the first graduating class at Noble Street. She has since graduated from the University of Illinois in psychology and Latino studies, and is now back working for Noble as the alumni coordinator. She says that as a student at Noble she always had a hard time remembering the 7 *Habits* in the right order, but that she constantly found herself using them while in college. She is the first in her family to go to college and admits that many times she wanted to give up, but insists that the mission statement she wrote as a freshman, "Never Give Up," is what kept her going.

So how is all this impacting test scores and other key success measures? Obviously, not everything can be attributed to the 7 *Habits* alone, but the ACT scores at the original campus are always among the highest of all non-selective schools in Chicago, which includes all public schools. Daily attendance rates are also high. And even better, students speak far more about which college they plan to attend rather than about whether they will attend college in the first place.

And that is not all. Only one fight has broken out in four years. Restrooms are noticeably void of graffiti. Students treat each other with respect. They also treat adults with respect, in large part because *they* are treated with respect. The waiting list of students wanting to attend one of the campuses has grown to more than two thousand names. Furthermore, several parents drive their student long distances to get to school each day, while other students catch early, early public transportation. All this, I believe, says a lot not only about what parents and students think of Noble Street Charter Schools, but about what they want in a school.

Mar Vista High School

As noted previously, most middle and high schools do not integrate the *7 Habits* as fully across their cultures as does the Noble Network. Instead most of them find ways to embed the habits into one-time special events or slip them into existing courses. One such example is Mar Vista High School in Imperial Beach, California.

Dr. Louise Phipps is a very innovative principal and educator. Named principal of the year by the Association of California School Administrators, she has a track record of success at challenging schools. She has spent more than a decade now in her current adventure at Mar Vista High School, and under her tutelage the school has seen significant academic improvement and, according to the teachers, a "phenomenal" change in its culture.

Not long after arriving at Mar Vista, Dr. Phipps took the teachers and staff to Coronado Island, just off the coast. There they experienced the *7 Habits* as a staff. Dr. Phipps viewed it as a positive way of letting teachers know she cared about them as individuals and wanted the best for them personally. One result of that experience was that Dr. Phipps and some of the teachers began looking for ways to take the habits to students.

Their first attempt was to teach the habits as part of ninth-grade English. That proved to be difficult, as they felt it was too much to cover along with all the other required content. But seeing the value of what the students had gained out of that first experiment encouraged Dr. Phipps to work with two of her teachers, Mary and David Holden, to design a stand-alone course that all students would be offered during their freshman year.

For more than seven years, the Holdens and a few other teachers have been teaching the 7 *Habits* as part of an innovative course they designed called Crossroads. It entails a potpourri of life and career skills and uses the 7 *Habits* as the foundation and glue for the course. Seven periods are taught each day, with about thirty-five students per class—all freshmen. Students in the class are allowed to keep their copy of the 7 *Habits for Teens*, as well as their *Student Activity Guide*.

The Holdens report that students enjoy both the class and the habits. They particularly like tackling fun projects such as producing videos of skits they have written around the habits. The Holdens say the few students who resist the 7 *Habits* are those who tend to need them the most, but several of those students have come back during later grades and thanked them. The students had come to see how the habits helped them get through not only school but life.

Though their efforts are not a schoolwide culture initiative per se, Mary insists that the habits have impacted the school's culture. The school has seen a drop in the number of discipline referrals since Crossroads was implemented, and the number of students completing college prep has gone up. Mary also reports a notable decline in the use of bad language in her classes. But what delights her most is that students openly bring their challenges to Crossroads because they know it is a safe place to talk about them. "The students need a framework for working through their challenges in a mature manner," she says, "and the 7 *Habits* provide that for them."

Roosevelt Middle School

Now for a middle school example.

The old saying is that one does not fully understand another person until one has walked a mile in their shoes. With Marilyn Vrooman it could be said that one does not fully appreciate her until one has walked a mile in her school, which is about the distance through the hallways and across the grounds. What makes the walk worthwhile is that her school is also a fire station, an ice cream parlor, a '70s dance hall, and an oasis complete with fish, rabbits, and waterfalls.

When Marilyn received the phone call letting her know she had been selected to take the lead at Roosevelt Middle School, a grade 6–8 school in Oklahoma City, Oklahoma, she literally cried, and not out of joy. Her heart had been set on a high school position, and she was not sure middle school was her best fit. Besides that, she knew the school to be riddled with serious behavioral issues that went along with an outdated building in a gang-ridden neighborhood. As she describes it, "Its halls were filled with young students whose academic lives were drowning in social issues they were not equipped to handle." She knew she did not have to take the job; other opportunities were sure to arise. Yet the thought that kept going through her mind was "If this is what God wants me to do, I'll do it."

Roosevelt has eight hundred students with 100 percent on free lunch. About 15 percent of the young men have gang ties. So when she accepted the assignment seven years ago, the question she had to ask herself was "Where do I begin?" The first two places she determined to begin her crusade were, one, the facilities, and two, the faculty.

The school's hallways were as gloomy as the test scores. Jutting in and out of each hallway were murky, low-lit cubbyholes littered with graffiti and broken student lockers. The lockers were the perfect cavities for students to hide drugs and contraband. So Marilyn enlisted the aid of a few student leaders, and over the summer they removed the lockers. They unbolted the steel casings and hauled them out to the school yard where they were retrieved for scrap. The lockers had been mounted on cement slabs, so Marilyn rented a jackhammer and blasted away while the students shuffled the residue off in wheelbarrows. I imagine that seeing the new principal roaming the hallways with a jackhammer in hand was enough to reduce at least a few discipline problems at the school.

In working with the students, Marilyn established friendly relations and won their respect. Word spread. "The new principal cares." Marilyn recognized that many students had very little in the way of social skills. Attached to video games during daylight and afraid to go out by night, many of them had little opportunity to develop even basic interpersonal skills. So where the lockers once stood, she and the student leaders set up areas where students could hang out and talk. South Oklahoma City is a large recruitment area for firefighters, so one area they turned into a mock fire station, complete with a fire pole, hydrant, and photos. Other students were into classic cars, so another area was designed around a car theme, while another area was turned into a '70s-themed ice cream parlor. Another area was turned over to teachers who transformed it into a science haven complete with a large fish tank and a waterfall, both of which are used for class projects. Marilyn heard the word *crazy* more than once when she began creating the areas. "Students will vandalize them in no time," people said. But she put her trust in the students and seven years later nothing has been harmed. Students are proud of the areas. They own them.

The second area Marilyn focused on was the faculty. Several of the teachers had been around for a long time and were taking archaic approaches to academic instruction. Rather than throwing a fit or "cleaning house," Marilyn acted on the advice from a book she had read, *If You Don't Feed the Teachers They Eat the Students!* Some of the teachers wanted an exercise area so Marilyn transformed an unoccupied area into a faculty exercise room. She also brought in content experts to speak on various education topics. That is how the *7 Habits* came into play. She and the teachers decided as a group to go through the *7 Habits* course. Part of the reason was Marilyn's philosophy that "if teachers don't feel effective or feel good about themselves, they will not be able to relate well with the students, and without relationships, students will not embrace learning."

Marilyn uses the *7 Habits* in her everyday role as principal. She is big on creating the "end in mind" and then empowering people to pursue that end as they best see fit. "Teachers know what my 'big rocks' are in making classroom decisions," she says, "but beyond that they are fully empowered to use their own judgment."

As the *7 Habits* became ingrained in the teachers, it seemed natural for them to begin looking for ways to take the habits to students. Several teachers found this easy to do, no matter what subject they taught. As for Marilyn, she determined to create a yearlong leadership course that she would team-teach with one of the faculty. In that course, students are taught basic leadership topics from a variety of sources, with the *7 Habits* providing the core. Additionally, students are involved in leading projects that benefit the school, and Marilyn also uses them as peer mediators in helping students resolve moderate disputes. That course has now expanded to six periods.

During one of her first years, Marilyn had some students she considered to be high risk. Many principals, if not most, would have simply found ways to remove them from the school, but Marilyn sensed they just needed time to mature. She received a $10,000 donation to fund the building of a ropes course for teaching leadership skills and hired a contractor to work with fifteen at-risk boys to design, build, and install eight low-level rope elements. The experience allowed the young men to gain a confidence in themselves that they were then able to transfer to their coursework. A team of students, including a few of the at-risk boys, were trained and certified to be ropes course facilitators. One of the boys said afterward, "I never ever imagined myself standing in front of any group as the leader."

Marilyn is clearly in favor of finding ways to empower students to be leaders and smiles big when she declares, "I believe in child labor." If a large shipment of student supplies arrives, the students are the ones who will be using them, so she has them do the unpacking and assembly work, especially if it involves technology—which she sees as the "native tongue" of many students. When the school faced a space shortage, Marilyn determined to repurpose a former storage area into four new classrooms. But as you might expect, she had students help design and build the new area. Students had to figure the square footage, determine how to partition off the different areas, research the building codes, and calculate the materials needed. A few teachers even taught the students how to frame walls and hang wallboard. Naturally, the district's facilities management crew oversaw the work and could have done it all on its own, but what would that have taught the students about math, architecture, construction, teamwork, or leadership?

Now, if you are beginning to imagine Roosevelt Middle School as a scintillating garden paradise with nothing but waterfalls, fish tanks, and flowers around every corner, you may be disappointed. Students still enter the school each morning through metal detectors. Driving to the office, Marilyn still passes through the housing projects to see if there is any gang graffiti left over from the previous night that might signal trouble for one of her students. So, no, Roosevelt is not yet paradise. But one by one, students' lives are being changed. And while Marilyn knows she may never get the glittering accolades some of the high-scoring schools in her district might receive, she had already accepted that fact before she proactively chose to take on the task of being principal. She is at peace with the direction the school is heading in and is quick to pass credit to others. "Hardworking people want to work with hardworking people," she says. "And that's one of the reasons I like working here."

Singapore

As noted in the previous chapter, the Singapore Ministry of Education initiated 7 Habits training for teachers in the late 1990s. Though approximately half of Singapore's twenty thousand teachers were being trained in the habits, it was not until the year 2000 that, in response to repeated requests from teachers and parents, the habits began to trickle down to the student level.

One of the early supporters of students receiving the habits was the Clementi Town Secondary School, which is under the direction of its principal, Mrs. Tan. In choosing to take on the 7 Habits, the school had a very clear objective, which was to help first-year students transition from their lower secondary school to the upper secondary level (that is from middle school to high school). They recognized that students needed greater self-discipline and more independent learning capabilities at the upper level and felt the 7 Habits would help in that regard. They also sensed the habits would aid students in their preparations for college exams and with learning basic creativity, teamwork, and interpersonal skills.

So, in concert with FranklinCovey's Singapore office and educators from a few neighboring schools, a course was developed titled HEY, which stands for Highly Effective Youth. HEY is similar to what other high schools are doing in terms of teaching the habits as part of a stand-alone class. However, one thing that makes Clementi Town's approach unique is the way they spread the concepts across the school and across the curricula. All teachers have been trained in the 7 Habits and each week at the schoolwide teachers' meeting the HEY teachers announce what 7 Habits concept the students will be focusing on that week. The other teachers then come up with pragmatic ways to use and reinforce that same concept in their lessons during that week, regardless of what subject they teach. For example, if Habit 2 is the week's focus, the science teacher might ask when conducting an experiment, "What is the end in mind for this experiment?" That way the habits become a living part of the school's culture, and the principles come to life for students and teachers alike in all subjects.

Nestled beneath Singapore's residential high-rises is Clementi Town Secondary School, one of the pioneers in teen programs in Southeast Asia.

On top of the classroom experience, posters garnish the school's hallways and large *7 Habits* banners hang outside their buildings. Tips for the *7 Habits* are shared during weekly assemblies, and parent nights have been set up to train parents in *7 Habits* basics. But there are also three other novel approaches—*signatures*—that Clementi Town has integrated into their efforts and that I want to mention. One is that they have dedicated rooms for the HEY program that are decorated with *7 Habits* themes. This creates an appropriate environment for student learning and enables all certified facilitators to have ready access to common materials.

Second, they have created what they call a "HEY Day." On this day, students in the HEY courses conduct a daylong workshop for students who are one or two levels below them in age. HEY students teach the habits in blocks, with the younger students rotating from session to session—habit to habit—throughout the day. Clementi Town sees this as a great way not only to introduce the habits to forthcoming students, but as a way for HEY students to review and solidify their understanding of the habits.

Having introduced over two thousand students to the habits, Clementi Town is now pursuing ways to apply them as a faculty and school and use them to assess their performance, which is its third signature. Recently, for example, it conducted an internal culture audit where staff members rated how well they felt the school as a whole exemplified each of the habits, for example, how proactive they felt the school was, how well it begins with the end in mind, and how well it puts first things first, thinks win-win, and so forth. They see it as a way of holding themselves accountable and leading by example and found the first round of the feedback process to be quite revealing and helpful.

Guatemala

This is a story that I have come to love through personal experience. I believe the approach holds tremendous potential, not just for Guatemala but for other countries as well.

In 2003, María del Carmen Aceña, the newly appointed minister of education for Guatemala, began visiting schools. She interviewed teachers, students, and parents, and came away alarmed that no one was talking about the future—neither their own futures, nor the future of Guatemala.

For thirty-six years, Guatemala had suffered through a painful civil war, leaving thousands dead and the economy in shambles. By 1996, when the warring factions finally laid down their arms, something of inestimable value had vanished from the country, namely the hope and optimism of its youth. Only two out of ten youths were managing to finish their schooling. María described them as "asleep, disconnected, and with very little interest in helping their country."

With the average age of Guatemalans at just eighteen, and with over 40 percent of the population under the age of fourteen, María knew that if its youth had no hope, then Guatemala as a country had no hope. So she helped form a group devoted to making Guatemala a better place. One of their first targets was educational reform. They had already made a few efforts with less than desirable results when during a trip to Finland, María learned of an innovative program in which high school students were being taught to dream of a better country and a better life. She wanted to implement something similar for her country, but how?

In June 2005, María attended a presentation I gave in Guatemala. Afterward she spent several days pondering Guatemala's future. She came out of that experience committed to press ahead with a new "Path of Dreams" program for students. She read *The 7 Habits of Highly Effective People* and became convinced that the habits provided a foundation to help young people overcome their doubts. The more she and her team synergized, the more María came to believe that the habits would empower both teachers and students to "relearn how to dream" and provide them with the tools to make their dreams become a reality.

After decades of academic and social turmoil, Guatemalan teens are finding their dreams with the government's Path of Dreams program, founded on the *7 Habits*.

A team was assembled, headed by Dr. Angélica Sátiro and supported by FranklinCovey consultants. Almost overnight, manuals, games, music, and other resources were in place. By fall 2006, over 2,500 high school teachers from public and private schools across the country had been trained in the *7 Habits,* and those teachers left motivated to launch the Path of Dreams program, for high school seniors. And while there was some strong initial opposition to the program from some professionals and politicians, the results of the first courses with students were so positive that the opposition quickly died down.

Amazingly, by the end of the 2006–2007 school year, a total of 175,000 high school students had been through the Path of Dreams program and had developed meaningful "life plans." A significant component of the program requires students to work in teams to develop action plans that are intended to help remedy such social problems as child abuse and AIDS. Some teams created plans for helping the elderly, while others developed plans for improving school libraries, restoring deforested lands, and sustaining businesses in poor communities. "Dreaming for a better Guatemala" was the theme. A recent graduate declared, "Now that we know exactly what we want to do with our lives, nothing can stop us."

High school seniors in Guatemala are honored at a ceremony celebrating their Path of Dreams projects.

During 2007, another four thousand teachers were introduced to the *7 Habits* and Path of Dreams program. According to María, "The program has thus far been a success. Youth, teachers, and parents have undergone a process of change. Today the youth leave school with skills for life, and committed to changing Guatemala. They are agents for change, and leaders of their communities with goals and plans. They are inspired and convinced that they are the owners of their lives and that success and happiness depend on themselves."

The vision is for one million students to become aware of the values embedded in the *7 Habits* over the next ten years. Programs are also under way to bring the habits to students at an earlier age. Soon all tenth-grade students will be given a copy of the *7 Habits for Teens* as part of a required curriculum. I cannot say enough about how impressed I am with María, who I have visited with on many occasions. She is a true leader with a vision.

When we started working on this project, we [teachers] had to begin by hoping in our own future before we could teach the youth to have dreams. When we began the *7 Habits* training, we began to discover that we had a treasure within us that we had allowed to lie dormant for some time. This affected our performance as well as the performance of our students.

I am very grateful because the *7 Habits* have had a profound impact on my life. I believed that I had arrived at the limit of my potential and that I didn't really have anything else to give. I had come to believe that I wasn't a creative person. Today I am not the same person that I was two years ago. I believe in myself and I believe this has been a direct benefit for my students. I act with a new conviction that I can still improve and that I can do something for my country. I will see this reflected in my students because they will grow as I grow.

—Guatemalan Teacher

Japan

Each year in Japan, more than thirteen thousand teens are taught the *7 Habits*. The origins of this are twofold. In Funabashi, Chiba, Mr. Takahisa Watanabe was teaching elementary students at Gyoda-nishi Elementary School. Mr. Watanabe had been personally impacted by the *7 Habits* and so he began passing bits and pieces of the habits on to his students. The results were enough to catch other teachers' interest, so much so that a popular book was written about his successes.

Meanwhile, in Tokyo, a successful company by the name of Venture Link was aggressively training its consultants in general business skills. However, the more they worked to train their consultants, the more they felt that what the consultants needed most were basic life skills, such as interpersonal skills, time management skills, and conflict management skills. Sound familiar? One of the company's executive board members, Mr. Ishikawa, suggested they look into *7 Habits* training. They did and that training turned out to be successful. But the question Mr. Ishikawa and his chief training officer, Mr. Suzuki, kept asking themselves was "Why are we needing to train these skills?" In other words, "Why haven't our consultants been taught these skills earlier in life?"

To make a long story short, soon Mr. Ishikawa and Mr. Suzuki were on their way to observe Mr. Watanabe's class. They were so impressed that they left with the conviction that all students in Japan should be exposed to the habits. They knew the intricacies of Japan's public education system and felt it was unrealistic to try to convince all schools in Japan to teach the habits. Yet, deep inside, both had a vision of what it could mean not only for Japan but for each individual student. That vision was so fixed in their minds that eventually they approached FranklinCovey's Japan office and urged them to take on the challenge. Though FranklinCovey, Japan, shared the same interest in taking the habits to students, they were so inundated with their corporate clientele that what little they were able to devote to education was limited to adults. Fortunately, however, the combined passion of the two companies for helping teens proved to be strong enough that ultimately they agreed to create a separate company focused solely on students. Mr. Suzuki was placed at the helm.

Competition to get into Japan's best schools is fierce. Some parents will sacrifice almost anything to get their son or daughter into a highly rated school. By the thousands, therefore, many parents send their sons and daughters to what are called "cram" schools. These are after-school programs for students to get advanced tutoring in subjects such as math and reading. The emphasis is on one thing—raising test scores so students can get into higher-rated schools.

Knowing how difficult it is to get new content inserted into Japan's public school systems, Mr. Suzuki strategically decided to focus on taking the *7 Habits* into the cram schools. At first it was a hard sell. After all, the *7 Habits* are not exactly national exam categories. But as more cram schools took on the habits, research revealed that students who had taken the *7 Habits* course there were indeed scoring higher on their exams. This caught many people's attention, but most particularly the parents'. Today more than ten thousand students a year receive the *7 Habits* via cram schools, while another three thousand receive training in the habits from private schools. Since parents must pay for cram schools and private schools out of their own pockets, I believe this says something about what parents in Japan want from a school.

Business leaders the world over, such as Japan's Mr. Suzuki, are wondering why students are not taught these basic life skills earlier in their education.

Corporate and Community Ties

Scores of other schools across the globe are taking the 7 *Habits* to middle and high school students in unique ways. For example, Arab High School in Arab, Alabama, noticed that a lot of students were graduating from high school and going straight into debt after buying a new car or taking out college loans and then dropping out. So they set up a course on financial management to provide students with basic skills for handling finances. The first three weeks of the course are dedicated to 7 *Habits* training. Lemon Bay High School in Englewood, Florida, reserves the first week of school for teaching all incoming freshmen the 7 *Habits* as a transition course to help students adapt to high school. Indeed, I could tell you of various ways that many high schools are implementing the 7 *Habits*, including schools in Korea, the Netherlands, the United Kingdom, Malaysia, Costa Rica, and elsewhere. I have just scratched the planet's surface. But instead I want to share two short stories that also involve high schools, but in a different way—one driven by community and corporate ties.

The first involves Lousiville, Kentucky. On the surface, the Louisville story appears much the same as those I have already described. Two high schools, Central and Iroquois, are teaching the 7 *Habits* though taking slightly different approaches. In the case of Central High, alma mater of famed boxer Muhammad Ali, students learn the habits in a law and government magnet program taught by Joe Gutmann. Across town, at Iroquois High, Sara Sutton teaches the 7 *Habits* as part of a sociology class for freshmen and sophomores. Some light follow-up to the 7 *Habits* is provided at both schools.

But what makes the Louisville story unique is how it got started and who is behind it. Dr. Tom Crawford knows that history well. Tom is a retired chemistry professor, former provost, and Hall of Fame inductee of the University of Louisville. As Tom neared retirement, he came across the 7 *Habits* as part of a book club. The thought that kept stirring in the back of his mind as he read it was "I wish I had come across this when I was a teen."

About that same time, Tom kept coming across some very disturbing statistics in local news sources, not the least of which was that in various parts of the community, cases of serious violence were up significantly from previous years, and about one-third of those cases involved teens. Many retirees in Tom's shoes would have simply looked at those numbers in disgust and then gone golfing or pursued some other relaxing hobby, and Tom admits he tried golf at first. But his wife will tell you that it just did not fit his style, which according to her "is all about thinking of others." So he gave up the links and started working with the University of Louisville to develop youth leadership initiatives.

Those efforts brought Tom in contact with other "comrades at heart," including William McKinley Blackford, IV, a local minister. William is a charismatic former star football player for the University of Louisville. But his past experiences with being homeless and living out of his truck provide him with a "street-smart" perspective on teen life and lets kids know he understands. He spends a lot of time counseling young men, many of whom come from single-parent homes, and several of whom have either never met their fathers or were abandoned by them at a young age. Tom was glad to have William join him in becoming a *7 Habits* facilitator, since he provided a walking role model of the *7 Habits* principles for young men.

Another contact Tom came across was Joe Gutmann, the teacher at Central High. Joe had for years been a prosecuting attorney for the Commonwealth of Kentucky. In other words, his career was focused on putting young men behind bars. But as he did his duty to keep the streets safe, he could not help but think how much better it would be if more were done on the preventative end of things. That is what led him to quit his attorney job and become a teacher at Central High.

Along the way, Tom, William, and Joe came across other adults interested in the community's youth, such as Barbara Sexton Smith, an extremely successful businesswoman who also had experienced life's hard knocks. As a team, they joined forces with a number of local banks, the city's mayor, and local community groups such as Hispanic Achievers, Urban League, Black Achievers, Youth Alive, Canaan Community Development Corporation, Lincoln Foundation, and Visions of Hope. At the core of their efforts was finding ways to take the *7 Habits* to Louisville teens. To date, they have raised about thirty thousand dollars, with which they have certified sixteen facilitators, taken the *7 Habits* in various formats to over 2,600 teens, and distributed over two thousand *7 Habits for Teens* books.

Of course, the proof of what impact the training will have on the youth and the community lies primarily in the future. But Joe, for one, senses that it is making an immediate difference. He cites as an example a student who came to him on the first day of school and asked for directions on how to find the bus that would get him back to the homeless shelter. When that same student a few weeks later was given a copy of the 7 *Habits for Teens,* Joe says, he would not put it down. He was glued to its pages until he had read it cover to cover. Joe has witnessed a whole new confidence in the young man, and takes great satisfaction in listening to him talk about college and a meaningful career. He knows there is at least one young man who will never see the inside of a courtroom—unless he becomes a lawyer.

William and Barbara are finding similar rewards as they work with young people at various community events throughout Louisville. As for Tom, at seventy-seven years of age, instead of dropping putts, he gets his kicks from traveling around the region introducing the 7 *Habits* to teen audiences in the form of seven science experiments. Yes, you guessed it. Each experiment represents one of the habits. Young people especially love his version of the "pop bottle," and if you ever experience it you may want to be wearing ear plugs. And, judging from the fire in Tom's eyes, his new career appears to be just getting started in Louisville.

Now for the second short story. Not far from Louisville, in Indianapolis, Indiana, two business executives, Mike Melichar and Bill Campbell, are pursuing similar teen-focused goals with the support of their employer, Dow AgroSciences. The company had arisen out of a 1990 joint venture between the Dow Chemical Company and Eli Lilly. Both companies had very strong heritages and deep cultural roots, and everyone knew that such joint ventures often do not work out largely because employees cannot let go of past ways of doing things. So shortly after the joint venture was solidified, Dow AgroSciences started looking for something that would tie the two cultures together, and ended up latching on to the 7 *Habits* and training three thousand of its employees throughout the world.

Mike and Bill were two of the company's original in-house facilitators. The pace at which they were training the 7 *Habits* across the corporation was quite time-consuming and even draining. So they were quite surprised when one of their fellow facilitators, Tom Wright, informed them that he was spending his Saturday mornings with local high school administrators brainstorming ways to take the habits into schools. Mike and Bill could not imagine where Tom got his energy, but they learned that he had a vision of every teen in the state of Indiana receiving the *7 Habits*.

Tom's efforts came to a tragic halt when he was killed in a plane crash. Yet some of his friends at Dow AgroSciences, including Bill and Mike, knew of his vision and determined to carry out at least a portion of it. For more than a decade now, they have annually been bringing forty-nine students from seven local high schools (seven students from each school) to Dow AgroSciences' corporate training center, along with a teacher who acts as a mentor and a Dow AgroSciences employee who acts as a corporate sponsor. There they engage the students in an intensive—but fun—one-day immersion in the *7 Habits*. The program emphasizes the concepts that will most help students to be effective in their relationships with others and to create future professional opportunities. At the end of the day, students are rewarded for their participation.

Though Bill has now been retired for some years, each October he enthusiastically returns as one of the course facilitators. Michael is lead coordinator for the program, which has taken on the name of Community Leadership Initiative. Their passion for helping students and their early memories of what the habits did for them personally is what drives them forward. Who knows, perhaps someday every teen in Indiana will have the opportunity to experience the habits after all.

I share the Louisville and Dow AgroSciences stories—and single out their activities—to emphasize how interested community and business groups are in the well-being of today's young people and how important they find these basic life skills and principles to be. Did you notice that the business and community leaders were not content to be idle spectators, sitting back and waiting for the schools to do something? As was the case in a few of the elementary schools and in Japan, an increasing number of businesses and nonprofit organizations are taking a more active role in what is happening with today's young people and their education—at all ages and in all cultures.*

* For more information on how your business or community organization can sponsor a school in your area, see page 231.

Students in Malaysia pose with their certificates of completion following a *7 Habits of Highly Effective Teens* program.

. . . and Beyond

This chapter is titled "Moving Upward and Beyond." *Upward* took us from the elementary level to the middle and high school levels. I could also share what is happening at the college/university level, but that is a topic for another book. So for the purposes of this one, *Beyond* will be limited to what is happening with the *7 Habits* at the adult level in K–12 education, with a specific focus on districtwide efforts.

Many districts are using the habits as a training option to expand the individual skills of teachers and administrators. According to Dr. Susan M. Baile, it is happening with good success. Dr. Baile conducted extensive interviews of adult educators at six locations in Georgia, Pennsylvania, Indiana, and California. All of them had participated in *7 Habits* training. Her findings report improvements in workplace satisfaction, better communication between employees, more teamwork and goal focus, and greater skills for conflict management. But while the training of individual educators has led to some overall organizational improvements, the best results occur when the training is attached to an intentional, culturewide initiative, such as what is happening in Texarkana, Texas.

The Texarkana Independent School District has one high school, one middle school, and eight K–5 elementary schools. Combined it has 1,800 students at the middle and high schools, and another five hundred or so students at each of the elementary schools. Nearly half the students come from low-income backgrounds.

When Larry Sullivan took over as district superintendent, the district was on the brink of bankruptcy—both financially and academically. Larry is a seasoned educator who credits much of his educational philosophy to William Glasser, with whom he studied and worked early in his career. He is also a staunch believer in the 7 *Habits,* and when he took over as superintendent he saw immediate need for them. He describes the situation as "needing to stop the bleeding."

But in Larry's assessment, "Just because a district may be bleeding, does not mean it is the right time to drop the 7 *Habits* on everyone." Given the district's empty pocketbooks, he saw his first order of business to be economic triage. A number of teachers and students, for example, were practically withering without air-conditioning, and he deemed it prudent to handle a few such matters before spending any budget on the 7 *Habits*. He also wanted to wait long enough to assemble a leadership team that he knew could get the job done while modeling the habits.

It was in his second year that Larry introduced the 7 *Habits*. The biggest need he saw was that people were working in isolation. They were not thinking as a team, nor doing things as a team. They had their own agendas and were emblazoned in turf fights with open hostilities. One man, whom Larry describes as a "sniper," attempted to shoot down any change attempt and "threw an anchor on anything" that required change. Some of the elementary school principals were squabbling over teachers and were extremely irked if a teacher transferred to another school within the district.

Larry wanted people thinking out of the box, synergizing, and focusing on the future of students—not engaged in infighting. He began with his leadership team by taking them off site, a step he highly recommends. He explained to them what the 7 *Habits* meant to him personally, and that he felt the habits would benefit the entire district and them as a team. But above all he wanted them to see it as a gift to them personally. And so to this day, many staff members see that experience as a key turnaround point, not only for the culture of the district but for them individually. A lot of synergy went on during those few days.

But, according to the team members, what opened up the power of the *7 Habits* for the district even more than the course was Larry's modeling of the habits. He is a big-time believer in Habit 5: Seek First to Understand, Then to Be Understood. So he spent a lot of time during the initial months listening in depth to teachers and parents. He recognized that some of his most valuable contributors were not the boisterous ones who made a lot of noise, but the quiet workers who minded their own business and stayed on task, and so he sought out their opinions. He was also a big believer in Habit 4: Think Win-Win. Parents came to believe that he saw and wanted them as customers. If he could not meet their needs, they knew that he at least wanted to, and worked with him to come up with third alternatives to solve problems.

Habit 6: Synergize, and the notion of valuing differences was also a big part of his style. He did not try to do other people's jobs; he valued their skills. He recognized that his assistant, Brenda, had a gift for calming people. When irate parents called in, Brenda had a talent for listening, not accusing; for getting the facts and boiling down the issues so that before the call was passed on to Larry, the parent was calm. Larry recognized that gift, so instead of telling Brenda to immediately pass such calls to him or to someone else, he encouraged her to first use her empathic talents.

Autumn Thomas, the district's chief people officer, has an M.B.A. and is one of several people Larry hired from outside the education field. In her words, "We are in the people business—the business of building people. In that business, you've got to have strong relationship skills, and that's one thing the *7 Habits* have brought to us." She says, "Prior to *7 Habits*, everyone was on their own island. Principals were upset at each other. Now they work together." She adds, "Part of the new pay structure we have is based on working together, on how the district as a whole does. So people are far more willing to try to understand a situation and to help each other out." She also notes that employee grievances have dropped dramatically.

James Henry Russell, the district's deputy superintendent under Larry, attests to what the habits have done for him personally. "For me," he says, "the 7 *Habits* training was a reawakening. I personally homed in on Habit 7: Sharpen the Saw. I weighed 275 pounds, worked ninety hours a week, and had cholesterol ratings higher than the top students' tests scores. Habit 7 gave me the conviction to take time for myself one hour a day to exercise." Today, James's slimmed physique speaks to his level of discipline. But when he speaks of the 7 *Habits*, his comments are mostly directed toward what has happened to the district. He describes the pre–7 *Habits* era by saying, "It used to be that you would go to the retirement dinner and be delighted to wave good-bye to people. Now you go and it breaks your heart to see people leave. Win-lose was the name of the game ten years ago. The district has now gone from several islands to one win-win thinking team. We're family."

The success at the district level is now trickling down to the students. At the high school, students have been receiving the 7 *Habits* as part of elective class for some time, but now the district school board has mandated that all high school students have a leadership course as a requirement for graduation. The 7 *Habits* are embedded into that offering and the word from students is "Hey, this class is about me—my life." And after seeing the results of what has happened at the district level and hearing students speak the language, all 150 teachers and administrators at the high school voted to go through the training as well. As Principal Paul Norton describes it, "We are now a *leadership* campus." Meanwhile, Bertie Norton, who came out of retirement to lead Nash Elementary, has now taken a team to A.B. Combs and brought Muriel Summers out for a school visit. They have since completed their first year of the leadership approach.

So it truly is becoming more of a districtwide effort. In fact, it is becoming a community effort, since Larry has now transitioned to a new role as city commissioner for Texarkana. It was not his idea. He was approached by business leaders and civic leaders to take on the job because they saw what he had done for the district and the students. Larry's interest in accepting the position was that he felt the role would involve him more with the business and university community, and that to him spelled more opportunity to be of help. James Henry Russell now heads the district, and the 7 *Habits* continue to be a significant source of his leadership philosophy.

NASH ELEMENTARY
Building the Foundation of Tomorrow's Leaders

Principal Bertie Norton came out of retirement to lead the leadership initiative at Nash Elementary. Educators like her are finding the process well worth the creativity and heart it requires.

> The *7 Habits* provide a framework for change. As a superintendent of schools, I knew that if I only went as far as to instill the spirit of Habits 1 and 2, that alone would move the district well in the direction of where it needed to go.
>
> —*Pedro Garcia, Professor, University of Southern California*

In the case of Texarkana, it was bleeding culture. There was a definite urgency and need for change, and everyone knew it. But I do not want to leave you with the impression that such culture efforts are only for dire cases. There are other districts using the habits as a part of planned, strategic culture initiatives that are without the urgency, such as the Charlotte County School District in Florida. In that district, there is no story of a huge turnaround because the district was already strong before the habits arrived. Nonetheless, Dr. Dave Gayler, District Superintendent, will tell you that the *7 Habits* are a big part of his district's culture. His approach is more "pull" than "push" since he does not want anyone to feel forced into participating in the *7 Habits*. Nevertheless, over five hundred district employees have now been trained in the habits. Sessions are taught by district personnel, as well as by two school board members who are certified trainers. "It is rare to have an open seat at a course," says Chuck Bradley, District Training Coordinator. "And we do up to sixteen sessions each year."

Dr. Gayler's hope is that at least one out of every two employees will take up the offering. If that happens, he feels the 7 *Habits* will become engrained in the district's culture to stay, well after he is gone. He notes that the 7 *Habits* are the basis, the cornerstone, for how the district operates. "It's part of the culture—soaked in," he says. "You hear the language in board meetings, in union discussions, and in the hallways. The language and colloquialisms are everywhere." Even part of principals' performance appraisal is connected with the habits. So, again, a district does not need to be in dire straits to take on the 7 *Habits* as a culture initiative.

Wrapping Up

Even if your emphasis is elementary schools, it is important to get a glimpse of what is happening "Upward and Beyond." One reason is that parents of graduated students are coming to Muriel and the other elementary leadership schools and saying, "I sure wish they did more of this at the middle school." Or "What's going to happen when they hit high school? Will they remember what they have learned?" In fact, some of the students are disillusioned when they arrive at middle school and find that students from other elementary schools have not been taught the 7 *Habits* or other leadership skills as they were. It is almost a shock to their system to find that other students do not know what it means to seek first to understand, or how not to be reactive, or why to respect differences.

> I work with the science teachers at the middle school that A.B. Combs funnels into. Teachers can tell if a student has been at Combs almost as soon as they meet them, and when the kids get to whatever middle school they go to, they truly miss the leadership theme they enjoyed at A.B. Combs.
>
> —*Dr. Laura Bottomley, A.B. Combs Parent and Professor*
> *at North Carolina State University*

You may already be in a role that has you involved at the middle, high, or district levels, or will soon be in such a role. So although I have not gone into detail about how these middle and high schools and districts have implemented the *7 Habits,* I hope that what you have read has at least sparked your interest. I hope you have also observed how these leadership principles apply at all levels of education and across all cultures. They are timeless and universal.

An unsolicited email from a teen at the Yorkshire-Forward Presentation in Rotherham, England:

February 13, 2008

Dear Mr. L. Moore,

I was one of the pupils from Castleford High School that came to your very powerful talk about *The 7 Habits of Highly Effective Teens.* I went into the class feeling as an invisible 15-yr-old, like a brick that has been overlooked many a times and not needed in that wall. But my life has definitely changed and I now know how my life should work, to be proactive, to plan life, and to rise when I fall.

Thank you so much.

Yours faithfully,

Stephanie

8

Making It Happen, One Step at a Time

Don't be afraid to give up the good to go for the great.
—*Jim Collins,* Good to Great

Anyone interested in implementing the leadership theme must by now be wondering, "Where do I begin?" "Do we as a school have the right people and the right energy to pull it off?" "Do *I* have what it takes?"

Change is difficult even when only one person is involved. I compare it to a trapeze act where the stunt artist launches from the safety of a lower platform in an attempt to reach a higher platform. It may be somewhat of a daring feat, but if the artist hangs on and exerts the necessary effort, coordination, and timing, he or she will inevitably achieve the higher height. There are timeless laws of physics that assure this.

But if change is difficult for a solitary individual, how challenging must it be for an entire school? To answer that question, try imagining fifty teachers and administrators attempting the same trapeze stunt as a team. Envision them all gathered on the lower platform preparing to launch. Some are excited, some are nervous, and some are outright resistant. Just the act of getting everyone to launch at the same time will be a major undertaking.

Yes, creating change in a school setting can be a circus. But as formidable as the task of implementing the leadership theme may appear, it is possible. It will happen when people are willing to put forth the necessary commitment, creativity, and coordination—and when timeless, universal principles are followed.

Perhaps the biggest challenge is that there is no one-size-fits-all process for implementing the leadership theme. Each school and classroom must design and tailor the approach to fit the unique needs of its students and culture. Nevertheless, there are four sequential, principle-based steps that can help guide such an effort. In this chapter I will briefly describe those four steps and provide a series of questions, insights, and hints to consider when getting started. In our training with organizations, these steps are called *The 4 Imperatives of Leadership*. As you consider these four steps, if you are a parent I want you to keep in mind that the same four steps, as well as all the processes mentioned in this book, can be implemented in the home.

Step One: Inspire Trust

My son, Stephen M.R. Covey, points out in his book *The Speed of Trust* that when there is low trust in an organization, change is slow to happen. Of course, the type of change he is referring to is "change for the better." "Change for the worse" can happen very quickly and with almost no effort, like growing weeds.

Trust must be present for desirable change to happen in a school. If a school's culture is filled with internal backbiting, a history of broken commitments, a staff of scarcity mentalities, weak competencies, or a ritualistic pattern of micromanaging, change for the good will be slow to happen— real slow—if it happens at all. So prior to instituting the leadership theme, a school will first want to consider the trust levels that are in existence at the school, and look for ways to resolve or remove areas of mistrust. Recall that when A.B. Combs started out with the leadership theme, it began the initiative as a pilot since there were concerns about some teachers not buying in. The pilot brought credibility and trust. Larry Sullivan likewise needed to build trust and hire the right people before he could introduce the *7 Habits* in Texarkana. So it is important first to ensure that there is a solid core of trust.

A favorite model I like to use is what I call the "Pyramid of Influence."

The base of the pyramid is *Modeling,* or example. Example is what is *seen.* Good example is what creates leadership credibility. Good example is what allows a teacher to believe what a principal has to say, or a student to trust what a teacher has to teach. Indeed, if there is one thing my entire professional experience has taught me about inspiring trust in an organization it is that the leaders themselves must first be trustworthy. Change works best and occurs fastest when it comes from the inside out. Only when leaders are trustworthy—which requires having both character and competence, or primary greatness—are they in a position to inspire trust in others. The same is true for teachers who hope to inspire trust in students. If a teacher or administrator only talks the talk, and does not walk the walk by exhibiting primary greatness, others will see right through them—especially children.

The next level of the pyramid, *Relating,* represents the quality of relationships we have with others. Relating is what is *felt.* It is represented by the amount of care, consideration, and empathy that exists in a relationship. It harks back to the old adage that people will not care how much you know until they know how much you care. So much of leadership and teaching is all about relationships. Again listen to Muriel: "One of the rea-

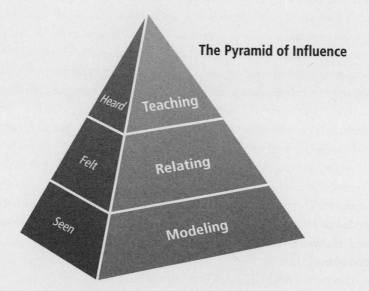

The Pyramid of Influence

sons we know our students are going to do okay on their core tests is that they are so connected with everybody at the school. The students that tend to do the best in this school are the ones whose teachers have never forgotten that the most important thing they can do is to have a positive relationship with their students."

> If a teacher has a good relationship with students, then students accept her rules, procedures, and disciplinary actions.
> —*Robert J. Marzano*, What Works in Schools

The pinnacle of the Pyramid of Influence is *Teaching*. Once students feel understood and accepted they are then more open to influence—to listening to what a teacher has to say. Likewise, once teachers see a principal's good example and have a good relationship with him or her, including feeling valued, they too become more open to influence. Teaching, therefore, is the culmination of what is seen, felt, and *heard*.

For example, the Pyramid of Influence has been applied within the Singapore prison system for juveniles. The system is a year into its program for teaching the *7 Habits* to hundreds of teen offenders, but so far only the adult security personnel have been taught the habits. Their sense is "How can we expect the teens to accept the habits if we as adults do not understand the habits or are not living them?" Their logic makes sense. When an outside consultant teaches the *7 Habits* in a corporate setting, he or she typically downloads the content to participants and then flies off, seldom to be heard from again. But in the prisons, security personnel will be the ones teaching the habits to the young offenders, and, rather than flying off, they will instead be interacting with the young offenders every day. So it would greatly help if they were living the *7 Habits,* and that is why they have dedicated year one to learning and living the habits themselves.

So it is with teachers. They in many cases spend more time with the students than any other adults do including parents. It is imperative that they be models of what is being taught. No, perfection is not required, but a strong semblance of "making an effort" certainly is. It is all part of inspiring trust, which is the vital core of any change initiative.

As teachers model the *7 Habits* and leadership principles, students begin incorporating the same manner of thinking into their everyday repertoire. Consider this example from Rowlett Elementary in Bradenton, Florida:

When a new student arrived from Ecuador in the middle of fourth grade, he spoke absolutely no English. He was completely wide-eyed and quite nervous. But the students in his class saw the situation, and took it upon themselves to help him out. The words they used were things like "Let's make this a win-win. We'll help him learn English, and he can teach us about his country and help us with our Spanish." Or "We can synergize and do this as a team." They practically made helping this boy learn English their class mission and goal for the year.

When time came for state exams at the end of that first year, the boy scored "above average" in reading. To hear him read, one would never guess what his situation had been only a few months earlier. As the school's principal, Brian Flynn, described it, "To see him stand in front of the class and talk and read, and to see how the students pulled together on his behalf was a total inspiration, and evidence of how the habits can make a difference."

Step Two: Clarify Purpose

One of the biggest challenges in implementing the leadership theme is getting off the initial platform—that comfortable "this-is-the-way-we-have-always-done-it" pedestal. Any time the winds of change arise, doubt and courage collide. For courage to win out there has to be some compelling reason to let go, to lift off. Nothing works better to make that happen than having a meaningful purpose.

Clarifying purpose involves finding answers to four questions:

1: *What is our mission?* A mission is not a destination, but a reason to journey. In every school highlighted in this book, the question that got them started was the same that all kids ask, *Why? Why* would we want to do this as a school? *Why* would this leadership theme help students? *Why* would this be worth it to me as a teacher or administrator? *Why* would parents support this? The initial purpose at A.B. Combs was to increase enrollment, but after speaking with key stakeholders it declared its mission to be "To develop leaders, one child at a time." Their biggest *why* became helping students become more prepared for life in the twenty-first century, and soon increasing enrollment became a nonissue. The more a school's mission is directed toward building students' confidence and preparing them for life, the more stakeholders will support that school's efforts. The key is to keep the focus on the true end in mind.

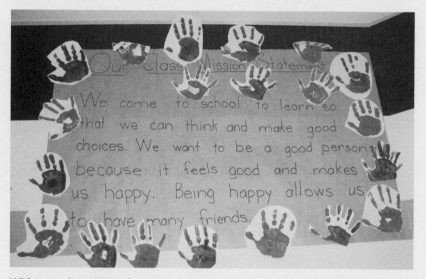

Without a clear sense of meaningful purpose—that of helping young people lead their lives—the leadership initiative would never take off or be sustained for long.

Hint: While eventually you might want to summarize your school's purpose(s) for doing the leadership theme into a concise mission statement, I suggest you begin simply by creating a list of the top three or four reasons why your school wants to embark on the leadership theme. Consider those reasons from the perspective of each stakeholder.

2: *What is our vision?* While mission is the purpose, vision is the destination. One way to think of vision is in terms of "results," the specific outcomes your school wants to achieve within a given time frame. For example, what does your school want to see in two or three years in the way of student behaviors, disciplinary measures, teacher satisfaction levels, parent participation, and, yes, test scores? The more clearly people can see what is included in the vision and what is not, the more focused they can become in their planning, in their purchases, in their lesson plans, and in their approach to classroom management.

Hint: Visions that lack at least some sense of urgency or targeted completion dates tend to be little more than daydreams, so it helps to translate your vision into a short list of realistic goals and time-specific milestones.

> When people comment on the joy they feel when they are in this building, and the happiness that we feel, it is because we are a team with a common vision and a common mission.
> —*Martha Bassett, Art Teacher, A.B. Combs Elementary*

3: *What is our strategy?* If vision is the destination, strategy is the path. Regardless of how compelling or promising a mission or vision may be, it makes no sense for a group of teachers and administrators to leap off their present pedestal without a plan. A strategic plan is the "how."

There are two general types of strategy: 1) the *hard* strategy and 2) the *soft* strategy. The hard strategy is the nuts and bolts of how a school will achieve its mission and vision, and how it will implement the leadership theme. It includes laying out logical, orderly, and manageable steps and timetables. It involves establishing rigorous answers to such questions as "What priorities will we address first?" "What will be the pace?" "What resources will be needed?" "Who will be involved?" and "How will we launch?" It also asks, "Is our plan reasonable; can we execute it?"

The soft strategy is represented by the school's *values*. "How will we treat each other on the journey? How will we treat students?" Some call it their Code of Conduct, or Code of Cooperation. In a sense, the soft strategy reflects the combined *character* of a school, while the hard strategy should reflect and be aligned with the combined *competence*.

Hint: Strategies, both hard and soft, lose viability if they become too detailed or lengthy. For implementing the leadership theme, the strategy should be summarizable in one or two pages. Remember, sometimes less is more.

4: *What is expected of each individual?* Clear expectations define each individual's role in navigating the path, or strategy. Are they to lead out? Are they to provide support? Are they to remove obstacles? Clear expectations fall into two categories: 1) general expectations that all people are supposed to take on and 2) individual-specific expectations. For example, A.B. Combs has a general expectation that anyone who sees trash on the floor is responsible for picking it up. They own the problem. The school then also has performance expectations and goals that are specific to each individual.

Hint: The more people can see how what is expected of them is directly linked to the mission, vision, or strategy, the more they will feel ownership and be fully engaged, and the less likely they will be to continue to engage themselves in activities irrelevant to the school's mission, vision, or strategy.

While all four of the above questions began with *What*, all four help answer the question of *Why*. And here is why. If a person does not know what the mission is, or what the vision is, or what the strategy is, or what his or her role is, that person will never fully know "why" they are being asked to do what they are being asked to do, nor will they feel a passion for it.

Before moving to Step Three, I will add that what happens at the school level must also happen at the classroom and individual level for the leadership theme to be most effective. Each classroom will want to develop its mission statement, goals, strategies, and expectations. Individuals, perhaps using the data notebooks, will then likewise want to set goals and identify what they need to do to accomplish those goals.

Step Three: Align Systems

Remember, this is the step where so many change efforts fail, often because it is ignored entirely.

Once a school has clarified its purpose(s) for adopting the leadership theme, the natural inclination is to want to jump in and get it started in the classroom—to implement. But one thing that even the corporate world is still learning is that *alignment* precedes implementation in the flow of success. Too many leaders ineptly think they can skip the alignment step and go straight to implementation. In fact, many do, and as I said earlier, that is why so many change efforts fail.

There are multiple systems to be aligned with the mission, vision, strategy, and expectations. However, four key systems—all of which are people systems—are most crucial to the success of the leadership theme. They have to do with 1) attracting, 2) positioning, 3) rewarding, and 4) developing people.

1. *Attracting: Who are the key people and stakeholders who can make this happen? How will you get their buy-in?* When creating change of this magnitude, people have to be recruited all over again—even the long-timers, if not especially the long-timers. Their hearts and minds have to be inspired as if they were starting anew. The best way to do this is to involve people early on. A foresighted leader will begin the process of bringing people on board *during* the creation of the mission, vision, and strategy, not after.

> The main thing about implementing the *7 Habits* is that the teachers have to take ownership of it. They have to make it a part of themselves after they are trained, and then teach it in a way that is most comfortable for them.
>
> —*Lauretta Teague, Principal, Chestnut Grove Elementary*

Part of achieving buy-in is anticipating and knowing what to do if certain individuals or groups resist. Teachers are a school's greatest asset, which also makes them the greatest threat. Pedro Garcia, a longtime district superintendent in California and Tennessee, talks about what he calls OBTs, or On Board Terrorists. These are people who attempt to drill holes in every effort to improve. They are the naysayers who sit in the back of the room and leak doom all over the place. One person alone can sabotage an effort if the situation is not handled correctly. If people see change as something you are doing *to* them, they might resist even if it is a good thing. But if they see it as something you are doing *with* them, they are far more likely to hop on board. One of the key decisions early on, therefore, will be how to launch the leadership theme in a way that maximizes the potential for buy-in.

Hint: When we reflect on the schools mentioned in this book, it is clear that one thing they all did well was involve parents early on. They invited them to planning meetings and included them in *7 Habits* training. Some even took them along to visit A.B. Combs. Parents have proved to be huge supporters of the leadership theme and have contributed some rather amazing talents to enhance the outcomes and success of the process.

2. *Positioning: What roles do teachers and administrators need to fill to make this happen? What leadership roles will students take on?* Positioning involves putting the right people in the right place at the right time. It answers the questions "Who will do what?" "Who will have authority to make what decisions?" "To whom will they be accountable?" This is often referred to as an organization's *structure.*

One thing that each principal who implemented the leadership theme did early on was assemble a team of decision makers and mentors. They included individuals whose opinions were respected and who represented multiple grade levels and specialty areas. Another important thing the principals did was design a structure that ensures collaboration. They recognized that the days of isolated teachers acting as hermits hiding in their classroom are over, and so they built collaboration right into the formal structure. This way the schools are team-oriented by intentional design, and collaboration is not left solely to haphazard encounters.

Another key to the success of the leadership theme is the role that the students take on. More than being given fun job titles, they are given responsibility. Robyn Seay, principal at Stuard Elementary in Aledo, Texas, says that this component of the leadership theme has had the greatest impact at her school: "What being referred to as leaders and being given leadership responsibility has done for the students is absolutely stunning."

Hint: Muriel says that one of the most frequent requests she receives from visitors is for a list of the student leadership roles. She is reluctant to share the list, however, because it is the students who help come up with the roles, and may not be what students at other schools might come up with. In other words, it is not that she is unwilling to share; she shares all

Meaningful opportunities to lead are what catapulted Stuard Elementary into so much success its first year.

the time. But in her mind, the process of involving students is more important than the list of job titles itself. Student involvement and empowerment are the keys.

3. *Developing: How will we train people in the* 7 Habits *and other leadership content?* Principals mentioned in this book determined early on how and when staff would be trained in the *7 Habits* and the quality tools. Most of the schools did this in a phased process, such as doing *7 Habits* training year one, quality training year two, and renewal training in years beyond. They also set up an ongoing process for training newcomers.

Plans also need to be made for training students. Will this be done at all grade levels or at just a few grade levels? Will the ubiquitous approach be used in year one, or will it be phased in, as a few of the schools did it? When will students be introduced to the quality tools? Again, there is no one right answer for each of these questions. It all depends on the specific goals and readiness of the school, its staff, and its students. But clearly one of the most effective ways to train the students is to involve them in leadership roles or to allow them to train other students.

Furthermore, consideration needs to be given to how to bring parents into the development process so that they too can become familiar with the habits and quality tools. Generally speaking, it is no secret that the home environment has the largest direct impact on student achievement. So why would a school ever think about implementing the leadership theme without involving the home? One of the best methods for doing this is to create opportunities for students to teach their parents, through small homework assignments. Other options might include holding special training sessions for parents, making up newsletters for parents, or simply highlighting the habits during school events where parents are in attendance.

Greta (in white) coaches other leaders of public speaking, such as this young man, while Muriel Summers takes her normal position, which is allowing students to take the lead.

Another factor is that students have varied learning styles. While teaching a lesson in a classroom setting is one effective way to teach the leadership principles, sometimes students will learn best through music, arts, service activities, leadership roles, or the like. One of students' favorite ways of learning about leadership occurs when outside business or community leaders are brought into the school and students are allowed to ask questions. The point is that the more the approach is varied, authentic, and tailored to students' learning styles, the more the content will stick.

Hint: It is in the actual "process" of teaching, creating lesson plans, designing displays, and leading school events that teachers, students, and parents best learn the leadership principles. So be careful not to take away from teachers the opportunity to be involved in the creation process by telling them how to do everything or detailing how exactly they must implement the leadership approach in their rooms. The greatest learning and sense of empowerment occurs while in the act of creating.

4. *Rewarding: How will progress and successes be rewarded? How will people be held accountable for inappropriate actions?* The leadership schools re-

When leaders of Lego Corporation visited, A.B. Combs turned it into an opportunity for students to learn more about leadership.

ferred to in this book reward often and in varied ways. They do not just do it for the "top achievers" or the "top achievements," but rather each child is rewarded for meaningful progress. They also look for ways to reward team, class, and schoolwide efforts, not just individual efforts. It is important that the way students, parents, teachers, and community volunteers are rewarded is meaningful to them. Therefore, a school will want to consider early on how achievements—big and small—will be celebrated at the school, classroom, and individual levels.

Of course, part of any reward system includes asking, "How will poor performance be handled? What will happen when a child does not adhere to the school values? How will a teacher handle student quarrels? How will the principal respond to a teacher who refuses to go along with change?" Too often, accountability is left to inconsistent, random, knee-jerk responses. Accountability is part of the reward system and should be proactively thought out prior to implementing the leadership theme.

Needless to say, the only way a reward system (including accountability) will be fully effective is if there are clear measurement processes and standards in place. Otherwise, how will a school know if success has been achieved? This includes finding ways to track academic progress and personal goals, such as using the data notebooks, or collecting other performance measures such as attendance numbers, disciplinary reports, and data on parent or teacher satisfaction. Regardless of which measures your school chooses, it helps to have as many of them as possible in place prior to implementing so that a benchmark can be set.

Hints: If the rewards, accountability actions, or measurement processes are not aligned with the mission, vision, strategy, and individual job expectations, do not expect the leadership theme to be sustained for long. Furthermore, in the case of the leadership theme, remember that while fun awards and public recognition have their place and value, intrinsic rewards tend to be the most motivating and reinforcing.

In summary, multiple systems need to be aligned with the mission, vision, and strategy, including the people systems of attracting, positioning, training, and rewarding. Other systems not covered are also important. Resource systems, for example, need to be aligned, including the budget, so that what little the school has to spend gets spent on the "main" things. Communication systems need to be aligned so everyone is receiving the same messages, on the same page. The point is that the more a school or classroom has its "arrows" aligned, the more its culture will resemble the illustration below. Notice how the biggest arrow involves getting the mission, vision, and strategy aligned with stakeholder needs. After that, midsized arrows can then be aligned with the big arrow. The small arrows, which include hundreds of minor things that teachers and the school as a whole have to deal with on a daily basis, can then be brought into alignment with the big arrow, or totally discarded if they are incompatible with its mission, vision, and strategy. Having the leadership theme embedded in the systems is what will create the culture. Having the leadership principles embedded in the systems is what will ensure that when the principal or other key people leave, the culture will remain.

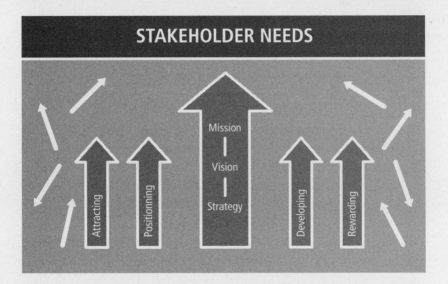

Step Four: Unleash Talent

This is the step where the launch from the lower platform truly takes place. It is where the leap of faith occurs. It is also where the culture comes to life. But before I explain more about this step, let me first go back to the trapeze analogy and add another dimension.

This time, imagine a group of forty to eighty teachers and administrators all clinging to one trapeze swing while sailing through the air. Can you imagine such an entangled, claustrophobic scene? Assume that only one of them is the leader. That leader knows the group cannot reach a greater height without flexing their bodies in unison to create enough thrust. So, "leading by example," he or she begins flexing his or her body and hollering, "Hey, everybody, do what I am doing!" As you might expect, several of the people are not even in a position to see what the leader is doing, while those who can see begin trying to contort their bodies in the same motion and rhythm as the leader. The result is that only a portion of the group is working while the majority is just hanging on for the ride.

Again, can you imagine that scene? If so, you have just envisioned what many change efforts look like in schools. Change never succeeds in this fashion.

> If you continue to do what you have always done, you will continue to get the same results.
>
> —*W. Edwards Deming*

So what does work? Consider a different approach. Envision the same group of teachers and administrators on the lower platform getting ready to launch. They have a clear vision and a strategy for achieving the higher platform and they buy into it. But the difference this time is that they each have their own swing. Yes, they are all still aiming for the same upper platform, but all are free and *empowered* to get there at their own pace and under their own initiative. The leader sets the example by leading out, but others joining in can also demonstrate their unique techniques, which in many cases may be better than the leader's. Feel better so far?

The reason this may feel better is because people are free to soar in their own way. They are subject to the same principles but now have the freedom to put those principles into practice in their own unique way. Some might even add a somersault or two. Of course, a few might also drop off to the nets below due to a lack of skill or desire, but when they do they will not drag the entire group down with them.

Habits 1 and 2 are where it all starts, not just for kindergartners, but for any change initiative.

What a wise principal will hope for in implementing the leadership theme is to become a leader of leaders, not a leader of followers. Leadership is the highest of all arts. It is the enabling art. Leadership is about unleashing the whole person toward inspiring and worthwhile goals. In a school, it is about finding teachers' and administrators' strengths—their gifts, their voices—and then letting them soar. It is about engaging their hearts, minds, bodies, and spirits. It is also about optimizing students' gifts and unleashing their talents. And that is what these schools are doing.

Some principals may hear the word *unleash* and fear losing control, especially if they have staff members who are not trustworthy. But because Muriel Summers, Beth Sharpe, Lauretta Teague, and the other principals have people on staff who have top skills and strong character, and who are "on board," they are able to unleash people's talents without fear. And, because they are able to unleash people's talents, they in turn are able to find time for visioning, reworking the strategy, visiting with stakeholders, meeting with students, and pursuing extra funding—things that many principals want to do but are seldom able to get to.

Some of the questions that need to be asked when unleashing people's talents: "How much will we trust teachers to be on their own?" "How will we know which teachers need more assistance?" "How much will we guide students versus telling them what to do?" "How can we utilize people's talents to create fun traditions or beautify the school?"

One point I want to emphasize in unleashing talents is that this applies to more than teachers. It applies to unleashing the talents of parents and community volunteers, but particularly to unleashing the talents of students. Consider what Gayle Gonzalez Johnson and Eric Johnson, parents of three students at A.B. Combs, had to say:

> At A.B. Combs, character comes first, then academics. I would not sacrifice the character training for better test scores. Yet our test scores speak for themselves.
>
> When our daughter was in elementary school, a new boy came to her classroom with significant anger issues. The way the teacher handled this student was inspiring. The teacher visited honestly with the children one afternoon when the boy was not in class. She said, "The recent blowups in our classroom are not working for us to make a good learning environment." She involved them in the solution. The children understood that much of the problem was this new student. On their own, they formed a support team. They said they could help this new boy even better than the teacher. This young man responded well and was making great academic progress for the first time in his life. When he later moved away the students in the class cried. They had learned to love him.
>
> Aneesa is a songbird and at A.B. Combs she has found her confidence to sing in public. This school helps each student excel in the area where they are full of natural gift.

It is intriguing that the Johnson's were not willing to sacrifice the character component, not even for higher test scores. But the point being emphasized here is who the true leaders were in the story of the classroom blowups. Did you catch how the teacher gave the students responsibility and respected them by involving them in the problem solving, using their gifts, and trusting them?

> The woods would be silent if no bird sang but the best.
>
> —*Henry David Thoreau, quote outside A.B. Combs music room*

The more everyone's talents are able to be unleashed and empowered, the more successful the leadership theme will be at your school.

Hint: If Step One: Inspire Trust, Step Two: Clarify Purpose (establishing mission, vision, strategy, and expectations), or Step Three: Align Systems have not been well thought out or clearly communicated, Step Four: Unleashing Talent has the potential to create more chaos than it will reduce.

Putting the Steps Together— A Progressive Framework

The four steps: 1) Inspire Trust, 2) Clarify Purpose, 3) Align Systems, and 4) Unleash Talent work in sequence, as is illustrated by the model below. Clarify Purpose is the natural starting place, with Align Systems and Unleash Talent being logical following steps. Inspire Trust is placed at the very core since it directly impacts all three of the other steps, and therefore takes

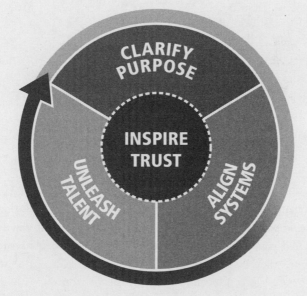

priority. The circular arrow in the model indicates that this is a progressive, ongoing process of continuous improvement and refinement.

Especially when first starting out, it makes sense to try to follow the four steps in sequential order. But, in reality, no change initiative is ever quite so simple as one, two, three, and four. I can assure you that A.B. Combs and the other schools mentioned in this book did not follow the four steps quite as cleanly and sequentially as I have made it appear here. In other words, at any given point a school might be working on all four steps at once, or they may even need to skip a step or work backward for a time. The reality is that once the leadership theme sets into full motion, it will become increasingly clear that the four steps work more in an interdependent fashion than they do in a nicely set sequence. But early on, I still suggest trying to follow the sequence as much as is possible.

As these students can teach you, Habit 1 means taking responsibility. Change in schools requires that teachers have more than an owner's manual; they must have ownership.

Another note to keep in mind in following the four steps is that A.B. Combs has built their approach over an eight-year period, and they are still building it. In other words, they have been through this cycle several times, and Muriel will tell you they are still in the process of tinkering and creating. Meanwhile the other schools that have taken on the leadership theme have been able to learn from the A.B. Combs template and as a result are successfully replicating the accompanying successes in far less time. So in getting under way, carefully decide how much your school can realistically take on during the first year, and then each following year revisit the cycle and determine what more you want to do, if anything, to expand or refine things at a pace that matches your needs and capacity.

Sustaining Change

As tough as creating change may be, it is only fair to warn you that the real challenge is not in creating change as much as it is in *sustaining* change. Any principal will tell you, for example, that it is far easier to jump to higher test scores than it is to sustain those scores. A.B. Combs found this out firsthand. Twice in the past few years their state exams have been drastically altered, making it hard to track progress. Furthermore, just recently some boundaries changes were set in place that dramatically altered the school's demographic –makeup, bringing to the school an even greater number of low-income students. As you might expect, Muriel see those new challenges as opportunities.

> One of the most damaging myths that aspiring school administrators often learn is that the change process, if managed well, will proceed smoothly. That myth amounts to little more than a cruel hoax, an illusion that encourages educators to view problems and conflict as evidence of mistakes or a mismanaged process rather than as the inevitable by-products of serious reform.
> —*Richard DuFour and Robert Eaker,* Professional Learning Communities at Work

To most successfully sustain any cultural change, including implementing the leadership theme, it is advantageous for a leader to understand why so many change efforts fail. Most often it is a matter of too little or too much, as indicated by the following list of some of the most common reasons why change efforts go awry:

Why Change Efforts Fail

Too Little	Too Much
No compelling purpose	Purpose not hitched to reality
Lack of a strong principal	Too dependent upon a strong principal
Not enough time spent getting buy-in	Excessive time trying to gain total consensus
People unwilling to change	People change too often, careen from fad to fad
Lack of strategy	Strategy too detailed—people not unleashed
Scope not big enough	Tackled more than could be handled
Jumped too soon into implementation	Always planning but never implementing
Moved too slow—people lost enthusiasm	Moved too fast—people overwhelmed
Not enough teamwork—individuals do own thing	Too much team focus—individual effort stifled
Successes not recognized or rewarded	Success declared too soon or overpraised
No accountability or feedback	Too much checking up—micromanaging
Give up too soon	Keep doing same things when they don't work

What this chart of failure paths implies is that leadership really is an art. It is a matter of testing, trying, analyzing, measuring, retrying, and recognizing that what worked yesterday may not work today. It is a balancing act.

So how does a leader go about sustaining culture change in a school?

I will answer that question by briefly referring to a sampling of research that has been carried out by educators for educators. I do this for two reasons. One is that it is right on track with what needs to be done. The second I will explain momentarily.

Robert Marzano, one of the most respected researchers in the field of education, points out in his book *What Works in Schools* three principles that he suggests are central to creating and sustaining change in today's schools:

- *Principle 1: The new era of school reform is based on the realization that reform is a highly contextualized phenomenon. Reform efforts will and should look substantively different from school to school.*

Is this not what we witnessed in each of the schools referred to in this book? They have placed their own signatures on the process. They own it. Remember Muriel's advice to David George in Canada: "Don't boil someone else's water." To sustain change at your school, that change needs to be matched to your school.

- *Principle 2: The new era of school reform is characterized by a heavy emphasis on data.*

Again, is this not exactly what the leadership schools are doing? Is it not the purpose of the data notebooks? This is why I state that the data component of what the schools are doing cannot be emphasized enough. This includes monitoring individual student data, classroom data, grade-level data, and schoolwide data.

- *Principle 3: In the new era of school reform, change is approached on an incremental basis.*

Muriel is fond of saying, "It is better to go slow in the beginning so that you can go fast in the end." A.B. Combs took the whole process slow—in increments. Year one was the pilot group. Year two, the whole school was on board. Year three, the quality tools were introduced. And so forth. Each year something new is added, or as Beth Sharpe at English Estates puts it, "the ante gets upped." In Muriel's words, "Excellence does not happen overnight. Excellence is a journey we will be on for the rest of our lives, reaching for the highest star and making great things happen. But you need to know that this is a process, and it takes time." So while English Estates and other schools were fortunate to move faster and harvest results at a quicker pace thanks to being able to learn from A.B. Combs, this is not a race. Schools should only move forward at a pace that matches people's ability to absorb change, all the while maintaining a pace that lets people know that "this is here to stay." Again, it is a balancing act.

Marzano's three principles for sustaining change mesh with what any school must do to sustain change of any magnitude. And we see what the schools mentioned in this book are doing is very much aligned with the methods and philosophies that respected researchers have been promoting for years in terms of leading change in schools. Remember the windows in the A.B. Combs schoolhouse model? All those researchers and all those

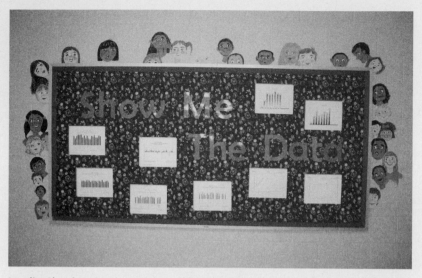

Leading by data is a key source of strength and accountability at the leadership schools.

philosophies weave together and are in direct alignment with what researchers have been saying, with what parents have been asking for, and with what today's realities are demanding. In essence, what these schools are doing is putting research into application.

Let me share one more example of how these schools are applying tested research from the field of education. Consider Larry Lezotte's effective schools research and his "Seven Correlates" for improving student achievement, as summarized below. Are these not the same types of things that A.B. Combs and the other schools are doing?

1. **Clear and Focused Mission.** In effective schools, the mission is clear and all programs and instructional strategies focus on its accomplishment.
2. **Opportunity to Learn/Time on Task.** In effective schools, every student is given adequate opportunity to master the required material, and those who struggle are given more time as needed.
3. **Instructional Leadership.** In effective schools, a strong leader with vision has tremendous impact on student achievement.

4. **Frequent Monitoring of Student Progress.** In effective schools, monitoring is more than annual standardized testing—it is the ongoing review of student work, accompanied by timely feedback.
5. **High Expectations.** In effective schools, a climate of high expectations includes the core belief that all students can learn, and that the teacher has the capacity to teach all students.
6. **Positive Home-School Relations.** In effective schools, active parent involvement yields improved student attitudes toward school, higher self-esteem, and increased achievement.
7. **Safe and Orderly Environment.** In effective schools, discipline, classroom management, and character education help create a climate that is both safe and conducive to effective teaching and learning.

Again, as you read through Larry Lezotte's "Seven Correlates," did you not think back to specific stories or steps contained in this book? In my mind, what researchers like Robert Marzano and Larry Lezotte are saying is exactly what these schools are doing. Indeed, a lot of good research, good philosophy, and good practices have been coming out of the education community for years, far more than what I have just referenced. They too are based upon timeless, universal principles, not merely the latest fads. That is why they keep showing up again and again in various journals and publications. The problem is that many schools have had a tough time implementing the principles—putting them into practice.

One of the things that researchers know about change is that you cannot rest on your laurels.

The implementation stage is difficult; it is hard work. Most schools go through an implementation dip. The thing that we have to do as leaders in that situation is make sure we provide the support so that people don't quit, put the process back on the shelf, and give up on the change.

And then after we get through that implementation dip and things are going well, we tend to forget all the good things that we did, and we as human beings just tend to relax a little bit. So to keep it alive, we have to keep bringing it to the forefront. One of the things we do at English Estates is talk about our leadership program on a monthly basis at staff meetings. We reevaluate, we adjust, we have writing teams that try to keep it fresh, and we also raise the bar a little bit each year.

Another way that we keep the 7 Habits fresh and our leadership program alive is by mentoring other schools. I think that is a very important thing for others to do, because when we invite people into our school, and tell them with pride about the things that we are doing, that makes a difference for all of us. It holds us mutually accountable, and it helps us go to the next level.

—*Beth Sharpe, Principal, English Estates Elementary*

In contrast, the schools described in this book have been making it happen. They are bringing the research to life, and they are doing it in a way that is making a difference in young people's lives in many parts of the world. And that to me is the key. Whether a school uses the four steps I have just described or some other existing framework or approach, the end in mind should never be anything less than helping young people to be better prepared to thrive in the twenty-first century through living principle-centered lives.

9

Ending with the Beginning in Mind

Have you ever been at sea in a dense fog, when it seemed as if
a tangible white darkness shut you in, and the great ship, tense
and anxious, groped her way toward the shore . . . and you
waited with beating heart for something to happen? I was
like that ship before my education began, only I was without
compass . . . and had no way of knowing how near the harbour
was. "Light! give me light!" was the wordless cry of my soul,
and the light of love shone on me in that very hour.

—*Helen Keller*

Education has been my career, and so has the field of leadership.
So you can imagine how fascinating all of this is to me.

I love what is happening with the students—at all grade
levels. I commend the teachers who have done so much to translate the
spirit of the *7 Habits* and the other leadership principles into language that
is friendly to today's young people. There is no question in my mind that
what these educators are doing is making a difference, and that is what
teaching—and *The Leader in Me*—is all about.

In summarizing the contents and spirit of this book, I want to return to
four phrases I used in the very first chapters. They are phrases that I mentioned so lightly that you might scarcely have thought about them. But research indicates that we best remember that which we hear first and that
which we hear last, and so I raise and reraise these phrases both at the start
and at the end because I so strongly believe that each is worthy of remembrance. It is my way of ending with the beginning in mind.

Phrase One:
"Modern-Day Miracle Worker"

You may remember that early on I referred to Muriel Summers and these other educators as being "modern-day miracle workers." That is a label that I am sure Muriel, in all her humility, will take open objection to, mostly because she and the others will be the first to say they did not do it alone. But I stick to the label, not just for Muriel, but for all the educators mentioned in the book, and this is why.

"Miracle worker" is a label often reserved for Anne Sullivan, the woman who mentored Helen Keller throughout most of her life. You may recall how Helen at a very young age became both deaf and blind through disease. The emotions attached to those physical losses resulted in her exhibiting wild, animal-like behaviors. Nothing, not even the best of advice from doctors, could calm her wildness. Nothing, that is, until the day Anne Sullivan entered her life in the spring of 1887.

What some do not realize is that Anne had already experienced more than her own share of life's hard knocks. Her mother died when she was but a child, and her alcohol-dependent father abandoned her and her younger brother. Relatives refused to take them in, so they were sent to an almshouse, a place where the diseased and unwanted souls of the day were housed. There Anne suffered more indignities. Her brother died of tuberculosis, and from disease she herself nearly lost all of her eyesight.

Through it all, the one thing that did not fail Anne was her spirit. One day, when a government inspector visited the almshouse, Anne lunged at him and clung on, begging desperately for an opportunity to go to school. She was fourteen before she finally was sent to the Perkins Institution for the Blind in Massachusetts. Unable to read, she was best known early on for her rebellious nature and temper tantrums. Classmates mocked her and some teachers were even less tolerant. But a few teachers saw potential in Anne and went out of their way to nourish her ambitions. They went so far as to help her gain access to a series of surgeries that restored much of her eyesight.

At age twenty, Anne was named class valedictorian, and at graduation she stood before her peers and declared:

And now we are going out into the busy world, to take our share in life's bur-
dens, and do our little to make the world better, wiser, and happier . . . Every
man who improves himself is aiding the progress of society, and everyone
who stands still holds it back.

Shortly after graduation, Anne responded to a call for a governess to
work with a young girl in Alabama named Helen. Helen was seven years
old at the time, so already she had struggled with her blindness and deaf-
ness for five years. But Helen too had a strong spirit, and her initial reaction
to Anne was no different from her response to all the others who had attempted to work with her. She was violent and obstinate. Yet there was
something about Anne that in a short time calmed Helen. Listen to what
Anne wrote in her journal two weeks after meeting Helen:

> The wild creature of two weeks ago has been transformed into a gentle child.
> She is sitting by me as I write, her face serene and happy . . . It now remains
> my pleasant task to direct and mold the beautiful intelligence that is begin-
> ning to stir in the child-soul.

Ponder those phrases one-by-one: "transformed into a gentle child," "sitting beside me," "her face serene and happy," "my pleasant task," "to mold
the beautiful intelligence," "beginning to stir in the child-soul." Are those
not absolutely inspiring words and phrases, particularly considering what
Anne had been through in her own childhood?

Soon Helen began to cling to Anne almost as tightly as Anne had grasped
on to the government inspector; Helen was literally begging for knowledge.
It began beside the water well, where the first word she learned was *water*.
From that point on she had an unquenchable thirst for exploration and
learning. Anne brought meaning to every smell, every touch, and every
breeze that drifted Helen's way. As an adult, Helen would reflect on those
early encounters by recording in her diary:

> A person who is severely impaired never knows his hidden sources of strength
> until he is treated like a normal human being and encouraged to try to shape
> his own life.

Again, contemplate the individual phrases: "hidden sources of strength," "treated like a normal human being," and "encouraged to try to shape his own life." Is it any wonder why Helen referred to Anne throughout her life as "Teacher"?

5ᵗʰ Grade Mission
2007-2008
To reach every child,
every day!

Just as Helen was to Anne, every child is important at A.B. Combs.

When I reflect on the statements from both Anne and Helen, I cannot help but be reminded of Muriel Summers and the other outstanding educators. Many of their students have been through tough challenges in life. Some have come to her with histories of rebellion; others have endured terrible emotional or physical tragedies. But no matter who they are or what life experiences they bring with them, when they walk through the doors of A.B. Combs, what Muriel sees in them are their unique "gifts." She accentuates the good that is in them and does whatever she can to develop them into leaders, "one child at a time." This Muriel does without bringing up her own array of disheartening challenges that she has experienced in life. For these reasons, I am not hesitant to place Muriel in the elect category of "modern-day miracle worker," or to use her as a model of what *The Leader in Me* is all about.

Any person who unlocks the unseen potential of others and inspires them toward noble causes is a modern-day miracle worker. So by this standard, Muriel is not the only miracle worker spoken of in this book. Many of the teachers and staff members at A.B. Combs are miracle workers. Beth Sharpe at English Estates is a miracle worker. Lauretta Teague of Chestnut Grove is a miracle worker, as is Donnie Lane. So too are many of the other teachers and administrators spoken of in this book. Think back to Joann Koehler, who spotted in Muriel the potential to become a great administrator. Consider what her spark ignited. Is she not also a miracle worker in the life of Muriel?

At the annual art show, every student at A.B. Combs has a piece of art on display. The message? Every child is important. Every child has gifts. Every child has potential. Every child can be a leader.

Like the teachers who saw through Anne's anger and hostility to spot her potential, these modern-day teachers are spotting potential in today's young people, one on one. They are spotting the leader in each child, and are helping them to unleash that potential, to find their voice. Every time they spark a new insight, a new ray of hope in a child—small as it may be—that to me is a miracle.

When literally hundreds of students arrive in unison each morning like a giant wave, or when they depart en masse at the end of the day like the tide going out, it must be difficult for educators to always keep in mind that ultimately, in the final analysis, every child is a one—a unique spirit with gifts. And lest anyone forget, every teacher and administrator is also ultimately a one, having their peculiar package of experiences and their own one-of-a-kind package of talents. What greater contribution can an individual teacher make than to enable an individual child to successfully lead his or her own life and to maturely respond to life's challenges?

Every teacher, each time he or she walks into a classroom full of students, is walking into an opportunity to be a miracle worker. When I think back on the definition of *leadership* that I shared early on—"Leadership is communicating people's worth and potential so clearly that they are inspired to see it in themselves"—I cannot help but think of these educators as not only miracle workers, but as true leaders—teacher-leaders.

Phrase Two: *"The Tradition of Caring"*

In chapter 1, I mentioned that during their first visit to A.B. Combs the Patels learned about the school's traditions, particularly "the tradition of caring."

School traditions are not solo acts. I sense that among the readers of this book there will be some very talented teachers who may be thinking, "There is no way this will ever happen at my school. The principal will never support it." Or there may be wonderful principals who read this book and sigh, "My staff is just not ready for this; only a handful of teachers will have the energy." What such teachers may be resolving in their minds is "I am going to do this in my classroom and do it so well that others will want to do likewise," while the principals may be considering: "I am going to pilot this like Muriel did with a small set of teachers and see if I can grow it from there."

I applaud such thinking of teachers and administrators. They are dealing with reality and looking within their Circle of Influence to see how they can eventually make it happen on a larger scale. I heartily encourage their efforts and wish them the best. But it is only fair to warn that if all a school has is one or two teachers doing the leadership theme, or a cluster of four or five, the results will not be the same as when the entire school is actively engaged. In no way can an entire school enjoy the same levels of success that the leadership schools represented in this book have enjoyed unless it becomes a schoolwide effort—a school tradition.

This is not to say, of course, that an individual teacher cannot get started alone, or that a principal should not try a pilot. It is just to recognize that even though teachers have an amazing knack for accomplishing amazing things on their own, the leadership theme will only flourish to its maximum potential to the extent that everyone—all stakeholders—are working together. To reap the full fruits of the harvest, the leadership theme needs to become a school tradition—particularly a tradition of caring.

Phrase Three: *"Not One More Thing"*

A phrase that arose more than once throughout the book in comments from educators is "This is not one more thing." At each of the leadership schools, the leadership theme is not one more thing; it is the "main" thing. It is all about helping students to see their own potential and then nourishing that potential in a way that prepares them for not just surviving, but thriving, in the twenty-first century—this new world we live in.

But in fairness, I point out that some of the schools do make this "one more thing." If nothing else, they set aside significant time at the beginning of each year to teach and reinforce the leadership principles. Some set aside specific time for it each week. Yet even those teachers would not speak of this as "one more thing." They love it, they see value in it, and so they make time to make it an important part of students' education.

Notice how I said they make time for it. Let me say something about this. Any time students are the forced recipients of meaningless facts, they are robbed of time they could have otherwise devoted to gaining mastery of knowledge and skills relevant to twenty-first-century living. Such thievery dulls their thirst for going to school and picks their intellectual pockets of valuable opportunities to progress and find enjoyment in life. And so I am stunned by what some of the leading researchers in the field of education have revealed in this regard. First, from Richard DuFour and Robert Eaker from their *Professional Learning Community*:

> It is time to recognize that the major flaw in the de facto curriculum of American public schools is not that schools do not do enough, but that they at-

tempt to do too much. Even though American students have fewer school days each year than their Asian and European counterparts, they are expected to learn far more curriculum content. Confronted with a curriculum that is "a mile long and one-half inch deep," teachers have become preoccupied with "coverage." They feel unable to teach for student mastery of knowledge and skills because of the race to cover content. One of the most meaningful steps a school can take to promote significant improvement is to develop a process for identifying significant curriculum content, eliminating non-essential material, and providing teachers with time to teach the significant curriculum.

"Significant curriculum" in my mind includes what educators are calling twenty-first-century skills. But is there really time or space in the current mass of required curriculum for those skills to be taught? Consider now what Robert J. Marzano reported in his acclaimed book *What Works in Schools:*

> . . . U.S. mathematics textbooks address 175 percent as many topics as do German textbooks and 350 percent as many topics as do Japanese textbooks. The science textbooks used in the United States cover more than nine times as many topics as do German textbooks and more than four times as many topics as do Japanese textbooks. Yet German and Japanese students significantly outperform U.S. students in mathematics and science.

Could it be that an unacceptable proportion of what our students are being taught falls on the borders of "too much" or "nonessential?" Could we be spending time on irrelevant content at the expense of neglecting twenty-first-century life skills and other relevant content?

With these kinds of questions in mind Marzano assembled a set of math standards that all U.S. students are expected to know by fifth grade. In all there were 741 standards. He then had a team of ten math experts rate each of the standards as to whether or not it was essential. Their findings were astonishing. Of the 741 standards, they rated 299 as "essential" and 143 as "nonessential," which means the rest fell somewhere in the debatable middle. If these numbers can be equated to time, what this says is that students spend 20 percent of their math hour studying standards that are irrelevant, and another significant portion of their time learning standards that are questionable. Ugh!

I am not going to prescribe what teachers should teach or what is or is not essential or relevant. I will do my best not to be one of those business-persons who act as if they know better how to teach students. But as a parent and grandparent and business leader, I do not want to hear that students are spending 20 percent of their time (one day per week) mastering irrelevance.

Put **Habit 3** First Things First

"Things which matter most should not be at the mercy of things which matter least."

Foremost in the heart of every educator is the desire to help students be successful in life. That includes reading, writing, and arithmetic. But today's world requires more if children are to continue wearing their smiles through life.

Today's young people deserve better. Let us not rob them of their precious time. Let us not spend time on things that do not matter. As Goethe said, "Things that matter most must never be at the mercy of that which matters least." This does not mean schools have to be strict, "put-your-brain-to-the-grind" work chambers. Trust me, at these leadership schools there is plenty of room for fun and games. But in many cases, even the fun has meaning. So let us make room to teach skills and character traits that will help students navigate the twenty-first century. If that means reconsidering some of the curriculum, then let that be the case.

The teachers at A.B. Combs have shown us a way to do this without adding "one more thing" or stealing anything essential from teachers' plates. By taking a ubiquitous approach, they are teaching twenty-first-century skills while doing what they were already doing. Granted, it may take some additional start-up time, but for the most part it is a matter of emphasizing a new focus. In fact, many teachers and administrators continue to report that the leadership theme saves them time. Not only are they more efficient and organized personally, but even ten minutes less each day of needing to halt the class to deal with discipline issues adds up to a lot of extra "essentials" time over the education span of a child.

Phrase Four: *"Universal Nature"*

The fourth phrase captures something that I hope you have observed and felt throughout the book. It is a reminder of both the universal nature of the principles and the universal nature of children. The *7 Habits* and other leadership principles will apply in any school and in any country. In fact, all over the world I have been told that I borrowed *7 Habits* from a particular culture or a particular religion or a particular guru. But that is not so. These principles are universal and do not belong to any one source. They are timeless and wonderfully self-evident. And I feel just as strongly about the universal nature of children. We all lead lives that are quite different and yet so very much the same. We all have four basic needs, for example. Children are the same. All can benefit from these universal principles. That is why in the beginning I said that these same principles and approaches can be implemented in a home. They apply everywhere.

A Final Word to Schools

Embedded in the four phrases I just briefly reviewed are the keys to the success of the leadership theme:

* Individual teachers unleashing the potential of students all over the world, one child at a time

- A schoolwide effort with all stakeholders engaged and contributing
- Emphasis on focusing on what is most important to be teaching
- Emphasis on teaching timeless principles and skills that are relevant to today's global reality and preparatory for what tomorrow will bring

Other key factors emphasized throughout the book:

- Listening to what stakeholders want in schools can provide valuable insight into what needs exist in the global economy.
- Parents and business leaders both want character and competence to be taught in schools.
- The leadership theme can help improve academic success by instilling self-confidence in students and by creating a safe learning environment.
- The ubiquitous approach can ingrain and reinforce both character and competence throughout a school's culture.
- Alignment precedes implementation in the flow of success.
- Data and accountability are significant drivers underlying the leadership schools' successes.
- Each school must place its own signature on its strategy to make it contextually relevant.
- Relationships, memories, and connectivity are a big part of what students take away from school and are vital contributors to student achievement and an integral part of *The Leader in Me*.

As you take these key points into consideration, I ask you to please accept this work as it is intended. It does not claim to have all the answers to today's educational dilemmas, nor does it claim that all the successes in this book are due entirely to the *7 Habits*. But what it does suggest is that it is profoundly important that we prepare students for the future by teaching them timeless principles of effectiveness—principles that apply in any culture and in any school, both today and in the future.

Each child is a gift, and each child has gifts. What is exciting is the opportunity we adults have to help them find, nurture, and unleash those gifts, to inspire greatness—primary greatness. So much of the literature on education implies that students will seldom have a better life than what their home offers them and that schools have little impact. Certainly the odds are against students who come from dysfunctional homes or social environments. But as an educator, I cannot accept that as my vision. I believe that good schools and good educators can and do make a difference. I also believe that students can indeed excel beyond their upbringing.

I admit that some of the content of this book may appear easier to apply than it really is. This will be a difficult challenge for your school if you do not have the level of competence and character—primary greatness—that it takes to sustain it. This is not an off-the-shelf program that is purchased and installed like a piece of software. Creativity is required. Effort is required. But implementing the leadership theme *is* doable, as these schools have demonstrated. If you sense that your school is not ready for it now, I challenge you to get ready. Start where you are, consider existing resources, and trust that you can make it happen.

As I asserted in the beginning, I believe that as a whole this generation of students is the finest to walk the planet earth. The turbulence we read about

By learning to be proactive and taking responsibility for their education and their lives, students take a significant step in creating the future that lies ahead of them.

and see on our campuses, caused by relatively few students, should not taint our vision of today's young people. Many of them are miles ahead of previous generations in both competence and character. They are part of a world that is full of challenges, but that only means that it is also full of opportunities. Unfortunately, however, too many of today's young people cannot see the opportunities, only the confusion. So it is critical that early in their lives they come in contact with adults who, in a principled way, can meet them at their critical crossroads to nurture all four of their basic needs: their bodies, their emotions, their minds, and their spirits—especially their spirits. They are worth it, and the quality of our future depends on it.

In today's world even the best of parents cannot expect to do everything all on their own for their children. Parents face heavy pressures from all directions, including complacency. It is difficult to be a parent. How grateful the parents of students at A.B. Combs and these other leadership schools must be for the noble teachers who have taken their children under their mentoring and enabled them to soar with new wings of self-confidence. What these educators are doing exceeds anything I could have possibly hoped for when the *7 Habits* book was released back in 1989. It is so satisfying to see and experience. So to these great educators I give full credit. I love them for what they are doing. I honor them.

This brings me to make a final challenge. There is a tradition at A.B. Combs that I have not yet mentioned: the "strategic pause." It involves having students pause for a few minutes, take a drink of water, stretch their bodies, look toward light, and think of something hopeful. It is a way of re-energizing and refocusing them. I invite you to try it. In fact, I challenge all adults who care about today's young people to take a "strategic pause." I call it "recompassing." Pause to reflect on what you have felt in this book. Does it match up with your view of what needs to be done in schools? Just about every time Muriel Summers stands in front of an audience or speaks to an educator or parent, one of the first things she says is "I know in my heart we are doing the right thing." Does this feel to *you* like the right thing to be doing? Is it something you would like to see in a school near you? I have sent a number of business colleagues to see A.B. Combs and in every case they have walked away thinking about how they might support the leadership theme in their community. A number have already taken action.

> We must be dreamers in action, not martyrs in wait.
>
> —*Thomas Friedman*, The World Is Flat

My hope is that within these pages you too have heard a personal call for action. I am not going to tell you what to do. That is for you to decide given your current desires and circumstances. It could be as simple as bringing the principles into your own home, or into your own life. Too many leaders lie at anchor—resigned to the status quo and confined by what worked in the past. Do not let that be you. Do not be a spectator. Work within your sphere of influence. Be a model—a light, not a critic. This is a new era. Today's young people need more than the steady diet of standard core subjects that they have been fed in the past. You could be the catalyst that brings it to them, even if only in your own home.

Donnie Lane took a proactive step in Decatur, Alabama, that may influence the culture of an entire community.

Many young people find themselves looking for direction—without compass. Borrowing from Helen Keller's words at the start of this chapter, they are walking "at sea in a dense fog," groping "toward the shore" and "without compass," begging "Light! Give me light!" All of us feel that way at times, no matter how old or young we may be. So it is no surprise that many of today's young people feel this way. Life is not always easy. And so there arises in that reality a challenge for all adults to step forward and get involved—to meet today's young people at that critical crossroads. Consider what you might do as you ponder the words of the poem that is sometimes entitled "At the Crossroads." It is a poem that has been printed and re-printed in several versions over many years and attributed to multiple au-thors. I believe it has survived for the better part of a century because of its permanently timeless and urgent message:

> He stood at the crossroads all alone,
> The sunlight in his face;
> He had no fear for the path unknown,
> He was set for a manly race.
> But the road stretched east, and the road stretched west,
> There was no one to tell him which road was best;
> So he took the wrong road and it led him down,
> Till he lost the race and the victor's crown,
> He fell at last in an ugly snare;
> Because no one stood at the crossroads there.
>
> Another boy on another day,
> At the selfsame crossroads stood;
> He paused a moment to choose the way
> That would lead to the greater good.
> And the road stretched east and the road stretched west,
> And one was there to show him the best;
> So he turned right and went on and on,
> And he won the race and the victor's crown;
> He walks today the highway fair,
> Because one stood at the crossroads there.

In today's global economy, we simply cannot afford to wait until young people receive their first promotion into corporate leadership before we show them the better road to getting along with others. We cannot stand by and wait for them to become CEOs or schoolteachers or parents before we teach them how to organize their lives, to set goals, or to be assertive.

We cannot afford to sit by idly and hope that they pick up on their own how to resolve conflicts, or how to be more responsible. We have done that for years and the approach is just not working. We must show them the upward path.

No, today's young people may not be ready to run multinational corporations upon graduation, but they should at least be able to effectively make basic life decisions, to feel a sense of worth, to walk with confidence, and to dream. What greater thing can we do than to meet them at their crossroads and do our part in enabling them to lead their lives?

10

Bringing It Home

A while back my daughter said to me, "Look, Mommy, we are synergizing. We are cleaning the kitchen together." I thought to myself, "Synergize, I just learned that word last week. How do you know what it means?" But she does understand what it means, and it is taught in such a practical way that she is able to use it in our home and with her friends. It is hard to be a parent nowadays, so to know that there is a system and a curriculum at school that is working alongside you in your parenting is wonderful. What an amazing impact it has had on our family.

—*Evelyn Alicea, Parent, English Estates Elementary, Fern Park, Florida*

I began this book sharing my conviction that our young people today belong to the most promising generation in the history of the world. I also shared my belief that they stand at the crossroads of two great paths—one that leads to mediocrity of mind and character and to social decline, and another, "less traveled" uphill path that leads to limitless human possibilities and restored hope for the world. As you have become a witness to this unfolding story of how schools, parents, and business and community leaders are partnering together to "inspire greatness, one child at a time," perhaps you have come to believe with me that every child *can* walk this path of personal leadership, if shown the way.

Now at the conclusion of this book, I want to share another conviction. As encouraging as the trends in these magnificent schools are, as much as these teachers and visionary administrators are inspiring a movement across the world, the work they are doing and influence they are having do not begin to compare to the influence that occurs inside the walls of a child's own home.

The home is a child's first school, first classroom, and first playground. Parents, grandparents, aunts, and uncles are a child's first teachers. Siblings and cousins are a child's first classmates and playmates. The home is the foundation of the education of the mind, the heart, the body, and the spirit. It lays the foundation of principles, values, morality, and fairness for a lifetime. In fact, the home provides education for life. It sets a child walking down one pathway or the other.

Given the immeasurable and irreplaceable role of parents and grandparents in the life of a child, I cannot set down my author's "pen" without offering one last chapter dedicated specifically to the idea that, no matter what is going on in your child's, grandchild's, niece's, nephew's, or "adopted" child's school, *you* can help these children discover the leader within and prepare them for a life of great contribution and service to their families, their communities, their places of employment, and the world.

Home: A Refuge from the Siege?

I am sure there are parents, including some who are teachers, who would argue that doing the leadership approach at home would prove to be more difficult than doing it at a school. I say this because I have spoken with CEOs who lead multibillion dollar organizations masterfully yet who in private confide that their biggest struggle by far is leading their own families. I have spoken with high-ranking military officials who command thousands with precision but who confess that the troops at home are in pitiful disarray. I have even spoken with teachers who say in essence, "I can manage any classroom size and gain the respect of students, but once I arrive home to my own children, all the glory and honor disappears. I get no respect. I have no control. There is no order."

Yes, parenting can be hard work—very hard, and often unpredictable. When I reviewed in chapter 2 some of the challenges parents across the world are facing in the new reality, I only remotely scratched the surface. Times have changed since Sandra and I raised our children. One of the biggest changes, of course, is the influence of technology and the media. Sandra and I had pretty good control over what types of language, scenes, and music entered the walls of our home. Children in those days had to go to extensive lengths to sneak something undesirable into the home and keep it concealed for long. But, nowadays, so long as a home is within reach of a wireless signal, every cubic inch of that home's airspace is infiltrated with potentially destructive messages and images that can steal away the identities— particularly the moral identities—of young people. All a child has to do is to click the right button and there it is. The cultural or social DNA is the great identity thief, not the person who steals and uses your credit card.

No institution is under siege in today's society more than the family. From the outside, families are being bombarded by pressures on young people to participate in drugs, premature sexual activities, or rowdy behaviors. They are being pounced upon by outside pressures to overachieve, to spend beyond their means, and to do things in overload. Even more threatening to families, however, are pressures from the inside. Often we hear of disharmony, heartbreak, infidelity, financial despair, abuse, loneliness, sibling rivalries, greed, and domestic violence—all having sources that come from within a home. Such inside and outside pressures can be disabling to a family's unity and progress.

But before I start sounding disheartened, let me say this. While I know the pressures and difficulties of being a parent, I also know the joys. Being a parent has brought me more joy, more peace, and more meaning than any other thing I have done in life—far more than any *secondary* greatness I may have achieved. I love my children for who they are, and thank them for the many moments of pleasure and enlightenment they have brought into my life. And I am now fortunate to be able to enjoy the same kinds of relationships with their children, and even their children's children.

I can think of no greater, no more important, leadership role than that of being a parent. So if you are a parent, I hope that you too are enjoying the pleasures of parenthood. I hope that you too can see great potential and gifts within your children. I also hope you see your own potential for being a "miracle worker" in their lives by enabling in them *primary* greatness— character and contribution—one son or daughter at a time.

Home is the great crossroad of a child's early life, the place where comings and goings are the most frequent. Do your children hear in your voice inspiration for whom they have the potential to become? Do your children find in their home a refuge from the siege?

One of the most profound results of the leadership theme is what happens when a child brings the principles home. Consider this e-mail that arrived as this book was being prepared to go to press:

Dear Ms. Summers: I want to share with you an incident that transpired at our home today that I think speaks to the power of the program you have established at Combs. Today was my daughter's second day at Combs. She is a third grader. When we arrived home, she and her sister began to argue. After less than ten seconds my daughter said, "I am not going to argue with you. I am going to be proactive, not reactive. We can think of a win-win solution." This was after only two days at Combs! I could not believe it. We are so grateful to be at Combs and to be a part of the amazing program that you have established there. Thank you!—Hardin Engelhardt

The Leader in Your Child

Not all parents want their children to grow up to be CEOs or a nation's president, but I cannot think of a parent who does not want his or her child to be able to lead his or her own life, to be a strong example for others, to live by principles, to be an influence for good. And that is what type of leadership this book is about: self-leadership in this new reality and doing the right thing even when no one is looking. Every child has that kind of leadership within. The challenge is how to bring it out, how to nurture it.

In considering how you might begin doing more to enable these leadership principles in your child, I invite you to return to three quotes referenced earlier: First, recall the fundamental premise of A.B. Combs's philosophy: "If you treat all students as if they are gifted, and you always look at them through that lens of being gifted in at least some aspect, they will rise to that level of expectation." Second, recollect Goethe's statement, "Treat a man as he is and you make him worse than he is. Treat a man as he has the potential to become and you make him better than he is." Third, reflect on the definition of leadership that I put forward: "Leadership is communicating people's worth and potential so clearly that they are inspired to see it in themselves." What do these three quotes suggest to you about your role as a parent and the powerful influence you can have on your child's feelings of worth and potential?

Pause from your reading for a moment and think of one of your children. If you have no children, think of a child whom you know fairly well. On a sheet of paper, write your answers to the following questions:

- What gifts does this child possess naturally?
- What talents or character traits does this child possess that if nurtured a little more could turn into gifts?
- What gifts, if any, did this child possess at an early age that have since been muted by his or her cultural DNA?

As you record your answers, consider in your thoughts: What have I said to this child within the past three days that has communicated my recognition of his or her gifts? What will I say to her or him within the next twenty-four hours that will communicate my recognition of and admiration for those gifts?

My mother, whom I consider my greatest teacher, was constantly affirming me right up until the day she died. Even when I was grown, had raised a family, and was enjoying a successful career, she still continued to commu-

My greatest teacher, my mother, always affirmed me, both when I was a child and as an adult.

nicate to me my worth, just as she had done over and over when I was a little boy. As she aged, I began calling her by phone nearly every day to check on her, and with each call I could expect one, if not several, affirmations.

So as a starting place for bringing the leadership principles into your home, I challenge you to look at what you have written on your piece of paper about your child's worth and gifts and determine how and when you will do more to communicate your belief in him or her.

Never underestimate the power of a sincere, positive affirmation of a person's worth, potential, and gifts—particularly in the life of a child.

The Power of Principles

No matter what kinds of protective barriers parents might try to erect, no matter how many times they attempt to limit time and programming on the television or set boundaries on the internet, cell phone, or other digital devices, once children step out of the home, parents are pretty defenseless in protecting them from the countless cruelties and negative influences that await them. A parent cannot follow their children everywhere or make every decision for them. Some have tried; all have failed.

The only approach I know of that gives parents any hope of truly providing their children with around-the-clock protection is that of instilling within them the internal desire to make right choices, even when no one else is watching. And the only way I know how to do that is to teach children correct principles—and the earlier the better.

The good news is that while the world has changed dramatically and will continue to change, the principles that can enable young people to make better decisions both today and in the years ahead will always remain the same. In other words, the same principles that Sandra and I tried to teach our children are the same principles that I would recommend to any parent today, anywhere in the world. The other piece of good news is that these principles do more than just protect children against negative social influences, because they are the very same principles that enable young people to succeed in the new reality, whether in school, in business, and at home or abroad. They are principles that have been around since well before I was born. They are present in every culture, and are applicable to any age, gender, race, or economic status.

And so I ask, whether a hundred years ago, a hundred years from now, or today, what parent would not want their children to *Be Proactive*: to take responsibility for their actions, to acknowledge mistakes rather than blaming others or making excuses, to show initiative, and to remain in charge of their emotions?

What parent would not want their children to *Begin with the End in Mind*: to have dreams, to have a plan for their lives or any project they are working on, and to focus on making meaningful contributions?

What parent would not want their children to *Put First Things First*: to focus their time and efforts on things that are most important, to avoid time wasters, to find time for planning and recreation, and to say no to things that will distract them from being their best?

What parent would not want their children to *Think Win-Win*: to have the courage to stand up for themselves while respecting others, to seek mutual benefit, to be willing to say no to situations that would harm someone?

What parent would not want their children to *Seek First to Understand, Then to Be Understood*: to truly and empathically listen to others' feelings, to not prejudge, to be open to input, or to know how to express themselves confidently and make a persuasive presentation?

What parent would not want their children to know how to *Synergize*: to be able to work with others, to optimize others' talents, to go after third alternatives, to be able to manage conflicts maturely, to be creative, and to value others' strengths?

What parent would not want their children to *Sharpen the Saw*: to renew their bodies by eating healthy, exercising, and caring for their physical and financial well-being, to be strong socially and emotionally, to grow mentally by reading good books and developing new skills, or to renew themselves spiritually by being involved in charitable acts, finding meaning in their lives by serving others, and living according to their values?

> This is more than character education. Character is a part of it, but these are real life skills of listening, how to express yourself, how to resolve conflicts, how to work in teams, how to value diversity, how to set goals. These are skills they will be able to use the rest of their lives.
> —*Holly Brown, Parent Volunteer and Board Member, Summit Academy, Draper, Utah*

I cannot imagine a parent who would not want these principle-based habits for their children. I also cannot imagine a child ever achieving his or her full potential without acting on these principles. Are they the only principles of effectiveness? No. Do the *7 Habits* solve every problem for every parent? No. But they are a great starting place, a great foundation.

Parenting comes with no guarantees of success. But the only approach I know of that comes close to providing a guarantee is to teach and instill principles into the hearts and minds of children.

Never underestimate the power of teaching principles.

The Power of Modeling

So how does a parent go about teaching principles?

I wrote a book on this very subject a few years ago that you can reference for more detail than I will be able to provide in this chapter. It is called *The 7 Habits of Highly Effective Families*. Or, you can go to www.TheLeader InMeBook.org for additional ideas. But I also strongly recommend that you go back through this book and reconsider what these schools have done to teach principles, and see if some ideas come to mind as to how you can apply the principles and practices in your home.

For example, reexamine the four steps:

Step 1: Inspire trust. Remember that the key to inspiring trust is *modeling*. The best way for your children to learn the *7 Habits* is to see you modeling the habits. There is no better way than modeling. *Relating*, letting them know you care about them, spending time with them, and letting them feel your love is also important. Once children see you modeling the habits and feel they can relate to you, they will be more open to you *teaching* them about these principles.

Step 2: Clarify purpose. Determine up front: Why are these principles of leadership so important for your child? What goals do you have for your child? What goals does your child want to pursue? When was the last time you asked? What family and individual milestones can be set in place to help you achieve your goals? What is your strategy for achieving your milestones? You may even want to consider working as a family to develop a family mission statement. (Practical suggestions for doing so will follow in this chapter).

Step 3: Align systems. "Systems" might be an unnatural term for the home, but they do exist. How will you get your children to "buy in" to learning these leadership principles? How will the principles be taught? Will they be taught directly, or in a ubiquitous manner, such as identifying them in movies, in books, during family vacations, or during sporting activities? Will the principles be evident in what hangs on the walls, or in the language that is spoken? In pursuing your family goals, what leadership roles will your children take on? How will adherence to the principles be rewarded? How will accountability for going against principles be handled? You see, in a fundamental sense, a home is no different than a school or a business. For the leadership approach to work in a home and to be sustained for more than a few weeks, it somehow needs to become rooted in the systems of that home.

Step 4: Unleash talent. What specific talents or "gifts" do you want to nurture or expand in your children? How will you nurture those gifts and set them free in your child? Will you do all the planning and goal setting in your family, or will your children be involved in planning family activities or in setting their own goals? Will they be empowered or micromanaged? How will you let them know you trust them?

All four steps contain ideas as to how you might bring the principles into your home. The true key, however, is in starting with step 1, particularly by modeling the principles. In fact, if you want a challenge—a personal challenge—try modeling the principles during a tough moment, a moment when you and your child are seeing things from different perspectives and you feel emotions warming up. Recall how the teachers and principals remarked how the habits helped students resolve conflicts? You too can choose to be the peacemaker in your home by using the habits to model a mature approach to resolving problems. Consider the following underlying paradigms of the habits and potential action steps you might take:

Underlying Paradigms and Principles	Key Actions
Be Proactive	
• You choose your actions and the "weather" of your mind.	• Stop and think. Ask: What is the *right* thing to do?
• You choose your response to how others treat you. In other words, your child does not "make" you angry; only you can choose to be angry.	• Gain control of your emotions. Walk away for a time if need be.
• Patience is a proactive choice.	• Focus on matters within your influence, not on matters outside your control.
	• Take responsibility for actions rather than blaming others or making lame excuses.
Begin with the End in Mind	
• The mental creation precedes the physical creation.	• Keep the bigger picture in mind.
• Your values and what is most important should guide your actions.	• Focus on how you want your child to perceive you as a parent once the disagreement is over.
	• Focus on what you want your relationship with your child to "feel" like once the disagreement is resolved.
	• Speak only words that will maintain your child's feelings of self-worth.
Put First Things First	
• "Things that matter most must never be at the mercy of things that matter least."	• Choose your battles. Do not engage in arguments over matters that have no relevance to what is truly important.
• Urgent matters are not always important.	• Act on problems at the right pace; do not allow them to fester or grow.
• Relationships are more important than things.	• Stick to your values. Do the "right" thing.
	• Seek to prevent future conflicts.
Think Win-Win	
• Lose-lose, lose-win, or win-lose are all undesirable outcomes.	• Make meaningful "deposits" in others' Emotional Bank Accounts.
• Fairness is the minimum starting point for an acceptable outcome.	• If you have made "withdrawals" from your child's Emotional Bank Account, apologize.
• "No deal" or agreeing to disagree are acceptable outcomes.	• Balance courage with consideration.
• The most acceptable outcomes are those where both parties "win" beyond what they previously perceived as possible.	• Seek outcomes that are mutually beneficial.

- Wise adults do not take unfair advantage of unwise children.

- Say no to outcomes that would not help your child in the long run.
- Avoid comparing your child with other children.
- Forgive.

Seek First to Understand, Then to Be Understood

- Giving people emotional "airtime" is the first step in allowing them to release and resolve emotions.
- Making your own thoughts and feelings understood in a calm, mature manner is just as important as listening.

- Listen with your ears, eyes, and heart until your child feels fully understood.

- Accept accurate feedback.

- Clearly, concisely, and calmly communicate your feelings.
- Correct inaccurate feedback.

Synergize

- Synergy values differences and seeks out third alternatives.
- Synergy creates solutions that are better than those either of the two parties might come up with on their own.

- Optimize your child's strengths and diverse perspectives to resolve the issue.
- Be humble. You do not have to have the right answer.

If needed, seek out another person who might have a more objective or educated view and who might provide a better solution than you or your child.

Sharpen the Saw (The great conflict preventer)

- Regularly sharpening the physical, social-emotional, mental, and spiritual saws goes a long way toward preventing future conflicts.
- Most conflict results from one or more of the four basic needs not being met.

Prepare Yourself Against Future Conflicts By

- Getting plenty of rest and exercise, and eating right so that you feel good. Fatigue feeds conflict.
- Taking time to build the relationship with your child in calm times. Learn stress reduction techniques.
- Studying life. Learn of basic human psychology to help you understand why a child might think or behave the way they do at different stages of life.
- Doing meaningful things that make you feel of worth so your confidence will be strong and your esteem impenetrable.

These are a few of the underlying paradigms, principles, and action steps you can take to model the habits during a potential volatile or pivotal situation with a child. Modeling is the most powerful way not just to resolve conflicts, but to teach a child the worth of principles as well.

The Significance and Power of a Family Mission Statement

One of the most powerful ways to model all seven habits is to go through the process of creating a family mission statement. I find it in some ways interesting, but in more ways alarming, that as I work with organizations across the world, many have some type of mission statement, most have some type of strategy or clear plan for what they want to accomplish as an organization and how they want to go about doing it, yet as I visit with families, relatively few have a clear plan or set of goals that they have established together, and far fewer have a mission statement. What organization in the world is more important than that of the family? It is *the* foundational organization of society. Why would any family not have a clear mission or strategy to ensure its success and progress?

I strongly believe that going through the process of creating a mission statement is the most bonding and important step a family can take. Think of taking the opposite approach, beginning with *no* end in mind. In other words, starting out with no proactive plan, to let life just kind of happen, to be swept along and governed by the flow of society's trends and values, to be without compass or map, with no vision and no purpose. In a sense, your family is just living out the scripts for life that someone else has given you. It just does not make sense, does it? That is why all highly effective organizations and athletic teams all have a game plan, a vision of their destination, and that is why it is so important that your family also have such a plan in place.

Whether the process results in a formal, written mission statement or not, the process of coming up with a family mission and game plan is by itself worth the effort, and it follows three general steps:

One, *explore what your family is all about.* Find opportunities and fun ways and activities to answer questions such as,

- What is the purpose of our family?
- What kind of family do we want?
- What are our family's highest priority goals?
- What are our unique talents, gifts, and abilities?
- What makes us the happiest?
- What do we want our home to look like, to feel like?

Specifically for children . . .

- What kind of home do you want to invite friends to?
- What makes you feel most comfortable when at home?
- What makes you want to come home?
- What makes you feel drawn to us as parents so that you are open to our influence? How can we as parents be more open to your influence?

Initially, you may find your children looking at you very strangely when you begin asking such questions, so you might need to find fun ways to do it or wait for the right setting or, better yet, "create" the right setting. You may need to do it over time; take a few months if needed. But I honestly believe that most children like to discuss such issues; they like to have a say in family matters. When they begin to open up, listen. Do not criticize. Keep the channels wide open; record thoughts and general themes.

Two, *write your family mission statement.* This makes some people nervous. They think it has to be a lengthy or perfectly written statement that will be displayed for the entire world to see. Not so. In fact, what is written is far less important than what is felt and what gets internalized. Nonetheless, I find it helpful to put it in writing in some form. A few suggestions include: 1) write it as though you intend it to be timeless, 2) consider all four basic needs: physical, social-emotional, mental, and spiritual, and 3) keep in mind the various ages so that it is meaningful to all members of the family. With younger children, you may want to keep it real simple and memorizable, such as one or two lines.

Three, *stay on course.* Once written, live up to the mission as parents first. Use the mission statement to make decisions. Schedule and follow through on activities that promote and reinforce the mission. Put wall hangings or notes around the home as reminders of the mission. Watch movies, sing songs, or read books that reinforce your mission, and course correct as needed. Is this not what the schools have done? Is this not exactly what has made them so successful? In other words, they do not just write a mission, hang it on the wall, and then go on to the next project. They live it. They keep it alive. They reward it. They are accountable to it.

All seven habits are utilized in these three steps—all seven. You model Habit 1 (Be Proactive) by taking the initiative to get the family talking about what matters most, developing the inner strength and security to be patient in the process, and hanging in there together even if there are complaints, bumps in the road, and negative emotion that rises to the surface; you model Habit 2 (Begin with the End in Mind) by the very creation of a family mission statement; you model Habit 3 (Put First Things First) by living according to the principles and values your family identifies in the mission statement and apologizing and getting back on track when needed; you model Habit 4 (Think Win-Win) by the way you respect and include the voice and feelings of each family member in the mission statement, mentally and emotionally accepting that it's all about going from "me" to "we"; you model Habit 5 (Seek First to Understand, Then to Be Understood) by empathizing, listening, reflecting back the feelings and ideas of your family members, and then communicating your vision as well; you model Habit 6 (Synergize) by being a catalyst to take what each family member shares, including different opinions, and developing a vision and language together that is better than what any one person started with; and finally, you model Habit 7 (Sharpen the Saw) by considering the needs and nature of each family member—body, mind, heart, and spirit—and by constantly creating family experiences that renew and deepen your commitment to your family purpose.

Perhaps you can see why the *process* is just as important, if not more important, as the *content* of the mission statement itself. It is a great way of modeling the habits. It is a powerful, practical family tool. I cannot overemphasize its importance. Give it the time it deserves.

Never underestimate the power of modeling.

Go at the Right Pace

At this point you may be thinking, "Stephen, you do not understand. I am a busy, busy person. I am overwhelmed as it is. I simply do not have time for this!" In other words, you may be like the teachers who exclaim, "I do not want 'one more thing' to have to teach my children!"

If that is the case, my first response would be to suggest that you find ways to integrate the principles into what you are already doing. Remember the teachers who said, "This is not one more thing, it is a better way of doing what we are already doing"? If, for example, you are already reading books or watching movies with your children, use those occasions to find incidences where the habits are exhibited and then make the points with your children.* Or, better yet, help them to discover and make the points on their own. If they are already doing a school project, such as writing a report on a historic person, help them to select people who exhibit strong leadership principles and discuss how they might apply the same principles in various situations. If you are redecorating your apartment, find inspiring pictures, quotes, or meaningful reminders of fun family activities to display on the walls. If you are already exercising regularly, take your children on a walk with you and tell them stories of people you know who exhibit leadership qualities. In other words, keep doing what you are already doing—just do it with a new lens.

Second, I would encourage you to examine what you are currently doing to see if there are things that you can remove from your schedule or "to-do" lists and to replace them with more worthwhile activities. Be honest. Are there things you are currently doing that in the grander scheme of things are a waste of time? Can they be replaced with more important activities?

Third, go at a wise pace. Sandra recently had back surgery. While some surgeries have rapid recovery rates, hers involved nerves, so the healing process is much slower. So slow that it is almost difficult at times to observe improvement. In fact, I call them "glacial" improvements because they seem to crawl at the pace of a glacier. But as she has done her entire life,

---

* For a starter list of excellent children's books that richly illustrate the *7 Habits,* go to www.The LeaderInMeBook.org. I also highly recommend my son Sean Covey's illustrated children's book, *The 7 Habits of Happy Kids* (New York: Simon & Schuster Children's Publishing, 2008).

Sandra patiently makes the daily improvements, however small, happen one day at a time. She perseveres. She works at it. She does not overdo it. She follows one exercise regime until she can incrementally add a little more. And that may be how it is for you in bringing the principles into your home—glacial change, little by little. For others the changes will be larger and faster. But either case, I promise that you will see and feel the difference—often immediately—as you reap the benefits of living by timeless and universal principles as a family.

Keep It Simple

Applying the leadership principles at home should not be more difficult than applying them in a school. And I honestly believe that applying them at home will make home life easier for you, not more difficult. The key is keeping the focus simple and simply keeping the focus. The main thing is to keep the main thing the main thing.

I know I have shared a lot of ideas throughout the book, but in the spirit of keeping it simple, if I were a young parent I would boil it all down to doing three things to prepare my child for the new reality. One, I would focus on building *independence* in my children. We hear more and more about the boomerang generation where kids in their twenties and thirties keep returning home because they do not have the wherewithal to survive independently in this new reality we live in. That, in most cases is because they have not been taught the principles of independence that are largely founded in habits one, two, and three (and habit seven, which is a *root* and fruit of all the habits).

Two, I would focus on helping my child become more *interdependent*. This means learning the skills of teaming with others, of getting along with others. The old saying is that no man is an island. Never has that been more true than today. People everywhere are increasingly connected. One cannot escape the need to work with others, so why not learn to optimize the process of working with others? If you are going to place them on a sports team, rather than simply helping them learn how to kick or throw a ball, emphasize and help them to learn about teamwork. That will bless them far longer than any trophy. Habits four, five, and six help in this regard.

Three, I would limit the focus to teaching and rewarding *primary* greatness—character and contribution. Often unintentionally, parents far overemphasize the value of *secondary* greatness—wealth, awards, positions, or fame. I have nothing against secondary greatness, but it should not come at the expense of a child not having primary greatness. So strive to channel a child's *proactivity*, their *ends in mind*, and their *first things*, toward achieving primary greatness. Work to make their greatest *wins*, their deepest *understandings*, and their greatest *synergies* centered around achieving primary greatness. Sharpen the four *saws* toward the goal of achieving primary greatness. Primary greatness is where the greatest rewards are to be found, both for the child and for the parent. So let it be your focus, and your children's focus.

In conclusion, no family is the same; they each come in different sizes, shapes, colors, and forms. No family is perfect; all are bent or broken at some point in time. Sandra and I surely do not claim to have done everything perfectly. But we also do not spend a lot of time dwelling on the past either. We look ahead. We plan ahead. We aim to move forward, particularly as we now set sights on building relationships with our grandchildren and great-grandchildren. This is a great world we live in, and we are excited about it. Yes, things have changed—not all for the better—but why focus on the negative when there is such an abundance of opportunities to make a difference? What good will dwelling on the downfalls of society do toward enabling your child to prepare for the future or make the right decisions today? No difference you make will ever exceed the difference you can make within your own home. Take advantage of it. Have fun with it.

Just as in schools, you will find that one of the hardest steps will be the launch—getting off the old comfort zone. But you have got to trust that you and your family can do it. You already have a lot going for you—just take it up a notch. I personally have embraced the motto, "Live life in crescendo," meaning the most important work you'll ever do is always ahead of you. Family is your most important work. I find it unleashes me both from past problems and from past successes and allows me to move forward in new ways. So look ahead. Let go. Start small. Make the leap. Enjoy bringing it home. Empowering your children with principles will empower you—it will free you up. A child who learns these principles both at home and at school will be even that much more rewarded.

Inspire a child to discover in themselves "the leader in me," and you change the child and, ultimately, the world forever.

Notes

Many photos appear throughout the book, the credit for which goes to several talented and generous photographers of both the professional and "learning" varieties. Special thanks go to Randall Miller of A.B. Combs Elementary, Lorie Lee of English Estates Elementary, Tom Trombley of Impact Photo, Medicine Hat, Alberta, Canada, and Sam Bracken of FranklinCovey.

An additional warm appreciation goes to the many sources cited including those below.

Chapter 1

7 "*The last few decades have belonged*": Daniel Pink, *A Whole New Mind: Why Right-Brainers Will Rule the Future* (New York: Berkley, 2006), p. 1.

Chapter 2

23 "*The research is clear*": Michael Fullan, "Broadening the Concept of Teacher Leadership," in S. Caldwell, ed., *Professional Development in Learning-Centered Schools* (Oxford, Ohio: National Staff Development Council, 1997).

24 *The shift was being tracked:* For more on Alwin's research on changing parent attitudes see *Psychology Today*, October 1988, an article by Anne Remley that refers to the "Middletown" research, started in 1924 by sociologists Helen and Robert Lynd and replicated fifty-four years later by sociologists Theodore Caplow of the University of Virginia and Howard Bahr and Bruce Chadwick of Brigham Young University. Surveys done by the National Opinion Research Center at the University of Chicago between 1964 and 1986 reveal a similar shift nationwide.

25 *In Asia, for example:* For an example of the trends in Asia and how they are impacting education in Taiwan, see Troy E. Beckert et al., "Parent Expectations of Young Children in Taiwan," in *Early Childhood Research & Practice* 6 (2004).

26   *Another reflection:* The Partnership for 21st Century Skills–sponsored Survey of American Adult Attitudes Toward Education was conducted by Public Opinion Strategies and Peter D. Hart Research Associates. The national survey involved eight hundred registered voters from September 10 to 12, 2007.

29   *Take for instance the U.S. Chamber of Commerce: Leaders and Laggards: A State-by-State Report Card on Educational Effectiveness* (Washington, D.C.: U.S. Chamber of Commerce, 2007).

30   *One of their responses:* The list of Top 10 Qualities & Skills Employers Seek given to Muriel was credited to the National Association of Colleges and Employers (NACE), which publishes such surveys each fall on their website.

31   *Daniel Goleman's research:* Daniel Goleman, "A Great Idea in Education: Emotional Literacy," in *Great Ideas in Education: A Unique Book Review and Resource Catalog,* no. 2 (Spring 1994), pp. 33–34. For more on how Emotional Intelligence impacts leadership in the workplace, see Daniel Goleman, Annie McKee, and Richard E. Boyatzis, *Primal Leadership: Realizing the Power of Emotional Intelligence* (Cambridge, Mass.: Harvard Business School Press, 2002), p. 39.

32   *"the good-to-great companies placed":* See Jim Collins, *Good to Great: Why Some Companies Make the Leap . . . and Others Don't* (New York: HarperCollins, 2002), p. 51.

35   *the following framework:* For a deeper description of the Framework for the Partnership for 21st Century Skills see their website at www.21centuryskills.org.

37   *"What students need to succeed":* Willard R. Daggett, quote provided by the International Center for Leadership in Education. For more on Dr. Daggett's work on rigor and relevance see *www.leadered.com.*

Chapter 3

61   *"When success in the classroom is defined":* Robert J. Marzano, *What Works in Schools: Translating Research into Action* (Alexandria, Va.: Association for Supervision and Curriculum Development, 2003), p. 149.

Chapter 4

71 *"Far and away the biggest mistake":* James C. Collins and Jerry I. Porras, *Built to Last: Successful Habits of Visionary Companies* (New York: Collins Business, 2004).

Chapter 5

90 *"If you don't know how to execute":* Larry Bossidy and Ram Charan, *Execution: The Discipline of Getting Things Done* (New York: Crown Business, 2002).

98 *"While organizations can pronounce a change":* Richard DuFour and Robert Eaker, *Professional Learning Communities at Work* (Bloomington, Ind.: National Educational Service, 1998), p. 133.

103 *"It always seems impossible":* Nelson Mandela, quoted in Roger Cohen, "Beyond America's Original Sin," *New York Times,* March 20, 2008, www.nytimes.com.

Chapter 7

158 *Dr. Baile conducted extensive interviews:* Susan M. Baile carried out her study in 1998. A more extensive review of the research can be found at www.franklin coveyresearch.org.

Chapter 8

166 *My son, Stephen M.R. Covey:* Stephen M.R. Covey, *The Speed of Trust: The One Thing That Changes Everything* (New York: Free Press, 2006).

167 *"If a teacher has a good relationship":* Robert J. Marzano, *What Works in Schools: Translating Research into Action* (Alexandria, Va.: Association for Supervision and Curriculum Development, 2003), p. 91.

185 *"One of the most damaging myths":* Richard DuFour and Robert Eaker, *Professional Learning Communities at Work: Best Practices for Enhancing Student Achievement* (Bloomington, Ind.: National Educational Service, 1998), p. 49.

186 *Robert Marzano:* For Marzano's three principles see Marzano, *What Works in Schools*, pp. 158–59.

187 *Consider Larry Lezotte's effective schools research:* Larry Lezotte's work on effective schools and his 7 Correlates for improving student achievement are pub-

lished and reviewed in many sources. For his most recent book and summary of the correlates, see Lawrence W. Lezotte, and Kathleen M. McKee, *Stepping Up: Leading the Charge to Improve Our Schools* (Okemos, Mich.: Effective Schools Products, Ltd., 2006).

Chapter 9

191 *"Have you ever been at sea"*: Helen Keller, *The Story of My Life* (1903).

193 *"And now we are going out"*: Anne Sullivan's entire valedictory address can be found at www.perkins.org/culture/helenkeller/sullivanvaledictory.html. For the other Anne Sullivan Macy and Helen Keller quotations, see Joseph P. Lash, *Helen and Teacher: The Story of Helen Keller and Anne Sullivan Macy* (New York: Merloyd Lawrence, 1980).

197 *"It is time to recognize that the major flaw"*: Richard DuFour and Robert Eaker, *Professional Learning Communities at Work: Best Practices for Enhancing Student Achievement* (Bloomington, Ind.: National Educational Service, 1998), p. 165.

198 *"U.S. mathematics textbooks address"*: Robert J. Marzano, *What Works in Schools: Translating Research into Action* (Alexandria, Va.: Association for Supervision and Curriculum Development, 2003), pp. 26–28.

204 *"We must be dreamers"*: Thomas Friedman, *The World Is Flat: A Brief History of the Twenty-First Century* (New York: Farrar, Straus & Giroux, 2005).

205 *"He stood at the crossroads"*: This version of the poem is a slight variation from the poem credited to Laura Soper and entitled "To Your Chum and My Chum." It appeared in Gertrude Frances Rowell, ed., *Guide Posts on the Highways and Byways of Education: The Public Schools of America, the Hope of Democracy* (no publisher listed, 1919).

Chapter 10

214 To provide insights into how to create a highly effective environment in your own home, Sandra and I wrote *The 7 Habits of Highly Effective Families* (New York: Golden Books, 1997).

221 A great resource for families with young children is *The 7 Habits of Happy Kids* (New York: Simon & Schuster Children's Publishing, 2008) by Sean Covey (author) and Stacy Curtis (illustrator). It is full of stories and discussion items.

Will Your School or Child Be the Next *The Leader in Me* Success Story?

The schools mentioned in this book all have something in common . . .
a culture and curriculum rooted in the principles of effectiveness.

Drawing from the best practices and thought leadership of successful educators around the world, FranklinCovey's *The Leader in Me* process will help schools develop students who are ready to succeed in the 21st century, with critical skills and characteristics such as:

- Trust and trustworthiness
- Strong work ethic
- Motivation and initiative
- Problem-solving skills
- Goal setting

- Effective interpersonal skills
- Sense of teamwork
- Valuing diversity in a global market

What's more, schools will enjoy a culture in which discipline referrals decrease, test scores improve, and engaged staff members contribute the highest and best of their talents and efforts.

What is the process for getting started with *The Leader in Me*?

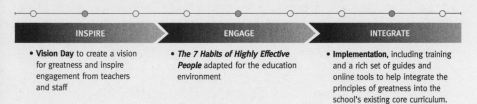

INSPIRE	ENGAGE	INTEGRATE
• **Vision Day** to create a vision for greatness and inspire engagement from teachers and staff	• *The 7 Habits of Highly Effective People* adapted for the education environment	• **Implementation,** including training and a rich set of guides and online tools to help integrate the principles of greatness into the school's existing core curriculum.

Put Your School on the Path to Greatness in the 21st Century.

For more information about how *The Leader in Me* can help put your school on the path to greatness, please contact FranklinCovey's Education Solutions by calling 1-800-272-6839 or by email at educate@frankincovey.com or visit www.TheLeaderInMe.org.
You can also visit www.franklincovey.com/education.

The
Leader in Me™

greαt hαppen∫ here

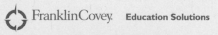

FranklinCovey **Education Solutions**

Version 1.0.6

Sponsor a School and Invest in Tomorrow's Leaders...Today

How does *The Leader in Me* prepare students to succeed in the 21st century?

FranklinCovey's *The Leader in Me* process directly addresses the skills and characteristics employers seek today, including:

- Analytical skills
- Accountability and responsibility for actions and results
- The ability to develop productive team relationships
- The ability to solve complex challenges and problems
- Valuing diversity in a global market
- Strong communication skills

Investing in today's learners—tomorrow's leaders—will help you create a pool of employees who are poised to thrive in your organization and contribute to the success of your organization in the future.

How will my organization's sponsorship of *The Leader in Me* initiative help schools?

This is a powerful way to invest in your community and future—one that has been proven to benefit schools in the following ways:

- Develops students who have the skills to succeed as leaders in the 21st century
- Decreases discipline referrals
- Teaches and develops character and leadership through existing core curriculum
- Improves academic achievement
- Raises levels of accountability and engagement among both students and staff

Help Put the Schools in Your Community on the Path to Greatness

For more information about how investing in *The Leader in Me* can help put the schools in your community on the path to greatness, please contact FranklinCovey's Education Solutions by calling 1-800-272-6839 or by email at educate@franklincovey.com. Or visit www.TheLeaderInMe.org. You can also visit www.franklincovey.com/education.

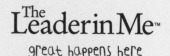

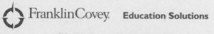

FranklinCovey. Education Solutions

The Leader in Me™
great happens here

Index

Page numbers in *italics* refer to illustrations.

A.B. Combs Elementary, 1–2, 3–4, *3,* 10,
  13, 14, *15,* 16, 18–22, 33, 36–37, *38,*
  40, 114, 182, *194*
  artifacts at, 95–98
  art show at, 95–96, *96, 195*
  changes at, 185
  class mission statements at, 56, 92, 97
  classroom management at, 87
  culture of, 19, 92–106
  data notebooks at, 61, *62,* 63–64, 92,
    187
  discipline at, 2, 87
  diversity at, 2, 5, *6*
  expectations at, 172
  folklore at, 101–2
  hiring of teachers at, 77, 80
  Inaugural Ball at, 98
  International Festival at, 2, 98
  language spoken at, 93–95
  Leader of the Day at, 93
  as magnet school, 19, 20–22, 27, *40,* 41,
    44, 71, 108
  morning news, 57, *86,* 94, 112
  music at, 53, 76, 95, 100
  parents at, 23, *24,* 26–28, 37, 41,
    203
  peer leaders at, 76–77, 80
  "pet projects" at, 72
  results at, 90–106
  science fairs at, 99
  Silver-Tray Luncheon at, 98–99
  traditions at, 2, 98–99
A.B. Combs Elementary, leadership
  principles at, 2, 16, 41, 43, *58,*
  67, 68, 73, 122, 132, 166

  alignment for success at, 71–89
  Baldrige principles and, 46, 49, 63, 67,
    68, 70, 75, 81
  benefits of, 4–5
  blueprint for, 45, 52, 64, 66–70
  bonus funds and, 112
  and business community, 28, 30, 37, 41,
    75, *177*
  Celebrate Success Day at, 99
  character taught at, 53
  enrollment and, 28
  focus of, 11, *12*
  Leadership Day and, 98, *99,* 109,
    118
  Leaders of the Week at, 85, 94
  Lego visit to, 64, *177*
  as magnet theme, *40,* 41, 44, 71
  mission statement of, 41, *42,* 44–45, 57,
    71, 90, 91, 96, 170
  as model for other schools, 10–11, 34
  Physical Fitness Leader at, 84
  rewards at, 86–87, *86*
  reward system aligned at, 83–87
  Service Projects at, *100*
  7 Habits and, 46–48, 53–54, 56, 57,
    63, 67, 68, *67,* 73, 74, 75, 77, 125,
    174, *184*
  and "Seven Correlates," 188
  strategic pause at, 203
  students and, 37–41, 75–80
  synergy at, 44, 54–55, 87
  teachers and, 34–37
  as ubiquitous strategy, 52–61
  vision statement of, 44–45, *45,* 57, 71,
    90, 91, 96

abundance mentality, 112
academics, *58, 59*
accountability, *35,* 92, 178, 201
Aceña, María del Carmen, 11–12,
  148–51
achievement, 79
adaptability, *32, 35*
Adequate Yearly Progress (AYP), 109
Africa, 24
African-American History Week, 54
agility, 49
Alberta Education, 128
Alfaro, Angelica, 140
Ali, Muhammad, 154
alignment, 71–89, 173–79, 183, 201,
  215
  of reward system, 83–87
  of standards, 49
  for success, 88–89
  training in, 81–83
Alisaya, Evelyn, 207
Almond, Pam, 100–2, *101*
Alwin, Duane, 23–25
analytical skills, 8, 31, *48*
anger issues, 182
anthropology, 91, 95–96
Arab High School, 154
Armstrong, Michael, 4
arts, 53, *57,* 95–96, 111, *195*
Asia, 24
attendance numbers, 178
"At the Crossroads," 205
attracting, 173–74
Australia, 13, 132

Baile, Susan M., 158
Baldrige, Howard Malcolm, 46, 49
Baldrige principles, 133
  at A.B. Combs Elementary, 46, 49–50,
    63, *67,* 68, 70, 75, 81
  creation of, 49–50
  as universal, 103
bar charts, 50
Barnett, Dyane, 53
Bassett, Martha, 55
Begin with the End in Mind, 21, *47*
  as aid to independence, 46
  for family, *216,* 220

in morning news program, 94
in physical fitness, 85
as universal, 213
Beijing Olympics, 127
Beyond the Three Rs, 26
Black Achievers, 155
Blackford, William McKinley, IV, 155,
  156
bone diagrams, 53
boomerang generation, 222
Bossidy, Larry, 90
Bottomley, Laura, 163
Bradley, Chuck, 163
brain, 7
Brenda (assistant), 160
Brown, Holly, 213
bubble maps, 50
business leaders:
  and A.B. Combs Elementary, 28, 30,
    37, 41, 75, *177*
  character and competence desired by,
    32, 34
  and education, xxi, 3, 4, 8, 28–34, 35,
    42, 127–28, *127,* 157, 177, 201

Campbell, Bill, 156–57
Canaan Community Development
  Corporation, 155
Canada, 13, 124–30
caring, 214
Carroll, Laura, 111
Catcher in the Rye (Salinger), 139
"Catch Somebody Doing Covey," 125–26
Central High School, 154, 155
Chamber of Commerce, Decatur, 117
Chambers of Commerce, U.S., 29–30
change:
  creating, *32*
  sustaining, 185–90, *186*
character, 27, 34, 123, 182
  business community's desire for, 32,
    34
  of school, 172
  ubiquitous approach to, 52–53, 58, 59,
    201
Charan, Ram, 90
Charlotte Country School District,
  162

Cherng, Andrew, 11, 32, *32*
Cherng, Peggy, 11, 32, *32*
Chestnut Grove Elementary, 13, 55, 115–17, 195
  culture at, 102
  7 Habits taught at, 115, 116–17, *116*
children, universal nature of, 14, 200
China, 49
Chinese Cinderella, 139
Chua Chu Kang Primary School, *16,* 22, 130–32, *131*
Chun, Ho Siow, 130
Circle of Influence, 196
citizenship, 49
civic awareness, 36
Clark, Ron, 66
Class Data Notebooks, 113
Clementi Town Secondary School, 146–48, *147*
Code of Conduct, 171–72
Code of Cooperation, 171–72
Cohn, Andrea, 55
collaboration, 26, *32,* 35
Collins, Jim, 32, 64, 71
"Color Me Covey," 125, 127
Columbine High School, 23, 41
communication, *35,* 47, 178
  skills with, 30, *47*
Community Leadership Initiative, 157
competence, 31
  personal, 31
  of school, 171
  social, 31
computers, *26,* 53
  literacy with, *35*
conduct, Code of, 171–72
conflict management skills, *31, 47,* 152
conflict resolution skills, 47
conformity, 24
connectivity, 201
Contos, Tony, 135–37
Cooper, Robert, 67
cooperation, 78
  Code of, 171–72
core subjects, 35
Costa Rica, 154
Covey, Sandra, 208–9, 212, 221–22, 223

Covey, Sean, xxii, 135
Covey, Stephen (author), 19–21, 41
  as father, 208–9
Covey, Stephen M.R., 166
"cram" schools, 153
Crawford, Tom, 154–56
creating change, *32*
creative minds, 30
creativity, 8, 26, *27,* 34, *35,* 47, *48,* 71, 84, 123, 202
Crestwood Elementary, 124–28, *127*
  culture of, 102
Criterion Catalysts and Technologies, 127–28
critical thinking, *26, 35*
cross-cultural skills, *35*
cultural DNA, 211
culture, 90–106

Daggett, Willard, 37, 66
data, data notebooks, 61, *62,* 63–64, 92, 133, 178, 187, 201
Decatur City Schools, 27
Decatur Public Works Department, 116
decision making, 34, *48,* 49, 174
DeGuia, Miss, 139–40
Deming, W. Edwards, 50
Developing Leaders One Child at a Time, 41–43, 68
developing others, *32,* 173, 175–77
Dewey Elementary, 10, 13, 118–24
  culture at, 102
  discipline at, 119
  7 Habits at, 118–24, *124*
Dickens, Christie, 10, 118, 119, 120, 122
differences, 56
Dinner-Data-Discussion, 113
Diogenes Laertius, 134
discipline, 4, 15, 68–69, 74, 79, 80, 87, 111, 178
  at Dewey Elementary, 119
diversity, in education, 2, 5, *6,* 24
Dow AgroSciences, 156
Dow Chemical Company, 156–57
dress, 138
Drucker, Peter, 64
DuFour, Richard, 66, 97, 185, 197–98

Eaker, Robert, 66, 97, 185, 197–98
eating, 213, *217*
eBay, 29
economics, 36
Ecuador, 169
education, xxii–xxiii, 1–5, 9–10
    adult attitudes on, *26*
    business community and, xxi, 3, 4, 8,
        28–34, 35, 42, *47, 48,* 123, 127–28,
        127, 157, 201
    and globalization, 6, 7
    in Guatemala, 11–12, 13, 148–51, *149,*
        150
    in information age, 6–7
    mental needs in, 38, 39, 47, *48*
    parents and, xxi, 4, 23–28, *47, 48,* 103,
        176, 201, 203
    physical needs in, 38–39, 47, *48*
    social-emotional needs in, 38, 39, 47,
        48
    spiritual needs in, 38, 39–40, 47,
        48
    students' desires in, 37–41
    sustaining change in, 186–87
    teachers and, 2, 3, 34–37, 43, *47, 48,*
        75–76, 103, 177, 180–81, 182
Effective Schools Movement, 66
efficiency, 50
8th Habit, The (Covey), 32, 48, 108,
    115
Eli Lilly, 156
Ellerman, Jerry, 122
Emma (student), 103
Emotional Bank Account, 136, *216*
Emotional Intelligence (EQ), 30, *67*
emotional stability, *48*
empathy, *31*
Enersolv Corporation, 115
Engelhardt, Hardin, 210
English, *53,* 58
English Estates Elementary, 13, 108–15,
    110, 116, 187, 190, 195, 207
    culture at, 102, 113
    discipline at, 111
    morning news at, 112
entrepreneurship, 36
environment, safe, 189
ethics, 8, 27, *35*

Europe, 24
Everett, Paula, 48, 92
excellence, 79
executive assistants, 102
exercise, 22, 38, 213
expectations, 189
    at schools, 172

fairness, *48, 216*
Falkner, Debbie, 54–55
family, 209
    mission statement for, 218–20
    7 Habits for, 214–15
    strategy, 218
    see also home
Farnsworth, Chuck, xxi–xxii, 135–36
financial management, 36, 154
Find Your Voice and Help Others Find
    Theirs, 48
Finland, 149
First Things First, 21, 46, 47, 101
    as aid to independence, 46
    for family, 220
    in morning news program, 94
    in physical fitness, 85
    as universal, 213
fishbone diagrams, 50, *51,* 53
Foo, Francis, 22, 130
force-field analysis, *50*
foresight, 7
Foundational Principles, 125
Fowler, Gayle, 56
FranklinCovey, 93, 132, 135, 137, 146,
    152
Friedman, Thomas, 204
Fritz, Mike, 128–30
Fullan, Michael, 67

Gandhi, Mohandas, 64
Garcia, Pedro, 162, 173
Gardner, Howard, 66
Gayler, Dave, 162, 163
geography, 35
George, David, 124–25, 186–87
Germany, 198
gifts, 80, 201, 210
Glasser, William, 67, 159
global awareness, 25–26

globalization, 7, 25, 29, 42, 201, 205
goals, *47,* 172
  in data notebooks, 61
  see also purpose
Goethe, Johann Wolfgang von, 40, 199, 210
Goleman, Daniel, 30–31, 64
Good to Great (Collins), 32
greatness:
  primary, 9, 31, 209, 223
  secondary, 9, 209, 223
Greta (student), *176*
Guatemala, 11–12, 13, 148–50, *149*
Gutmann, Joe, 154, 155–56
Gyoda-nishi Elementary School, 152

habits, 21–22
Hamburger Rubric, 83
hard strategy, 171–72
hard work, 83
Hardy, Patrice, 69
health, *35*
Highly Effective Youth, 146–48
hiring, 32
Hispanic Achievers, 155
history, 35, 53, 82, 95
Holden, Mary and David, 142
home, 108–10, 189, 207–10
  leadership principles at, 5, 15, 212, 214, 224
  see also family
honesty, 30, *48,* 52
Hughes, Langston, 53
hygiene, 39, *48,* 93, 138

identity theft, 39–40, 70, 209
"I Did It My Way," 132
If You Don't Feed the Teachers They Eat the Students!, 144
Illinois Standards Achievement Test (ISAT), 120
implementation, 71, 90–91, 173, 201
independence, 46
India, 49
Influence:
  Circle of, 196
  Pyramid of, 166–68, *167*
information age, 6–7

information management, *35*
initiative, 24, 30, *31, 35, 47*
innovation, *26,* 49, 50
inspiration, of trust, 166–69, 182, 183, 214
inspirational leadership, *31*
integrity, 30
intelligence, 30
interdependence, 47, 222
International Food Festival, 2, 76, 98
Internet, 7, 29
interpersonal skills, 30, 143, 146
involvement, *48*
IQ, 30
Iraq War, 37
Iroquois High School, 154
Ishikawa, Mr., 152

Japan, 13, 152–53, 157, 198
Jeffers, Dan, 27
Johnson, Aneesa, 182
Johnson, Eric, 182
Johnson, Gayle Gonzalez, 182
Johnson, Sandi, 111
Joliet Township High School, 134, 135–37
Jones, Amy, 103–4
Jones, Gray, 103–4
Jones, Michael, 104
Jordan, Michael, 55
Joseph Welsh Elementary, 128–30

Kai, Arlene, 46
Keesee, Jacquie, 100
Keller, Helen, 191, 192–94, *194,* 204
King, Martin Luther, Jr., 64
Koehler, Joann, 19, 195

Lane, Donnie, 32, 115, 117, 195, 204
language, 35, 93, 136, 142, 208
Law of Harvest, 71, 93
LEAD, 79, 100
Leaders and Laggards, 29–30
leadership, 11, 26, 27, *35,* 49, 210
  as art, 186
  four imperatives of, 166–85
  as instructional, 188
Leadership is Elementary, 110, *110*

leadership principles, 12, 103, 105, 169, 177, 191, 212–14
  aligning systems in, 172–79, 215
  Cherng's sponsorship of, 10–11
  clarification of purposes in, 169–72, *170,* 182–83, 214–15
  expectations of, 172
  and greeters for guests, *78*
  in Guatemala, 11
  and hiring of teachers, 77
  at home, 5, 14–15, 212, 214, 224
  inspiring trust in, 166–69, 183, 214
  introduction of, 73–75
  mission and mission statements in, 41, *42,* 44–45, 57, 71, 90, 91, 96, 134, 140, 169–70, 172, 173, 178, 179, *179,* 218–21
  parents taught by students, 176
  peer leaders and, 76–77
  as right thing to do, 10, 11, 12, 203
  strategy for, 52–61, 71, 90, 91, 171–72, 173, 178, *186,* 218
  among teachers, 75–76
  universal nature of, 14, 47, 168, 200, 212–14
  unleashing talent in, 179–83
  vision, vision statements in, 44–45, *45,* 57, 71, 90, 91, 96, 170–71, 172, 173, 178, 179
  see also A.B. Combs Elementary, leadership principles at
Leahy, Thomas, 122
learning-centered education, 49
Lego Corporation, 64, *177*
Lemon Bay High School, 27, 154
Lezotte, Larry, 66, 188–89
life skills, 58, *58,* 59
Lincoln, Abraham, 64
Lincoln Foundation, 155
listening skills, 33, 47
lotus diagrams, 50, *51,* 53
Louisville, Kentucky, 154
loyalty, 79

MAGIC, 78–79, 100
Malaysia, 154

Malcolm Baldrige National Quality Award, 49
Mallory, Vicki, 36
Mandela, Nelson, 106
manners, 23, 84–85
Mar Vista High School, 141–42
Marzano, Robert J., 61, 168, 186, 187, 189, 198
mathematics, 26, 35, 53, 76, 95, 113, 120, *120,* 145, *199*
  essential vs. nonessential, 198–99
Max (kindergartner), *59*
media awareness, *35*
media literacy, *26*
Medicine Hat, Canada, 124
Melichar, Mike, 156–57
memorization, 7
mentors, 174
Meyer, George, 118
Michener, James A., 60
Michigan, University of, 23–24
Microsoft, 29
Middle East, 24
Milkie, Michael, 138
Milkie, Tonya, 138
Ministry of Education, Singapore, 130, 132
mission, as clear and focused, 188
mission, mission statements, 134, 139, 170–71, 172, 173, 178, 179, *179*
  at A.B. Combs Elementary, 41, *42,* 44–45, 57, 71, 90, 91, 96, 170
  for families, 218–21
Modeling, 167, 214–15, 218, 220
modern day miracle workers, 18, 192–96
monitoring of student progress, 189
multiple intelligences, 66
music, 53, 76, 95, 100, 111, 123

Nash Elementary, 34, 161, *162*
Nation at Risk, A, 29, 49
Netherlands, 154
Ng Boon In, Mme., 130
Noble Street Charter High School, 137–41, *139*
North America, 24
North Carolina Food Bank, 76

Northwestern University Settlement
    Association, 138
Norton, Bertie, 34, 161, *162*
Norton, Paul, 161
"Not one more thing," 197–200

obedience, 23
Olympic games, 127
On Board Terrorists (OBTs), 173
openness, *48*
opportunity to learn, 188
optimism, *31*
oral communication, *26*
organizational awareness, *31*
organizational skills, 30, *47*
Osterstrom, Justin, 79–80
Other 90%, The (Cooper), 67

pace, 221–22
Panda Express, 11, *32*
paradigm shifts, 126
parent buy-in, *24,* 74–75
parents, xxi, 3, 4, 23–28, 34, 37, 41, 103,
    121, 174, 175–76, 201, 203, 209,
    213
    7 Habits taught by, 60
Partnership for 21st Century Skills, 26,
    35–36
Patel, Dr. and Dr., 1–2, 96, 104, 105,
    107
"Path of Dreams" program, 11–12, 149,
    149, 150, *150,* 151
patience, *216*
Payne, Jeanne, 27
peer leaders, 77
people skills, 8, *35*
Perkins Institution, 192
personal competence, *31*
Phipps, Louise, 141–42
physical education, 53, 60, 95
physical fitness, 76
Pink, Daniel, 7–8, 66
planning skills, 33, 46, *47*
Plocica, Christian, 56
Poland, Denise, 121
Porras, Jerry I., 71
positioning, 173, 174–75
Post, Lori, 120

Powell, Debbie, 85
presentation skills, 33
primary greatness, 9, 31, 209, 223
principals, 103
principle of renewal, 47, *48*
priorities, 21
Private Victory, 46
Proactivity, 48, *48,* 125, *204*
    as aid to independence, 46
    with discipline issues, 87
    in disputes, 120
    for families, 104, 111, 210, *216,* 218,
        220
    in folklore, 100
    911 and, 121
    in physical fitness, 85
    with school photographs, *121*
    as universal, 213
problem solving, 26, *35, 48,* 50
productivity, *35*
Professional Learning Communities at
    Work, 66, 97, 185
Professional Learning Community
    (DuFour and Eaker), 197–98
PTA, 77
public speaking, 76, *82,* 103, *105,*
    176
Public Victory, 47
purpose, clarification of, 169–72, *170,*
    172, 183, 214–15
    see also goals
Pyramid of Influence, 166–68, *167*

Random Acts of Leadership, 113
Readers are Leaders, 112
reading, *26,* 36, 77, 113, *120,* 199
Reagan, Ronald, 49
receptionists, 102
recompassing, 203
Red Cross, 77
Red Deer, Canada, 128
Redmond, Rick, 128
regret, 11
Reilly, Leslie, 1, 34, 109, 114
relating, 167
relationships, 49, 201
renewal, principle, of, 47, *48*
respect, 25, 78

responsibility, 8, 24, *35,* 52, 78, 79
rewarding, 173, 177–78
Ricky, Mr., 75
Roosevelt Middle School, 142–46
Rotary Club, 113
Rowlett Elementary, 124, 169
Russell, James Henry, 160–61

Salt in His Shoes, 55
Sam, 103
Sátiro, Angélica, 150
Saw, Sharpening of, 22, 114, *114*
    for family, 103, *217,* 220
    principal of renewal in, 47, *48*
    Russell's homing in on, 160
    as universal, 213–14
Schaffner, Dede, 112, 114
Schollie Research and Consulting, 129
science, 26, *26,* 35, 53, 59–60, 76, 95
seashells, 56
Seay, Robyn, 174
secondary greatness, 9, 209, 223
self-assessment, *31,* 33
self-awareness, *31*
self-confidence, 4, 10, *31, 47,* 74
self-control, *31*
self-direction, 26, *35*
self-esteem, 4
self-leadership, 46
self-motivation, 30
Seminole County Public Schools, 1, 34,
    109, 112
service, *31*
7 Habits for Families, 126
7 Habits of Happy Kids, The (Sean
    Covey), xxiii
7 Habits of Highly Effective Families, The
    (Stephen Covey), 214–15
7 Habits of Highly Effective People, The
    (Stephen Covey), xxi–xxii, 20–21,
    23–24, 41, 61, 70, 87, 92, 93, 95, 101,
    103, 108, 110, 111, 112, 163, 164,
    168, 191, 201, 203, 214
    at A.B. Combs, 46–48, 53–54, 56, 57,
    63, 67, *67,* 68, 73, 74, 75, 77, 125,
    174, *184*
    Aceña's reading of, 149–50, 151
    in Chestnut Grove, 115, 116–17, *116*

    at Clementi Town Secondary School,
    146–48
    at Crestwood Elementary, 124–28,
    127
    at Dewey Elementary, 118–23, *119*
    in Japan, 152, 153
    at Joliet Township High School, 135,
    137
    at Joseph Welsh Elementary, 128–30
    and leadership principles at A.B.
    Combs, 46–48, 53–54, 56, 57, 63, 67,
    67, 68
    at Mar Vista High School, 141, 142
    in music, 48
    at Noble Street Charter High School,
    137–38, 140, 141
    in play, 131–32
    at Roosevelt Middle School, 144, 145
    in songs, *116,* 125, 127, *137*
    stretches choreographed to, 56
    as taught by parents, 60
    as taught to parents, 121
    in Texarkana Independent School
    District, 158–62, 166
    ubiquitous method of teaching, 55, 57,
    59
    as universal, 47, 103
    for young people, xxii, 20, 46–48, 60
7 Habits of Highly Effective Teens, The
    (Sean Covey), xxii, 134, *137,* 138–39,
    142, 155, 156
7 Habits Trail Mix, 113
"Seven Correlates," 187–89
Sharpe, Beth, 108, 109, 110, 112, 113,
    114, 181, 187, 190, 195
simplicity, 222–24
Singapore, 13, *16,* 130–32, *131,* 134,
    146–48
    prison system in, 168
skills, 30–31, 33, 43
Smith, Barbara Sexton, 155, 156
Snow White and the Seven Dwarfs,
    131–32
social competence, *31*
social DNA, 209
social responsibility, 26, *26, 35*
social skills, 143
soft strategy, 171–72

South America, 25
Southern California, University of, 162
South Korea, *137,* 154
Southwest Airlines, 29
Soviet Union, 49
Speed of Trust, The (Stephen M.R. Covey), 166
spider matrices, 50
sports, 222–23
stakeholders, *72*
stay on course, 219
storytelling, 100–101, 103
strategic pause, 203
strategy, 171–72, 173, 178, 179, *186*
   for family, 218
   hard, 171–72
   soft, 171–72
   ubiquitous, 52–61, 69, 201
strong work ethic, 30
Stuard Elementary, *77,* 174, *175*
Student Activity Guide, 142
students, 37–41, 104
Sullivan, Anne, 192–94
Sullivan, Larry, 8, 159–60, 161–62, 166
Summers, Ms., 210
Summers, Muriel, 18–22, 37, 41, 64, 70, 106, 161, 163, *176,* 181, 185, 186–87, 194–95, 196, 203
   advice from, 125
   alignment accomplished by, 71–72, 73, 76, 78, 89
   appreciation by, 85
   on blueprints, 67–68
   business community and, 30
   on character education, 44
   and discipline problems, 68–69, 80
   on introduction of leadership theme, 73–74
   on leadership implementation, 90–91
   as modern day miracle worker, 18, 192
   parent focus groups of, 23
   as Principal of the Year, 2, 85
   at professional conferences, 107
   school changes as opportunities for, 185
   as storyteller, 102

on student leadership roles list, 174
on test scores, 9
at Washington seminar, xxii, 19–20, 41, 46, 108
Summit Academy, 124, 213
sustaining change, 185
Sutton, Sara, 154
Suzuki, Mr., 152, 153, *153*
synergy, xxi, 22, 207
   at A.B. Combs, 44, 54–55, 82, 87
   as aid to interdependence, 46, *48*
   with discipline issues, 87
   as family, 103, 111, *217,* 220
   Larry Sullivan's belief in, 159
   in "Path of Dreams," 150
   at Rowlett elementary, 169
   at Texarkana Independent School, 159–60
   as universal, 213

Take a Kid Fishin' Day, 113
talent, 179–83, 196, 215
Talking Sticks, 112
Tan, Mrs., 146
teachers, xxiii, 2, 3, 34–37, 43, *47,* 75–76, 177, 180–81, 182
teaching, 168
Teague, Lauretta, 115, 117, 181, 195
teamwork, 26, *26,* 30, 31, *32, 48, 86*
teamwork skills, 33, 47
technical skills, *48*
technology, 6–7, 25–26, *26,* 42, 145
technology skills, 30
Teresa, Mother, 64
test scores, 9, 10, 11
Texarkana Independent School District, 8, 159–62, *161,* 162, 166
TheLeaderInMe.org, xxiv
TheLeaderInMeBook.org, xxiv, 13*n,* 33, 214
third alternatives, 21, 87
Thomas, Autumn, 160
Thoreau, Henry David, 183
Timboon Elementary, 132
Time, 55
time management skills, 33, 46, *47,* 152
time on task, 188
tradition of caring, 2

transparency, *31*
Trueman, Katie, 76
trust, 166–69, 182, 183, 214
Tuesdays with Morrie (Albom), 139

ubiquitous strategy, 52–61, 201
Understanding, 21
  as aid to interdependence, 46–47
  for family, *217, 220*
  honesty and, *48*
  Larry Sullivan's belief in, 159–60
  in Texarkana Independent School
    District, *161*
  as universal, 213
United Kingdom, 154
United Way, 13, 123
universal nature:
  of Baldrige principle, 103
  of children, 14–15, 200
  of leadership principles, 14, 47, 168,
    200
  of *7 Habits,* 47, 103
Urban League, 155

values, 32, *216*
Venn diagrams, 50, 53
Venture Link, 152
vision, vision statements, 170, 171, 172,
    173, 178, 179
  at A.B. Combs Elementary, 44–45, *45,*
    57, 71, 90, 91, 96
Visions of Hope, 155
Vogel, Bill, 109, 114
Vozzo, Steven and Helen, 82

Vozzo, Walter, *82*
Vrooman, Marilyn, 142–43, 144–45, 146

Washington, Booker T., 70
Washington Elementary, 123
Watanabe, Takahisa, 152
Waterman, Cheryl, 123
Watkins, Barbara, 63, 99
We Beat the Street (Davis, Jenkins,
    Hunt and Draper), 139
What Works in Schools (Marzano),
    168, 186, 198
Whole New Mind, A (Pink), 7, 66
Winters, Gailya, 22, 66, 76, 107
Win-Win, 21, 56
  as aid to interdependence, 46–47
  with bonus funds, 112
  with discipline issues, 87
  as family, 210, 220
  for family, 104, 111, *216*
  Larry Sullivan's belief in, 160
  with playground disputes, 120
  at Rowlett Elementary, 169
  in Texarkana Independent School
    District, 160–61
  as universal, 213
Wong, Harry, 92
work ethic, 32
World Is Flat, The (Friedman), 204
Wright, Tom, 156–57
writing, 35, 53–54, 113, *199*
written communications, *26*

Youth Alive, 155

About FranklinCovey

Mission Statement

We enable greatness in people and organizations everywhere.

FranklinCovey (NYSE: FC) is the global consulting and training leader in the areas of strategy execution, customer loyalty, leadership, and individual effectiveness. Clients include 90 percent of the Fortune 100, more than 75 percent of the Fortune 500, thousands of small and midsized businesses, as well as numerous government entities and educational institutions. FranklinCovey has forty-six direct and licensee offices providing professional services in 147 countries. For more information, please visit www.franklincovey.com.

About Stephen R. Covey

Stephen R. Covey is an internationally respected leadership authority, family expert, teacher, organizational consultant, and author who has dedicated his life to teaching principle-centered living and leadership to build both families and organizations. He holds an MBA from Harvard and a doctorate from Brigham Young University, where he was a professor of organizational behavior and business management.

Dr. Covey is the author of several acclaimed books, including the international bestseller *The 7 Habits of Highly Effective People,* which was named the #1 Most Influential Business Book of the Twentieth Century and one of the top ten most influential management books ever. It has sold more than 18 million copies in thirty-eight languages throughout the world. Other bestsellers include *The 8th Habit: From Effectiveness to Greatness, First Things First, Principle-Centered Leadership, The 7 Habits of Highly Effective Families, Living the 7 Habits,* and *Everyday Greatness,* bringing the combined total to more than 20 million books sold.

As the father of nine and grandfather of fifty, he received the 2003 Fatherhood Award from the National Fatherhood Initiative, which he says is the most meaningful award he has ever received. Other awards given to Dr. Covey include the Thomas More College Medallion for continuing service to humanity, the National Speakers Association Speaker of the Year in 1999, the Toastmasters Golden Gavel Award in 2004, the Sikh's 1998 International Man of Peace Award, the 1994 International Entrepreneur of the Year Award, and the National Entrepreneur of the Year Lifetime Achievement Award for Entrepreneurial Leadership. Dr. Covey has also been recognized as one of *Time* magazine's 25 Most Influential Americans and has received eight honorary doctorate degrees.

Dr. Covey is the cofounder and vice chairman of FranklinCovey Company, the global consulting and training leader in the areas of strategy execution, customer loyalty, leadership, and individual effectiveness. FranklinCovey shares his vision and passion to enable greatness in people, organizations and societies everywhere.

www.StephenCovey.com
www.TheLeaderInMeBook.org